Joanne Howl, D.V.M.

Your CAT'S Life

Your Complete Guide to Raising Your Pet

from Kitten to Companion

PRIMA PETS
An Imprint of Prima Publishing

Interior photos © Artville
Color insert photos © Isabelle Français and Joan Balzarini
Chapter 1 breed photos © Isabelle Français
Cover Photos © Photodisc, FPG, Tony Stone

Library of Congress Cataloging-in-Publication Data Data on File
ISBN: 0-7615-1361-2

99 00 01 02 HH 10 9 8 7 6 5 4 3 2 1
Printed in the United States of America

How to Order
Single copies may be ordered from Prima Publishing, P.O. Box 1260BK, Rocklin, CA 95677; telephone (916) 632-4400. Quantity discounts are also available. On your letterhead, include information concerning the intended use of the books and the number of books you wish to purchase.

Visit us online at www.primalifestyles.com

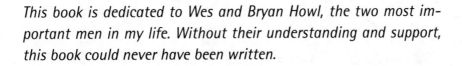

This book is dedicated to Wes and Bryan Howl, the two most important men in my life. Without their understanding and support, this book could never have been written.

Also Available from PRIMA PETS™ _____

Your Cat's Life by Joanne Howl, D.V.M.

Your Chihuahua's Life by Kim Campbell Thornton

Your Dog's Life by Tracy Acosta, D.V.M.

Your German Shepherd's Life by Audrey Pavia

Your Golden Retriever's Life by Betsy Sikora Siino

Your Rottweiler's Life by Kim D.R. Dearth

Contents

Introduction

My first memory is wrapped around a cat, or rather a small calico kitten. She wriggled deep into my heart one crisp spring morning. She was barely seven weeks old, and I was almost three. I remember that my mother bundled me up in a jacket for a brisk walk to a neighbor's house. I've no memory of what happened inside, but I emerged the proud owner of a tri-colored, mewling ball of fur.

Although nearly forty years have passed since that day, my joyous walk home with my prize kitten is nearly as clear in my mind as the walk down the aisle on my wedding day. I stuffed the kitten in one of my father's tall white sport socks. As I clutched the top of the sock protectively, the kitten peered out over the top. She squealed and wiggled as her head bobbed with each of my steps, while her clinging claws turned the sock as prickly as a porcupine. Her eyes were as clear as sunshine, and her patch-work colors amazed my own young eyes. The lasting impression of that day was how I felt inside. I was, for the first time, completely in love.

Love is a wonderful feeling and a perfect first memory. But when it comes to caring for kittens, love isn't enough. To thrive, a cat must either be very lucky or have an owner with a good understanding of the cat's physical needs (proper food, safe shelter, and decent medical care), and her emotional needs (love and affection). Our family was utterly cat ignorant, but fortunately the little calico who I called Candy was packed full of luck. She became my teacher, leading me into a life of study of and delight in all things cat.

When God created the cat, he probably intended to document his creation with an owner's manual. He surely meant to write a book that was concise and easy to read, yet filled with insight on the form, function, and foibles of the feline species. A book that would have told me that wetting out of the box meant Candy was ill, not spiteful. A book that suggested vaccinations to prevent a lifelong battle with upper-respiratory infections. And surely such a book would have warned me that neglecting to spay a female early in life might lead to breast cancer, the disease that stole Candy's life from her in early old age.

Given the impatient nature of man, Adam probably demanded delivery of his cat before the documentation was complete. After all, what would Eden be without a cat? Or perhaps Eve beat on heaven's door the moment she heard the kitten was weaned and was so excited about carrying it home in a sock that she overlooked that manual, leaving it forever locked inside heaven. Whatever the reason, cats don't come with explanations. That may add to their mystique, but it doesn't do much to improve their life on earth.

This book, inspired by the love of several felines who have shared their lives with me, is designed to be a quick, handy, up-to-date review of details for cat care that should come attached to every cat. It's not a bible, just an earthy and usable manual on how to care for a kitten or cat. Whether you're contemplating a future feline housemate or, suddenly smitten, have just woken up with a ball of purring fluff tucked contentedly on your chest, this book should give you insight into the mind, body, and heart of the beast inside your house.

As we follow the life of the cat from kittenhood to adulthood, we'll learn what makes a cat tick, how to keep her healthy and happy, and how to save money doing it. And yes, how to make the relationship fun and fulfilling for the people involved, too.

I've learned much from the experience of living with and loving cats over the last forty years. As a veterinarian, I've also invested most of my adult life studying medicine and science and ministering to the ills of both cats and dogs. Others more knowledgeable than I have also generously shared their insights, experiences, and scientific perspectives to help me create this book.

The following pages are a guide to raising a healthy kitten and keeping a happy cat. You'll also find fun facts and up-to-the-minute, hard-core scientific information in a readable style. You'll learn what makes a feline function physically, mentally, and emotionally and take a look at the spiritual bond between cats and the humans they own.

Cats are too complex to be explained in a single book, so I don't try to cover everything in these pages. If you're hungry for minute details on the anatomy, physiology, reproduction, or genetics of cats, you won't find it here. Likewise, this isn't a treatise on cat shows or cat breeding or an encyclopedia of cat breeds. If you need more details, you'll see where to find them in the Where to Go to Know More sections.

These pages are not in any way intended to substitute for the advice of a competent, caring veterinarian who knows your cat. Although the knowledge in this book can help you make informed decisions, it is general information. Because each feline is incredibly individual, what you read here—or in any book—is only a guide. Consult your personal veterinarian for proper care of your unique and beloved cat.

Why buy this cat book? Because it's packed with hot topics, scientific facts, and updated medical material you won't find anywhere else on the shelves. On top of that, it's filled with fun tales of cats, their owners, and the special bond they share.

Candy, my very first cat, instilled in me a basic understanding of a cat's needs. She introduced me to a wonderful world of feline love, lore, and science. If this is your first cat book, I hope it will guide you in the same way. Even if it's the fifth or fiftieth cat book you have on your shelves, it should bring you fresh insights into the life of a cat. In either case, I'd like to share with you a fabulous feline world full of love, beauty, and long, healthy lives.

Let's embark on our adventure through a cat's life. Turn the page, and let the fun begin!

So, You Want a Cat

In This Chapter

- To Cat or Not to Cat, That Is the Question
- Making the Decision
- Matchmaker, Matchmaker, Let's Make a Match
- Top-10 Cat List

Do you dream of romping with a kitten or cuddling with a cat? You're not alone. Cats are now the number-one pet in America, outnumbering man's former best friend, the dog, by more than just a few whiskers. Recently the American Veterinary Medical Association estimated that 70 million cats were owned as pets in the United States, compared to 55.9 million dogs.

You'll find almost as many reasons to own a feline friend as there are cats. Some people prize cats for their mouse-hunting skills. Others bask in their beauty, whereas some enjoy having a little tiger, independent and only partially tamed, in their house. Simply petting a cat can help you relax and actually lower your blood pressure, an important factor that can lead to a longer life. But the real reason that people invite a feline into their house is simple: Cats are good company.

There are few greater joys than staring into the innocent eyes of a kitten unless it's a beloved cat purring on your lap on a cold winter morning. But those wonderful moments are tied to needs that you must meet day in and day out if you want to share your life with a healthy, happy cat. Before you set your heart on the pitter-patter of little paws in your house, it pays to consider the whole picture.

To Cat or Not to Cat, That Is the Question

Let's talk to Fred, who is considering getting a kitten. He lives in a small, tidy house with an expensive leather sofa tucked between two ficus plants. Behind the couch, finely woven drapes billow gently in the breeze. Fred hands me a soda, sinks into his tan overstuffed chair, and starts to talk. "I'd love to have a couple of kittens," he says. "They'd make the place more alive, and they'd be so much fun. What do you think?"

"Well," I hedge, "do you think you're really ready?" I envision kittens dangling from the curtains and sliding down the couch, leaving claw-lacerated leather in their wake. While Fred expounds on his preparedness to own a cat, images of overturned plants and mounds of half-eaten leaves upchucked on his chair keep coming to mind. What if he discovered a warm, wet hair ball on the seat of his chinos one morning just as he sits to sip his morning Gevalia?

Fred's a great guy, warm and compassionate, but I happen to know that he works long, long hours at his weekday job as a computer engineer. And when he's not typing on keyboards, he's traveling the world, hiking and enjoying the wilderness. What's more, when he becomes enthralled with a new female companion, he may not see his own house for weeks. Fred's voice stops, then drops a little. "Maybe this isn't the best time for a kitten," he admits. "I guess I'd better settle down a little first. Yeah, and maybe redecorate."

Fred has a feline-shaped hole in his heart, and one day he'll fill it with the kitten of his dreams. But for now, trying to fit a kitten into his no-strings lifestyle and immaculate home would only make both him and the cat miserable.

Making the Decision

Responsible cat ownership means never having to say "You're outta here" for nine cat lives—roughly 15 to 25 human years. When both you and the cat match, years pass in the twitch of a kitten's whisker. But when you aren't ready, cat ownership can be a challenge, not a joy.

So how do you know if you're ready for live-in feline affection? The following questions should help you decide.

1. *How much free time do you have?*

Compared to dogs and horses, cats are undemanding pets. In about half an hour a day you can meet a cat's basic needs: fresh water, healthy food, a clean litter box, clipped claws, and a tidy coat.

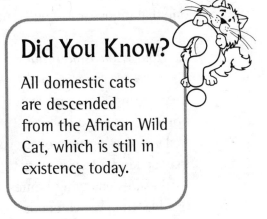

Did You Know?

All domestic cats are descended from the African Wild Cat, which is still in existence today.

Throw in an extra two hours once a year to take care of a healthy, full-grown cat's medical needs. Sounds easy, right?

Well, cats have one more need: affection.

For years experts have claimed that cats are solitary creatures. But that's not exactly right. Given half a chance, cats form very strong bonds with their owners and with other cats. Most of today's behaviorists describe cats as having a complex social order. In other words, cats enjoy a nice stroll alone on occasion, but they need love and interaction with others, too.

> Cats enjoy a nice stroll alone on occasion, but they need love and interaction with others, too.

How much affection does a cat need? It depends on the cat, but most would appreciate a minimum of fifteen minutes in the morning as you get ready for work plus a half hour or more each evening for petting, play, and purrs. Of course, a cat can easily handle stretches of solitude when your boss demands overtime. But loneliness shouldn't be a permanent way of life.

If you're tied to a job all day and then burn the social candle most of the night, you might prefer an aquarium instead of a cat. Likewise, people who travel extensively may not be cat ready unless they choose a sociable cat that can bond with a caretaker or one that enjoys traveling along.

2. How stable is your home?

Cats are creatures of habit. Although adaptable, they much prefer to grow roots and stay put rather than roam from home to home. If you're a college student nearing graduation, have a job that requires a move every year, or live at "no known address," it may be kinder to put off getting a cat until life slows down a little.

Besides changing homes, instability within a home can bring trouble, too. Are you about to be married to a great guy who's allergic to cats? Or does your wife want to start a family but believes the old wives' tale that a cat will suck the breath out of a baby? Worse, do you live with an abusive person? Often abusers will make a cat suffer to hurt you. If there's any question that someone else will hurt the cat or force you to get rid of it, then be kind and don't get one in the first place.

3. How much disposable income do you have?

There's no such thing as a free cat. That's a mantra you should chant each time you stare into the heart-melting eyes of a give-away kitten. Not that spending money on a cat is a bad thing or that keeping a cat will bankrupt you. Just don't expect your little angel in a fur suit to come completely without dollar signs.

How much dough do you need to support a cat? Although a few toys and a litter box aren't big-budget items, over time, a cat can be costly. Food, accessories, kitty litter, and well-cat veterinary care bring the cost of owning a cat to $300 to $600 a year. Health emergencies and serious illness can be expensive, so it's wise to set aside at least $500 in a medical savings account as well.

While these aren't break-the bank expenses for most people, they can be a burden, especially if you don't plan for them. If your ends barely meet, especially if you have children to care for, think long and hard before rocking the checkbook with another financial responsibility.

4. Can you say "commitment"?

Americans are a get-it-now, leave-it-later society. We buy a new car every three years and replace our computers about as often. We even make prenuptial agreements, planning our divorce before the words *until death do us part* leave our lips. *Disposable* is one of America's favorite words today. Disposable razors, disposable diapers, and disposable pets.

Disposable pets? Oh, yes. It's almost a fad to get a kitten and get rid of the cat. And why? Recently the National Council on Pet Population Studies and Policy reported that the top eight reasons an owner took an animal to a shelter were sick or old pet, owner is moving, pet was found as a stray, landlord won't allow, too many animals, can't afford to own, family allergic, and not using the litter box.

It's no fun being disposable property, especially when you're a living, feeling being. Emotionally sensitive, easily stressed, and capable of giving great love, even to the people who abandon them, one-fifth of all cats born in the United States—millions of cats—end up in shelters each year. Of these, about 71 percent are euthanized. If you can't commit to meet the needs of a cat, then don't make the mistake of getting one. It's the kinder decision.

5. *How's your temper?*

Are you pretty much in control of yourself, or do you tend to explode when tired or stressed? How do you think you'll respond when ten pounds of cat lands on your chest at five o'clock in the morning? For all their inherent wildness and natural resilience, cats are pretty breakable. I've treated broken legs from cats flung out of bed and mangled tails that were caught in a slamming door. The owners weren't mean people, but they had no idea their angry reactions could injure—or kill—a cat.

While a quick fit of temper can leave your cat injured and you saddened, it can also land you in jail. Recently a Maryland man was charged with cruelty in the death of a cat. The man was keeping a friend's cat, and

the cat leaped on the bed while the man was sleeping, then nipped him on the nose. He chased the cat and kicked him in the chest. The man noticed the cat couldn't breathe well, and he called his friend to notify her that it needed help. The cat died before the friend arrived. Was it wanton cruelty or a case of reflexes gone bad? If cruelty, the man is looking at a year in jail and a $5,000 fine.

6. Do you really like cats?

Most people adore kittens. A kitten is endlessly entertaining—willing to stalk, leap, and play at a moment's notice. On the other paw, cats are generally sedate. They hunt out a warm lap and shun laughter. They still play from time to time but generally prefer the dignified life.

Some people are simply kitten fanatics. A few can't stand to be without a kitten, so they adopt a new one each year. Meanwhile the previous adoptees become neglected, shipped off to the shelter, or grudgingly fed, then ignored. If you loathe the cat but love the kitten, take heart. You might enjoy fostering kittens for a feline rescue agency or working at a humane society shelter. Then you can relish each kitten without wondering what to do with the cat.

Matchmaker, Matchmaker, Let's Make a Match

If you've read this far, chances are you're ready to open your home to a kitten or cat. But how in the world do you know which cat is right for you? Since cats are like snowflakes—very similar but absolutely unique—there's no scientific way to sort out which one of millions is your dream cat. But you can improve your chances of the purrfect match by considering the following choices.

Kitten or Cat?

The heart-stopping cuteness of a kitten comes with a price: hyper-activity. A healthy kitten spends about 50 percent of his day in high gear. Curtain climbing, plant chewing, and leg chasing are part of a day's work. When they sleep, kittens may look like breathing Beanie Babies, but when they're awake, they demand attention, food, and activity. If you're energetic and tolerant, a kitten will re-ward you with some of the most fun to be had on four feet.

If you don't have the time or the temperament to devote to a three-ring circus in a fur coat or if the potential of feline interior redecoration unnerves you, then consider a cat. By the age of one year most cats have abandoned much of the kitten exuberance for the more contemplative life that comes with feline maturity. Not that older cats won't play—they certainly will—but you may have to initiate the game rather than throw away the ball to slow them down.

Expenses change with the age of a cat, too. A healthy adult cat is likely to require only an annual visit to the veterinarian. Kit-tens, on the other hand, must have a series of vaccinations, treat-ment for internal parasites, and usually surgical sterilization. Each, of course, costs money.

Longhair or Shorthair?

Just as in women, a cat's "big hair" can be beautiful, but it takes a lot of maintenance. Persians, with their cloudlike coats, are the consummate longhaired beauties, but they require a careful combing once a day to keep the mats away.

If coifing, brushing, and bathing Kitty isn't your idea of fun, shorthair cats are for you. A short coat may not turn as many heads as a big-haired beauty, but you might enjoy the short-coated cat more because you're combing her less. Most shorthair cats can look terrific with just a brush or a rub with a chamois every week—sometimes less.

Somewhere in between carefree and coifed lie the medium-hair cats. Some of these, like the Angora, have a heavy ruff and luxurious tails that are easy to care for and rarely mat. Others are cursed with a baby-fine fur that tangles without daily combing. If in doubt, ask a groomer, veterinarian, or experienced cat owner to help you pick out a nonmatting type of medium hair.

Needy Nelly or Independent Ernie?

Close your eyes and dream of your perfect cat. Let your mind drift, just imagining the enjoyable times you might share together. What did you see? A cat twined around your legs, chatting with you? Was she sitting on your lap, purring, or playing fetch? Or perhaps sharing your dinner and intimately involved in your life? If so, you probably would prefer a cat that needs—and de-mands—your love. A driving need for owner attention is one of the hallmarks of the Siamese and other thin-bodied Oriental breeds. Some alley cats are affection sponges, too. To improve your chance of getting a highly active, owner-bonded mixed breed, try picking a long-bodied cat with an Oriental look or a talkative cat. When a cat puts in the effort to try to speak to a per-son, it's a good bet they want to get involved in that person's life.

Did your perfect-cat fantasy tend to more serene moments, such as a glimpse of your friend asleep in the sunshine, rolling in catnip, or lounging in the garden?

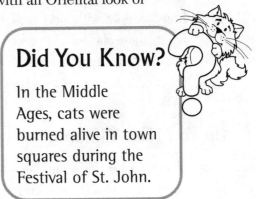

Did You Know?

In the Middle Ages, cats were burned alive in town squares during the Festival of St. John.

Or did you envision a few minutes of greeting each morning and evening but little other interaction all day long? If so, you may be more comfortable with an independent-minded kitty. The round-bodied British Shorthair or American Shorthair are lovable but relatively undemanding of an owner's time. Some mixed breeds can be quite self-sufficient as well. To increase your chances of getting a mixed breed that fits this bill, look for a barn cat background or the square and stocky body type.

Are You a Traveler?

If one of your greatest joys in life is travel, you'll need a special cat. Some cats absolutely love to tag along, but others literally drool in misery when they ride in a car, plane, or train. While our top-ten list of cat breeds can improve your chances of getting a travel-happy breed, the truth is that good travelers are more often made than born. You'll have more success at getting a kitten and teaching her to love travel early than in taking a stay-at-home older cat and dragging him along.

Travelers who spend time overseas (it can be difficult to get cats through quarantine in several countries) or who travel often on feline-unfriendly business trips need to be sure to pick a cat that will thrive in their absences. Avoid Siamese or Oriental breeds, which bond deeply with one person and wilt like an unwatered flower when their chosen one isn't around. Instead pick the more adaptable personality of a mixed-breed cat or British Shorthair type and practice leaving him with friends for days at a time from kittenhood.

Do You Have Children?

If you've got kids and haven't yet heard them beg for a kitten, prepare yourself—it's coming (especially if they see this book lying around!). Kids and kittens are picturesque, but they aren't always a perfect match. A playful, frightened, or angry feline can bite and scratch to flee the grasping hands of a child. On the flip side, a child can seriously injure—or kill—a kitten. Adult cats are a bit more resilient but are still no match for even the smallest toddler. Never leave young children and cats together without adult supervision.

Some cats learn to tolerate fast movement and yelling, squealing children, but others never will. The best child's cat is probably a good old mixed breed, although some purebreds can be child friendly, especially if raised with children from kittenhood. Two good kids' cats could be a Manx, which is energetic, enthusiastic, and sturdy, or the stoic, sedate, and tolerant British Shorthair.

> The best child's cat is probably a good old mixed breed, although some purebreds can be child friendly, especially if raised with children from kittenhood.

Loner or Life of the Party?

If you're a hermit, you may not need to worry about the sociability of your pet. But if Friday night is party night at your house, it's wise to choose a cat that is likely to relish strangers rather than vanish under the bed. Although many breed books tout Persians and British Shorthairs as calm and sociable but Siamese and other Orientals as skittish, these are just stereotypes. Sometimes the calm breeds quietly vanish when strangers arrive while the high-adrenaline types want to hang out and play.

If it's important to you to have a cat that adapts well to other people and pets, the key is to train him to the lifestyle from kittenhood. Ideally you'll pick a kitten that has been raised inside a home and handled daily by the owner from birth. You'll want to take him into your home before he's twelve weeks old and invite cat-friendly people over frequently. With this sort of upbringing most cats will learn to love company.

Boy or Girl?

Either a male or a female kitten has an equal chance of being a wonderful pet. If you plan to spay or neuter by six months of age, then the biggest gender issue is merely the cost of surgery. Spaying a female usually costs two to three times as much as neutering a male.

If you want to keep your cat intact, you'll have to deal with several unpleasant side effects. Indoor female cats can come into season about once every three weeks all year round (outdoor cats sometimes skip cycling in the winter). Because a female in heat yowls, rolls, and cries all day and all night long, she's not a very pleasant pet. And it's likely she's pretty miserable herself unless she's bred. That, of course, brings kittens.

While an intact tomcat can't dump a litter of kittens in your lap, he can father hundreds of kittens each year if allowed to roam. And he'll want to roam. An intact male's main goal in life is to look for love, not hang out quietly at home. In catdom, lovers have to fight off other toms, so count on your boy coming home with scratches, scrapes, and cat bites—if he comes home at all.

Bite wounds often get infected, requiring medical attention. Bites can also expose your cat to feline immunosuppressive virus, a deadly disease that affects a cat much like AIDS affects humans.

Keeping your intact tom inside will preserve his health, but he'll still be tough to live with. Tomcat urine is one of nature's most pungent fragrances. Because cats use urine as markers of territory and during times of stress, almost all intact cats—male or female—are likely to spray their urine on walls, doorways, or furniture.

The only good reason to own an intact cat is for breeding purposes. And the only good reason to breed is to improve a specific pure breed of cat. Fifteen cats are born for every person born in the United States. Most of these kittens are destined to end up destroyed simply because there are too many cats in the world. Please don't litter.

One Cat, Two Cat, Three Cat, or More?

Cats don't like being crowded, but they don't particularly relish a solitary life either. Given a choice, cats will form loose societies based on family groups with plenty of room to interact—or not—at their own whim. When cats become crowded, you're more likely to have behavior problems with them, such as urinating out of the box or fighting. When numbers get high—ten cats or more—the chance of behavioral problems increases to almost 100 percent.

Single-cat households often do quite well as long as there's plenty of affection available from humans or other pets. Solitary cats, however, are much more likely to destroy furnishings and play aggressively. It's not deliberate meanness. They have a real need to play, and if there's no pal in sight, they turn to whatever else is handy.

Two compatible cats are a joy to watch as they curl in each other's paws to sleep or sit in the sunlight, purring and grooming each other. And raising a pair of

Did You Know?

Contrary to popular belief, cats are not color blind. Studies show they can see blue, green, and red.

kittens can be easier than raising one. Because a running, pouncing playmate is much more interesting than lifeless home furnishings, your home will be spared the brunt of a kitten's energy. Tired kittens seem drawn to warm laps, so even though they look to each other as primary playmates, chances are excellent they will still come to you for affection.

Three cats are similar to two and not a whole lot more trouble. If they're compatible, they'll tend to spend more time together and less with you. On occasion one can be labeled an outcast and the two-against-one teaming can result in bickering and behavior problems.

From a cat's point of view, the best living situation most likely is two cats per house. One or three cats are also good choices. Avoid higher numbers.

Pedigree or Just Plain Cat?

Experts estimate that nearly 93 percent of cats are mixed breed, whereas only about 7 percent of cats sport "papers," which prove they belong to a registered breed. Mixed breeds rise to the top of the most popular list for several reasons. They are easy to find and inexpensive. Every newspaper in the country has a long list of spring kittens looking for new homes. Also, an American mixed breed tends to be a very healthy, robust animal. They aren't subjected to intense inbreeding, so hereditary defects are relatively rare unless the neighborhood tom is allowed to breed with generations of his own offspring.

On the downside, it's hard to predict exactly what your mixed breed is going to look like or act like when he grows up. Purebreds are popular among people who don't want just any cat but a specific look and personality type. If you've met a Persian that thrills your heart, you have an excellent chance of being captivated by most other Persians as well.

If your dreams of cats include raising kittens, you'll want to purchase a pedigreed cat—a cat whose ancestry is written down and accepted by a breed club, such as the Cat Fanciers Association. And not just any pedigreed cat will do. You'll need to get one from healthy, high-quality parents so that your kittens stand a chance of actually improving the breed. Breeding should never be taken lightly since so many unwanted cats end up euthanized in shelters. Even if you find a home for each of your kittens, each one takes up a home that another is literally dying to find.

If you can't swallow the thought of paying hundreds, possibly thousands of dollars for a cat or if you're content to take a feline in one of many forms, colors, or personalities, then an alley cat is your best bet. As a beginner's cat, inexpensive to own and generally healthy, a mixed-breed cat is hard to beat.

Which Breed for Me?

If you're contemplating a pedigreed cat, you'll have some homework to do. You'll have to sort through breeders until you find one who seems ethical and caring and has a cat you like. Then you'll have to search the mother's and father's line to make sure that none of the cat's ancestors have shown signs of any serious genetic defect. Detecting these defects is especially important when purchasing cats meant to be shown or bred.

But first things first—you need to find a breed you love. Gray or black, striped or spotted, furry or flat coated, the choices seem endless. They aren't, really. Only 37 breeds are recognized by the Cat Fanciers Association (CFA), the major cat registry in

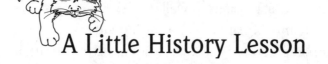

A Little History Lesson

Although cats moved in with people over 6,000 years ago, purebred cats are a new phenomenon. Certain regions bred cats that looked similar to one another even in ancient times, but that was more natural selection than planned breeding. Only since the mid 1800s have people mated cats to get kittens bred for looks alone. By the end of the eighteenth century raising fancy cats documented by papered pedigrees was the rage.

The first official cat show took place in 1871 in London, the bastion of the papered-litter crowd. Today the Cat Fanciers Association recognizes 37 breeds and the International Cat Association recognizes 41. These numbers won't hold for long: it's estimated that at least one new breed is founded per year.

the United States. Another handful of breeds are considered rare, new, or experimental and have not yet received official sanction. The best way to find your breed is to get out to cat shows, talk with breeders and owners, and read as much as you can about your breed. After using logic to narrow the field, choose the breed that twangs the heartstrings the hardest.

Top-10 Cat List

The following breeds are the 10 most popular breeds registered with the CFA in 1998. If a purebred cat is in your future, you may want to consider one of them.

As you read the breed descriptions, remember that these thumbnail sketches describe an average member of the breed. Cats take great pride in being utterly unique, and even though purebreds are more similar than different, they are hardly clones.

The cat you end up with will fit the sketch in many ways, but he'll also undoubtedly be his own singular self.

1. Abyssinian

This loving and personable breed was founded as a result of unrequited royal love. It's said that the emperor of Abyssinia (now Ethiopia) fell in love with Queen Victoria of Britain. He wrote her a long letter, asking for her hand in marriage. Victoria refused to respond to the emperor's inquiry. In retaliation for the snub, he began to arrest British citizens abroad in his country. Victoria sent 32,000 troops to ensure the safe release of her people. The emperor, in an extreme gesture, shot himself in the head as the troops arrived. War was avoided, and the troops had a holiday in which they exchanged gifts with the locals before being called home. Several soldiers collected beautiful ruddy red native cats, which were the foundation of the Abyssinian breed.

Purrsonality: This is a lively, playful, tireless, highly intelligent breed. Abyssinians need a lot of room to exercise and a host of interesting things to do to be happy.

Attention needs: The Aby thrives on attention! If the owner ignores this cat, she's likely to become depressed and unsociable.

Leave-at-home ability: Most Abys will be very unhappy separated from their master. Some will consent to be cared for by a substitute, but only if they have hours of attention each day.

Travel ability: Most Abys much prefer travel to being left home alone.

Purrsonability: Abys choose their owners carefully but love them intensely once chosen. Rehoming these cats might be a problem.

Trick ability: This cat can often be trained to walk on leashes and do tricks. The Aby is considered a very trainable cat if she bonds with her trainer.

Coat length: Short and thick.

Body style: The Abyssinian is a medium-sized cat with a long, muscular build.

Colors: The accepted colors are ruddy, red, blue, and fawn. The coat should be ticked, which means each individual hair has bands of black as well as the primary coat color. This same ticking is common in nondomestic animals, such as the rabbit, so it gives the cat a wild look.

Grooming: The coat is low maintenance but is best groomed by hand stroking or a fine comb. Avoid rubber brushes or chamois, as they can damage this breed's uniquely resilient coat.

Medical considerations: Abys have several serious inherited health conditions. Although many are vigorous and robust, carefully select a cat from a line free of the following diseases:

Amyloidosis: This disease is caused by a buildup of abnormal protein, called amyloid, in the kidneys and sometimes other organs. It causes progressive and usually fatal kidney failure. Signs of the disease usually appear before five years of age. It's similar but not identical to amyloidosis in the Siamese—Siamese more often suffer whole-body failure.

Retinal atrophy: There are at least two types of inherited retinal disease in Abys, and both generally lead to blindness. One form affects young cats, and the other is slowly progressive, affecting older cats. There is no treatment and no cure. Blind cats can make acceptable indoor pets.

Slipped kneecap and hip dysplasia: These congenital problems may cause lameness, arthritis, and the inability to jump.

2. American Shorthair

A favorite American Shorthair legend places the cat, like other American bluebloods, on the Mayflower. Whether or not that particular ship carried cats, it's certain that colonists brought cats to America in its earliest years. These hearty, shorthaired, amiable felines became an important part of every farm and homestead. They were even sold as essential companions to prospectors in the gold rush years. By the late 1800s, when purebred cats became the rage, the rustic heritage of the native American cat became a disadvantage. Breeders were accused of getting their stock out of the pounds and off the street. A "papered" feline from Britain was actually the first American Shorthair to be recognized in America. By the 1970s, however, true American-bred cats became the norm in this robust and popular breed.

Purrsonality: American Shorthairs are generally affectionate, easygoing, and quick to purr. They can be an excellent companion for children.

Attention needs: While this breed loves to play, they are relatively undemanding.

Leave-at-home ability: Because they are adaptable, amiable cats, they will normally accept care by strangers.

Travel ability: As befits a cat whose ancestors sailed to America, the breed often travels well.

Purrsonability: The American Shorthair loves its own family but can be outgoing and friendly to strangers.

Trick ability: Although not a circus cat, some American Shorthairs will learn a few tricks to amuse their master or to earn tasty treats.

Coat length: The coat is short, thick, and slightly hard to the touch.

Body style: This cat is medium sized, solid, and powerfully muscled.

Colors: All colors except pointed are accepted.

Grooming tips: A hard rubber brush helps remove dead hairs. Even though the coat is short, American Shorthairs should be brushed regularly during the spring shedding season.

Medical considerations: This breed has a wide genetic base (it's not closely inbred) and so is still relatively free from the intense inbreeding that tends to accentuate genetic problems. It's considered one of the healthiest of the purebreds.

3. Birman

The origin of many breeds is steeped in legend, but the tale of the Birman may be the most mystical. The story starts in ancient Burma, many years before the time of Buddha. In the sacred Khmer temple of Lao-Tsun lived a hundred yellow-eyed white cats. The statue honoring the goddess of the temple was golden, with sky blue eyes. The goddess was able, among other things, to order the transmigration of the souls of priests into

the bodies of holy animals. The white cats were seen as the spiritual pathway of the priests to heaven, and they were carefully cared for and protected. The high priest of the temple had a particular favorite cat named Sinh. They were devoted companions. When the temple came under attack by Siam, the good priest suffered a heart attack. Sinh leaped on his chest, allowing the priest's soul to enter his body. As he did so, the cat turned a golden color, and his eyes turned as blue as the goddess's. His feet stayed the purest white, honoring the touch of the holy priest. The other priests, bolstered by this miracle, defended the temple. When the cats returned to their normal places, they had all been transformed into the colors of the goddess. From that day onward, goes the legend, the sacred cats of Burma retained their holy colors and have been held in the highest esteem.

Purrsonality: The Birman is affectionate, gentle, and faithful. Their gentle natures make them good with children.
Attention needs: Birmans aren't demanding cats, although, as befitting temple cats, they thrive on human adoration.
Leave-at-home ability: This is a placid, adaptable cat that will usually do well under the care of a stranger.
Travel ability: While they probably prefer to stay put, many learn to travel without complaint.

Purrsonability: This breed generally gets along well with other people and pets.

Trick ability: The average Birman would much prefer to be worshiped than asked to perform tricks.

Coat length: The coat is medium long to long and is always silky in texture.

Body style: The Birman has a long, stocky body.

Colors: The cat still has the sacred colors: a golden body with dark points, pure white paws, and crystal blue eyes.

Grooming tips: The fur is thick and long and needs regular grooming. Unlike the Persian, the Birman's coat isn't prone to matting and is reasonably easy to care for.

Medical considerations: The Birman is generally a healthy breed, but some lines do have medical problems, including

> Epibulbar dermoids: These are small pieces of skin and hair that grow on the cornea of the eye. They are usually easily treated with surgery, but the condition may be inherited. Affected cats should not be bred.

> Slipped kneecap and hip dysplasia: Both congenital problems can cause lameness, arthritis, and the inability to jump properly.

4.   Exotic

Cat owners have always adored the sweet disposition and cute face of the Persian, but few people enjoy the daily grooming that its long, thick coat demands. In order to get an easy-care, short-coated Persian, breeders mixed Persians with American Shorthairs and nonpedigreed cats. As a result, the Exotic Shorthair, whose coat needs only a quick brush instead of a 15-minute session daily—was born in the 1960s. Today the breed is more often known as simply the Exotic.

Purrsonality: This breed loves home and comfort. They are affectionate and sweet.

Attention needs: The Exotic needs daily affection from his owner, but he's not overly demanding.

Leave-at-home ability: Most will adapt to caretakers other than their owners.

Travel ability: Some may make happy traveling companions.

Purrsonability: Although many Exotics are slow to warm to strangers, they can be won over by gentle petting and soft words.

Trick ability: This breed isn't fond of learning tricks.

Coat length: Exotics have a short, plush coat.

Body style: The breed is cobby, with a square chest and round head. They're a medium- to large-sized cat.

Colors: All colors and patterns of the Persian are acceptable in the Exotic.

Grooming tips: Although the hair is short, it's thick and should be brushed daily.

Medical considerations: Because this breed was founded from so many unrelated cats, inherited diseases don't crop up as often as in the founding Persian breed. But any of the medical conditions found in the Persian may affect some lines of Exotics. The primary medical problems in this breed are related to the flat face and include *tear-stained eyes* due to abnormal tear ducts, *difficulties breathing* through badly formed, small nostrils, and *dental problems* from mouths that are too small to contain a normal set of teeth.

5. Himalayan

People have always adored the Persian type of cat, but by the 1920s some thought that a longhair breed with colored points would be absolutely irresistible. To get the pointed coloration, Siamese blood was deliberately introduced into Persian lines. One important foundation queen was Himalayan Hope, a non-

pedigreed cat of perfect type that was rescued from an animal shelter. By 1957 the breed was officially recognized in the United States.

Today it's considered a separate breed by all associations except the CFA, which, despite the cat's Siamese blood, considers the Himmie simply a color variation of Persian.

Purrsonality: As one would expect from her heavy Persian ancestry, the Himalayan is generally affectionate, docile, and sweet tempered. Because of the Siamese influence she tends to be slightly more outgoing, demanding, and active than the Persian.

Attention needs: This breed is relatively undemanding, but they do crave affection.

Leave-at-home ability: Some Himmies are happy to have a stranger care for them. Many will pine for their beloved person.

Travel ability: Many of these cats will make good travelers. They are generally calm and prefer to stay with their owner when possible.

Purrsonability: Most are willing to meet strangers as long as they are calm, friendly people. Some Himalayans are strictly single-person cats.

Trick ability: Although this breed is intelligent, tricks are beneath them.

Coat length: The coat should be long, thick, and luxurious.

Body style: Himmies have a rounded body and head. Their faces are flattened, some extremely so.

Colors: A wide variety of colors is accepted, but Himalayans must have a pointed pattern, which means they have dark faces, ears, feet, shoulders, and hips.

Grooming tips: A high-maintenance cat, the Himmie must be brushed or combed daily and bathed occasionally.

Medical considerations: Since these cats are from both Persian and Siamese stock, any disease that is common in either breed may affect the Himalayan. Some lines, however, are a great deal healthier than either parental breed. Notable medical problems include

Hereditary cataracts: Although hereditary cataracts have been found in a fair number of Himalayan cats, these cataracts are usually rather small and don't result in blindness. Affected cats should not be bred.

Psychogenic dermatitis or hair pulling: Some Himalayans will chew, lick, and rip out their hair, with no medical reason for doing so. When physical causes, such as fleas and allergies, are ruled out, it's considered an emotional disorder that can be treated with a variety of drugs or sometimes with behavior therapy.

Cutaneous asthenia: This uncommon disease shows up as thin, stretchy, extremely fragile skin. At its worst, it can be life threatening. It's inherited, so affected cats should not be bred.

Polycystic kidney disease: See *Persian,* below.
Vision disorders: Crossed eyes, nystagmus (quivering eyes), pigment abnormalities, and defects of the visual nerve system can affect the vision of some Himalayans. These disorders also occur in the Siamese.

6. *Maine Coon*

In colonial times large, ring-tailed tabby cats prowled the Maine woods at night. Their large size and sometimes uncatlike habits, such as enjoying a romp in shallow water, gave rise to the popular

legend that they were descended from both house cats and rac-coons. (That's an impossible cross, of course.)

The breed doesn't lack for other legends about its origins. Some say that Marie Antoinette sent her Turkish Angoras to New England for safekeeping during the French Revolution, where they lent their longhaired genes to colonial house cats. Others insist that the Vikings brought their very similar Norwegian Forest Cats to America many hundreds of years ago. While the dawning of the breed is cloaked in lore, it's a documented fact that early New England natives loved their big cats. They even exhibited them in an annual show at the Skowhegan State Fair in Maine at least a decade before the first "official" cat show in London in 1871. After the introduction of the Persian, however, the giant north woods breed languished. In 1976 the International Society for the Preservation of the Maine

Coon was founded, and a revival of the nearly extinct breed was under way.

Purrsonality: Coon cats are loving, affectionate, and playful.
Attention needs: They love to be involved in their owner's life but are not overly demanding.
Leave-at-home ability: Most will adapt well to being cared for by strangers.
Travel ability: As befits a seafaring heritage, many Maine Coons learn to love a traveling life.
Purrsonability: Some Maine Coons are reserved around strangers, but given time, almost all are quite adaptable to grown people, pets, and children.
Trick ability: A Maine Coon will happily watch you try to train him.
Coat length: Heavy, smooth, and long. A ruff around the neck is desirable.
Body style: Maine Coons are large, long cats. Males weigh in at 12 to 18 pounds, and females are only slightly smaller at 10 to 14 pounds.
Colors: The traditional tabby coat is the most popular, but any color except lavender, chocolate, or pointed is acceptable.
Grooming tips: The long coat is somewhat easier to care for than the Persian's, but it still needs a thorough combing twice a week to keep it mat free and healthy.
Medical considerations: Although they started out as very vigorous cats, many lines of Maine Coons are now closely inbred and hereditary problems are becoming more common.

Heart disease: Some families of Maine Coons are plagued by hypertrophic cardiomyopathy, a serious disease in which the heart muscle, for unknown reasons, grows very thick. This can cause sudden death or severe illness before a cat is three years of age.

Gum disease: In several lines of Maine Coon, serious gum disease has caused a painful mouth and early loss of teeth despite good dental care. Although currently no proof exists that gum disease is hereditary, it does tend to run in family lines. Diet may also play a role.

Slipped kneecap and hip dysplasia: These congenital problems may cause lameness, arthritis, and the inability to jump.

7. Oriental

When the original Siamese was introduced in the West, many of them were actually solid colored. These cats were looked down on and removed from the breed. In the 1950s cat fanciers decided to re-create the solid-colored Siamese, and the result is the Oriental. There are now both short- and longhaired varieties. The Oriental has been called the "greyhound of cats" since it is lean, lithe, and fast moving.

Purrsonality: Much like Siamese, Orientals are devoted, loving, intelligent, playful, athletic, and very vocal.

Attention needs: The Oriental thrives on human attention and wilts when ignored.

Leave-at-home ability: This breed craves the presence of its chosen person and will often do very poorly in the care of strangers.

Travel ability: The average Oriental would prefer travel with his person rather than being left behind.

Purrsonability: The Oriental often greets strangers affectionately and may get along well with other pets.

Trick ability: Some Orientals can be coaxed into learning a few tricks.

Coat length: The Oriental may have a short or long coat.

Body style: The cat is long, lean, and lithe with a small, wedge-shaped head and very large ears.

Colors: Almost any color is accepted except pointed.

Grooming tips: Even the longhaired coat isn't prone to matting. Periodic combing is required for the long coat, whereas rubbing with terry cloth or chamois will keep a short coat glistening.

Medical considerations: The Oriental was created by outcrossing the Siamese with other breeds, such as the Russian Blue and American Shorthair. As a result the breed has less risk of inherited disease than the Siamese. No specific medical problems are attributed to Orientals, but some lines may have any of the problems listed under *Siamese,* below.

8. *Persian*

In the late 1600s Italian traveler Pietro della Valle wrote: "There is in Persia a cat of the figure and form of our ordinary ones, but infinitely more beautiful in the luster and color of its coat. It is of a blue-gray, and soft and shining as silk. The tail is of great length and covered with

hair six inches long." How a cold weather cat came to live and thrive in the warm Middle East is a mystery, but the exotic, heavily furred Persian was adored wherever it was introduced. Early Persians didn't have the extremely flat face that we know them by today. Indeed, in 1903 some writers considered the Persian and the Turkish Angora, with its high cheekbones and medium-length nose, to be almost identical cats. The flat face of today's Persian may be adorable to look at but isn't necessarily suited for healthy teeth or easy breathing.

Purrsonality: One of the most placid breeds, the Persian is described as docile, gentle, lovable, and sweet natured.

Attention needs: The breed is generally undemanding, although most love to be petted and adored.

Leave-at-home ability: Many Persians will thrive in the care of a stranger while their owner is away; a few will pine until their owner returns.

Travel ability: These quiet cats are often good travel companions. But Persians with flat faces may have trouble breathing when stressed or overheated. Avoid sending these cats by air cargo.

Purrsonability: Variable. Some adore strangers, some will ignore them, and some will hide whenever an unknown person or pet appears.

Trick ability: This is no circus cat and rarely performs tricks.

Coat length: The coat should be long, flowing, and thick.

Body style: The Persian has a distinctly rounded shape with a flattened face.

Colors: Almost all naturally occurring colors are accepted.

Grooming tips: Persians have thick coats that tend to mat and require daily grooming. A metal comb is the best tool to avoid mats and tangles. They may require bathing, which should be done only after a careful combing to minimize damage to the coat.

Medical considerations: Many Persians are quite healthy cats, but the breed is predisposed to many potentially serious conditions. Some of the most notable are:

Chédiak-Higashi syndrome: This syndrome is found only in blue smoke cats that have very light yellow-green eyes. Affected cats dislike bright light, their blood may not clot well, and they may be more likely than other Persians to get infections. Chédiak-Higashi syndrome generally isn't fatal.

Entropion (eyelids that roll inward): This painful condition can be cured with surgery but if left untreated can damage the eye and interfere with proper vision.

Excessive tearing: Usually caused by an improperly functioning tear duct, excessive tearing is common in Persians. Some cats with this problem can be cured by surgery.

Glaucoma: An inherited condition that causes a sudden, extreme rise of pressure inside the eye, glaucoma has been reported in the breed, and many affected cats go blind. If detected early, it can be controlled with medicine.

Small nasal passages: Many Persians have trouble breathing through their nose. This can be serious since it may be impossible for a cat to get enough air when upset, overheated, or excited.

Polycystic kidney disease (PKD): In some lines of Persians, PKD is a serious problem. The kidneys are large and spongy looking and don't

Did You Know?

The top five registered breeds with the Cat Fanciers Association are the Persian, Maine Coon, Siamese, Abyssinian, and Exotic.

function properly. Most cats with this disease die an early death. It's considered hereditary, so avoid buying a cat with this problem in her family tree.

Slipped kneecap and hip dysplasia: These congenital problems may cause lameness, arthritis, and the inability to jump.

Gum disease: Some lines of Persians suffer from serious gum disease, which causes a painful mouth and early loss of teeth despite good dental care. Although no proof currently exists that gum disease is hereditary, it does tend to run in family lines. Diet may also play a role.

Ringworm: Ringworm is actually a fungal infection that can cause minor or major skin disease in a cat. It's very common in Persian catteries and although treatable can sometimes be difficult to cure.

9. Scottish Fold

The first Scottish Fold appeared from humble barn cat blood on

a farm in Perthshire, Scotland, in 1961. Susie, as the folded-eared farm cat was named, lived for only two years (the average life span of any outdoor cat) and produced only one litter. Two of her kittens inherited the odd ears, but one was neutered and didn't produce kittens. Snooks, the lone remaining Fold, was bred and produced Snowdrift, the founding father of the breed. He claims 76 descendants, 42 of which bore folded ears. Although the breed was disdained in England as a deformed variety of cat, it became very popular in the United States because of its good looks and pleasant personality. Not all pure-bred Scottish Folds have folded ears. Many appear normal but are still purebred Folds.

Purrsonality: The Scottish Fold is placid, adaptable, optimistic, and good-tempered.

Attention needs: While he loves his family, the Fold is relatively undemanding of their time.

Leave-at-home ability: Most Folds will adapt well to other caretakers.

Travel ability: With their calm outlook on life, many Folds make good traveling companions.

Purrsonability: While they will never seek the center of attention, Folds usually adapt to visitors and willingly share their home with other pets or children.

Trick ability: These cats are known to enjoy a game of fetch but are generally unwilling to learn tricks on command.

Coat length: Scottish Folds can have either long or short coats.

Body style: The body is medium sized and cobby, with a rounded head. Most have neatly folded ears.

Colors: All colors and patterns are acceptable except for pointed patterns.

Grooming tips: The coat is easily cared for, needing only occasional grooming to look good.

Medical considerations: The folded ear is inherited and is linked to a defect in cartilage formation. As long as a cat has only one parent with folded ears, it's likely to have minimal or no health problems. But the offspring of two folded-ear cats can have very serious health problems, including painful, crippling deformities of bone and the cartilage of the joints, because the same genetic defect that causes the cute fold can also affect cartilage throughout the body. These health problems are so serious that many countries refuse to recognize the breed, claiming that it's inhumane to continue breeding for these damaging genetic traits.

10. Siamese

This long, lean cat wears a distinctively pointed coat and comes with a loud, raspy voice. The Siamese is considered an ancient breed, originating in Siam (now Thailand). It was one of 17 distinct varieties of cat that appeared in *The Cat Book Poems,* a book written in praise of felines sometime between 1350 and 1767 by an unknown author in ancient Siam. Many legends exist about the origin of Siamese cats, which are widely believed to have been sacred in their native land. The modern Siamese was exhibited at the first official cat show in London in 1871, and a Siamese cat club was in place by 1901.

Purrsonality: The breed is loving, devoted, demanding, vocal, active, agile, and playful. It can be an incessant talker.
Attention needs: Very high. These cats need close, sometimes constant interaction with their chosen human to be happy.
Leave-at-home ability: Siamese hate it when their master leaves them. Older Siamese are notorious for starving themselves, sometimes to death, when their beloved human must travel without them.

Travel ability: While they might voice complaints during the entire trip, most Siamese would prefer to travel than to suffer a single day of separation from their loved ones.

Purrsonability: Many Siamese are highly reserved with strangers. But some will happily bond with other pets and greet strangers like long lost friends.

Trick ability: Given enough time, a Siamese may consent to learn a few tricks from a sincere and devoted master.

Coat length: The Siamese coat is short and lush.

Body style: The modern Siamese is very slim, elongated, and angular with a small, wedged head. The earliest known Siamese had a round head and a heavy, strong body. Only since the late 1950s has the thinner, angular variety become popular. The Traditional Cat Association is reviving this older "apple-headed" variety.

Colors: Although Siamese can be a wide range of colors, they must all have a distinct pointed pattern.

Grooming Tips: The coat is easy to care for and requires only occasional brushing.

Medical considerations: Although individual Siamese may be robust and healthy, the breed as a whole has a long list of in-herited or common medical problems. Choose your lines care-fully, especially if you're interested in breeding Siamese cats.

Acromelanism: Acromelanism isn't a health problem but a trait of all Siamese. It describes the temperature-dependent pointed coat coloring peculiar to the breed. In other words, the cat's coat gets darker where the temperature of his body is cooler. Because the body is warmer than the legs, Siamese have a light body and dark legs. Likewise, when a Siamese is raised in cold weather, his coat is dark, whereas a littermate raised in a warmer climate would develop a lighter color. This trait can be a problem when the cat is subjected to temperature extremes because the coat can change color. Many owners find that simply bandaging a foot can result in a temporary lightening of the fur. Although this condition poses no health problem, a poorly colored coat can coast ribbons in the show ring.

Vitiligo: This condition causes loss of pigment around the eyes and nose, leaving white hairs mixed with the normal coat. Although it's not a health threat, it's undesirable in breeding animals.

Adenocarcinoma of the small intestine: According to some sources, the Siamese is three times more likely to develop this cancer than any other cat. Caught early, this malignancy can be well controlled or cured by surgery.

GM1 gangliosidosis and mucopolysaccharidosis VI (enzyme deficiencies): These serious syndromes caused by enzyme deficiencies have been reported in the Siamese. They may cause nervous disorders, abnormal body size and shape, and death. These syndromes have no cure, and affected cats should not be bred.

Congenital heart defects: Several types of heart defects have been linked to families of Siamese. Depending on the defect, the cat may die a very early death or live with the condition for several years.

Crossed eyes: This is a hereditary fault. Affected cats can't see well, and they should not be bred.

Glaucoma: This inherited condition, which causes a sudden and extreme rise of pressure inside the eye, has been reported in the breed. If detected early, glaucoma can be controlled with medicine. Many affected cats go blind.

Gum disease: In several lines of Siamese serious gum disease has caused a painful mouth and early loss of teeth despite good dental care. Although currently no proof exists

Pets in Public Housing

If you're one of the millions of people living in public housing, take heart! Your landlord can no longer forbid you to own a pet. On October 21, 1998, a Veterans Administration (VA) and Housing and Urban Development (HUD) appropriations bill became law. Part of this bill contains language that specifically allows "one or more common household pets" to live with a resident, provided that the resident keeps the pets responsibly and in accordance with local laws. This means that as long as you don't neglect or abuse your animals, you're entitled to share your home with a pet. You may be required to pay reasonable pet deposits or establish an escrow account for damage your chosen furry friend might do to the property.

This new law follows in the footsteps of 1983 legislation granting seniors and the disabled the right to own pets in public housing. Although naysayers initially said that allowing pets in these homes would create problems, lawmakers have recognized that this isn't the case. What's more, the benefits of bringing four-legged love home has had profound, immeasurable benefits on people's emotional health.

If you're renting VA or HUD property and your landlord says no to Kitty, ask him to take a look at Public Law (PL) 105-276, Title 5, Section 526. If that doesn't change his mind, a brief discussion with a lawyer should open the door for your pet.

that gum disease is hereditary, it does tend to run in family lines. Diet may also play a role.

Cystinuria: In humans, cystinuria is caused by an inborn error of metabolism that is inherited. It's presumed to be inherited in cats, too. Affected cats develop bladder stones made of cystine, which is a component of protein, and treatment is difficult.

Amyloidosis: In this slowly progressive, ultimately fatal disease an abnormal protein called amyloid is deposited throughout the body. Affected cats are often unthrifty

The benefits of bringing four-legged love home has had profound, immeasurable benefits on people's emotional health.

(simply fail to thrive) and thin and develop liver failure, kidney failure, or general ill health. Although there is no cure, some affected cats can live for years with the condition.

Vision disorders: Crossed eyes, nystagmus (quivering eyes), pigment abnormalities, and defects of the visual nerve system can affect vision in some lines of Siamese.

2

Choosing a Companion

In This Chapter

- Where Do I Find a Cat?
- Picking the "Pick of the Litter"

Most of the time ownerless cats can be found just about anywhere. They twine around your leg when you step into the street. Friends wave kittens in front of you, teasing you with feline cuteness. Farmers hang spray-painted signs along the highway, advertising the ripeness of their newest crop. Of course, that's when you don't have room for a cat. The moment you open your home, ready to welcome a cat, it seems as if the entire unfettered feline population disappears. Suddenly every cat and kitten is attached and loved. Now that you're ready, where do you find a cat?

The richest kitten adoption season is during the so-called spring tide, which occurs about 63 days after lengthening daylight triggers a surge in feline hormones. Queens, or mature female cats, come into heat by the thousands, and the kitten population naturally leaps shortly after. There's a smaller "fall tide," when shortening daylight trips the hormonal trigger again. Between the tides a steady stream of kittens are born year-round. And, of course, adult cats are always available. You just need to know where to look.

Where Do I Find a Cat?

If you're hunting for a feline friend, be assured that he's out there somewhere, just waiting for you to appear and bring him home. He might be hanging out in a friend's home, an animal shelter, or even a breeder's cattery. As you paw through your choices, looking for Mr. Purrfect, you'll find good prospects everywhere. As a general rule, stay away from pet stores, and buy your purebred cat from a top-of-the-line breeder. All the other sources can be a good—or bad—place to find your cat; it just depends on the facility and your tastes. Arm yourself with the image of a healthy kitten or cat (described later in this chapter) and go prowl around.

Newspapers and Neighbors

Newspapers not only bring daily events into your home but also can be an easy way—and often a good way—to find a cat. Word

of mouth, bulletin boards, and posters can alert you to potential pets on the prowl in your neighborhood. Over-the-back-fence adoptions work out well most of the time. According to a survey by the American Pet Product Manufacturers' Association, the vast majority of pets are found by word of mouth or local advertising.

Although it's possible to find a healthy kitten this way, it pays to be careful. Giveaway kittens are usually the result of "misalliances"—the polite term for promiscuous sex or unintentional breeding—rather than planned matings. Despite their cuteness, a litter of little darlings is de facto evidence of an owner's neglect to spay and neuter the parents. Such owners are likely to neglect other preventative health care, such as parasite control, vaccinations, and feline leukemia tests. Adopting kittens from people who ignore basic health care increases your risk of getting an unhealthy pet—and expensive medical bills. And it also encourages them to let their cats keep on having kittens.

Giveaway adult cats are a completely different story. Even the most caring owner might find herself forced to rehome a beloved pet. Finding a good home is a tough job, so the owner usually turns to newspapers, posters, and word of mouth. You should, of course, always ask if the animal has been spayed or neutered and check the vaccination records and feline leukemia test results before bringing your new cat home.

If you imagine you're going to find the next Cat Fanciers Association Grand Champion by shopping the neighborhood newspaper, think again. Sure, it's entirely possible the top-ranked cat in the country lives down the street from you. But those kittens aren't going to be advertised locally. The best breeders advertise by word of mouth, at cat shows, in breed magazines, and in general cat magazines. The purebreds in the paper are almost certainly from a hobby breeder or kitten mill. You might find a cute kitten

Did You Know?

A cat onboard a ship is a sign of good luck.

with registration papers, and if you're very lucky, he might be healthy, too. But don't expect show quality.

Your Veterinarian

Yesterday I walked into a friend's veterinary hospital and discovered the head technician leaning against a counter with a kitten in one hand and a warm bottle of milk replacer in the other. Three other small kittens wriggled and squealed in a box by her feet. Karen fed her hungry charge as she kept a watchful eye on the bustling hospital. "I guess you've got your hands full," I said, stating the obvious. "This is nothing," Karen countered, nodding at the box full of hungry kittens. "We've got six more just like them in the kennels. And two adults, too." A second technician overheard the conversation as she whizzed by from the autoclave to the operating room. "The good news is that we've already found homes for them all," she told me.

Few veterinary hospitals are quite so rich in strays or lucky in finding homes for them as my friend's. But most veterinarians see their share of cast-off cats. It's unfortunate that people dump strays at veterinary hospitals, because veterinarians don't have the manpower or money to care for abandoned animals. Because their cages are needed to treat the sick, most unwanted pets are sent on to the local animal shelter. However, almost every veterinarian will shoulder the expense of adopting out a fortunate few pets each year.

Veterinarians don't sell animals, but most do require that the new owner pay for some of the health care the pet has received. These charges may cover vaccinations, feline leukemia tests, and the cost of surgical sterilization. They don't begin to cover the actual costs of feeding, boarding, medicating, and taking care of the cat for days or weeks at time. Or the cost of the manpower to feed orphan kittens from a bottle every two hours round the clock for four weeks. In return for minimal health care costs, you'll receive a healthy kitten or cat who has had the best possible care during his life in the hospital ward.

Veterinary hospitals are also a great place to feel the pulse of the local cat community. In the waiting room you'll almost certainly find a bulletin board filled with cats for free or sale. If you don't see what you want, ask the staff. They usually know the best breeders and great clients who have nice cats in need of rehoming.

Rescue Organizations

A feline rescue organization is a grassroots group dedicated to saving and rehoming cats. These groups are usually run by a few dedicated people who donate energy, time, and more than a little of their own money to save as many cats as they can. Each rescue works a little differently from all the others. Some take in any cat at all, whereas others adopt only one specific breed. At least one rescue is dedicated to rehoming retired purebred show and breeding cats. To find out what types of rescues are operating in your town, ask your veterinarian or local humane society. If you're Internet ready, a Web search is likely to turn up several rescues within driving (or shipping) distance.

There are several advantages to adopting from a rescue group. The cats are normally fostered in homes, not kept in cages, so they are less stressed. This helps keep the cats healthy and allows their true personalities to shine. Because of this and because rescue groups often do extensive temperament tests, you'll know if your prospective adoptee is cuddly or cold, if he likes children or dogs, what he likes to eat, and other important details. Most rescues work closely with a veterinarian and take excellent care of their charges, so the chances of getting a healthy pet are high. Another advantage: Most rescues offer a one-week to one-month trial period. That means you can get to know your new cat before you make a lifetime commitment.

Because these groups put in so much of their own money, time, and energy into placing their cats, they are often pretty picky about the new home. If a rescue group asks you a lot of questions about your current pets, your reasons for wanting a cat, and your plans for this particular cat (indoors or out, declaw or not, etc.), don't be offended—they're trying to make sure their cats will be well cared for in their new life. A lot of questions—and even a home visit—might seem annoying, but it's a sure sign of a great place to get a cat.

> Most rescues work closely with a veterinarian and take excellent care of their charges, so the chances of getting a healthy pet are high.

Prices range from a few dollars to a hundred or more, and contributions are always welcome to help defray the costs of keeping and adopting cats.

Breeders

If you dream of show rings and kittens, plan on purchasing Puss from a breeder. Buying from a breeder can be a wonderful experience. A great breeder can teach you about the breed and find a particular line—a group of related cats with similar characteristics, such as extraordinarily blue eyes or an extra-sweet disposition—that suits you best. She can also open doors for you into the show world, where a savvy mentor can make the difference between ribbons and also-ran.

The problem is that top-quality breeders are a rare breed themselves. And buying from the masses of below-average breeders can be a nightmare. The two most common operations are backyard breeders or kitten mill operators. Kitten mill operators crank out kittens like popcorn without regard for quality or genetic defects—they just want to earn money. The breeding cats are often kept in small cages with unsanitary conditions and reproduce as many kittens as possible in their lonely lives. Kitten mill kittens often have serious physical and emotional defects from early malnourishment or genetic problems. Because they aren't handled much, they may not be able to grow into happy, healthy pets.

Backyard breeders are smaller versions of kitten mills. They usually have just a few mother cats, while kitten mills have dozens—or hundreds. Backyard breeders are also out for profit, but they don't take the business seriously, so the cats often breed erratically. These breeders rarely take the health of their cats seriously, either, so the kittens often suffer from worms, upper respiratory infections, or another serious disease.

Another group of breeders are the hobby breeders, who get into breeding for the love of their pets. Many hobby breeders try hard to do almost everything right but are so blinded by love for their cats that they lose perspective. In even the finest litters, only one or two kittens have the potential to grow into a winner in the show ring. If you hear the words "every kitten is pick of the litter," you've likely met a breeder blinded by love. Walk away before you get hurt.

So how do you find a top breeder? It takes time—and homework. Visit cat shows to see who's bringing home the ribbons.

Did You Know?

Over half of all cat and dog owners give their pets a human name.

Ask the owners of the breed you fancy to give you the address of their local club, then subscribe to the breed club magazine. Talk to as many breeders as you can and visit their catteries. Quiz your prospective breeder about hereditary problems and breed traits, then check the answers with breed books or your veterinarian. If a breeder swears her cats are completely free of genetic defects, make sure she puts that guarantee in writing.

While you're interviewing breeders, ask about the preventative health regime of the cattery. Ideally each kitten is examined individually, feline leukemia tested, and vaccinated by a veterinarian before it's sold. The cattery should also have a preventative health plan against feline infectious peritonitis, feline leukemia, and ringworm. A great breeder will let you discuss these issues with her veterinarian. Avoid breeders who do all the health care themselves or shun scientific facts in favor of less credible "fringe" treatments such as nosodes (a homeopathic vaccine substitute that relies on the "energy" of an illness to prevent disease) instead of vaccines. Although alternative medicine and holistic care can play a role in cattery management, if it entirely replaces conventional medicine—or common sense—avoid buying the kittens.

Many catteries with good bloodlines and healthy stock ignore the basic emotional needs of their cats. Kittens raised in lonely cages or basements usually turn into cold, unlovable adults. If you want a real cat—a sociable feline friend who's just as much fun to live with as he is to look at—make sure the breeder raises her kittens "underfoot," which means sharing the family's living space. They should also be handled daily. A breeder who exposes her kittens to friendly children, strangers, and other pets before they are eight weeks old creates a confident kitten who is comfortable with a variety of living situations. These earliest lessons in sociability stay with the kitten for life.

Breeders: The Good, the Bad, and the Great

If you're having a hard time sorting the dream breeders from the nightmares, don't feel left out. It can be very hard to know a great breeder at first glance. You can find a few helpful clues, however. If a breeder shows up in the "bad" category even once, it may be wise to look elsewhere.

Bad Breeder	Good Breeder	Great Breeder
Claims the breed has no negatives.	Willingly tells you the negatives of the breed.	Willingly tells you the negatives of her line.
Claims every line except her own produces genetic cripples.	Discusses any genetic defects in her line.	Gets out a genetic chart to show a single sick cat five generations back.
Shuns conventional veterinary advice.	Has a veterinarian design her preventative health plan.	Offers to let you discuss cattery health with her veterinarian.
Cattery is dirty and smelly.	Cattery is clean.	Cattery is spotless.
Kittens raised in cages, outbuildings, barns, or basements.	Kittens raised underfoot.	Kittens raised underfoot, with daily handling.
Will put the registration in the mail later.	Paperwork goes easily.	Has all documents plus extras.
Won't let you look or won't let you in all parts of the cattery.	Willingly lets you see her cattery.	Asks you to come in right now.
Lets you have the kitten before eight weeks or insists on keeping beyond 12 weeks.	Releases kittens between eight and 10 weeks of age.	Encourages adoption at about nine to 10 weeks and discusses socialization issues with you.
Contract states sales price but nothing protects the cat or you.	Fair contract.	Contract is very detailed yet readable and fair.
Has plenty of kittens to pick from; maybe several litters at once.	Might have one or two kittens available soon.	Rarely has kittens available now; usually you must wait for an upcoming breeding.

A good breeder is also handy with paperwork. He'll show you a pedigree for your kitten's parents and give you the forms to register your kitten at the time of purchase. He'll also give you a contract, which should be detailed. The contract should explain the purchase price of the cat, the intended use of the animal (show, breeding, or pet), and any obligations you have to the breeder (such as returning the cat if she doesn't work out or allowing her to show the cat herself). It should also give a health guarantee that allows you a week or two to discover any infectious problem and a year or more to discover genetic defects. It should also stipulate that you may choose to take a partial refund or return the cat if a health problem is found. The time frame for return or refund is usually within a month for illness and within one to two years for genetic defects. The best health guarantees give protection against genetic disease for the life of your cat.

Animal Shelters

If you want to choose from a lot of cats and kittens, visit an animal shelter. The thousands of shelters across the United States always have kittens and cats up for grabs. Because a cat has only two ways out of a shelter—adoption or euthanasia—your adoption literally saves a life.

Despite the desperate situation of the cats inside, you might find the local animal shelter surprisingly picky about letting you adopt a cat. Some shelters want to know more about your than the fussiest rescue operation. The people who work at shelters are strict because they are forced to kill a lot of pets due to the actions of irresponsible owners. It's a miserable job, so they

No-Kill Shelters

Several major shelters have recently vowed that they will refuse to euthanize any animal, regardless of how long it takes to find him a home. On the face of it, who can argue with the idea? No one is in favor of murdering millions of innocent animals each year, are they?

The no-kill concept may be laudable, but it has created a huge controversy in sheltering circles.

Proponents of no-kill point to the moral high road. They say that their existence is an expression of the value of all life. It's a stand against animals being killed by a random injection of euthanasia solution and disposed of like garbage. Only by refusing to be a part of the carnage, they say, can we educate our children and our citizens about a pet's right to live. The belief—and hope—is that when people come to value life, they will naturally act more responsibly toward their pets.

Despite the grand ideas, no-kill shelters draw a lot of criticism. They are accused of sidestepping the most miserable part of a shelter's job without regard for repercussions. When a no-kill has full cages, the shelter just quits accepting pets. Those animals end up at a kill shelter or abandoned to fend for themselves. And they might make quite a few kittens while they're out there, too.

It has also been said that no-kills tend to be very selective when they accept pets, taking only the most adoptable ones and sending the sadder cases to certain euthanasia at a neighboring shelter. At the same time, no-kills can capitalize on their heartwarming ideals in huge fund-raising campaigns. People love to donate money to such happy places. Unfortunately, this may mean that the neighboring shelters—the very ones facing an increased euthanasia load—begin to receive less public funding, so they have less resources to funnel toward adopting out the animals in their shelters.

Everyone embroiled in the argument over no-kill shelters agrees on one point: They would all love to hang up the euthanasia syringes and shut down the gas chambers. They also agree the only way that will ever happen is for people to take personal responsibility for pet overpopulation. Even if you don't own a pet, your tax dollars are paying for local animal control officers to destroy hundreds, thousands, or hundreds of thousands of animals each year.

The bottom line: Adopt from a shelter, no-kill or traditional as you please. Just make sure you do your bit to stop the carnage. Spay or neuter your pet.

are very motivated to make sure that every cat they send home stays happily adopted for the rest of its life.

Another surprise can be the cost of adoption from a shelter. The fees can range from a low of $50 per cat to a high of over $100. Although animal shelters are normally run as nonprofit organizations, it costs a lot of money to house, feed, and medicate stray and unwanted animals. Your donation rarely covers the cost of keeping the cat for more than a day or two.

> To maximize your chances of a healthy cat, find a shelter that quarantines new cats for a week or more and houses sick cats away from the adoptable pets.

Many shelter adoptees come with health problems. These are almost always treatable and mild, such as sneezing, ear mites, or intestinal parasites. Infectious disease can be extremely hard to control in shelter situations, but some shelters do a better job than others. To maximize your chances of a healthy cat, find a shelter that quarantines new cats for a week or more and houses sick cats away from the adoptable pets. The shelter should also vaccinate their cats and kittens and test for feline leukemia and feline immunosuppressive virus.

Pet Shops

Pet shops have a reputation as a bad place to buy a cat. And there's good reason. Most traditional pet shops purchase their "product" from kitten mills—breeders who turn out kittens in assembly-line fashion. These kittens often have serious physical and emotional defects from early malnourishment or genetic problems. Because they aren't handled much, they may not be able to grow into happy, healthy pets. The stress of shipping, processing, and warehousing in the pet store can also take a toll on their physical and emotional health. It's wise to walk away from the cute little purebred in the window.

A Better Way—Pet Store Partnerships

Today many pet stores are turning away from selling living "product." Instead they join forces with local humane groups to help place needy cats in loving homes. It's a win-win-win situation for you, the cat, and the store. The adoption group screens the felines for temperament and health, so you get a better pet. Meanwhile kitten mills no longer find it profitable to pump out "product," so fewer sick cats are born. And the pet store can make money by selling litter boxes and cat food even as they perform a valuable community service.

Pet stores who turn their cages over to humane groups are proud of their work. Expect to see big signs proclaiming that the cats belong to an adoption agency. A volunteer from the organization will be on hand to expedite adoptions or a contact phone number will be hung on the cage. If you aren't sure whether the kittens are truly adoptees or are owned by the store, ask the management. And make sure to call the humane group to confirm the store's story before you sign a check.

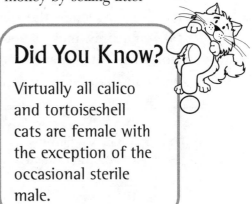

Did You Know?

Virtually all calico and tortoiseshell cats are female with the exception of the occasional sterile male.

When a Cat Adopts You: Taking in a Stray

Your dream cat may be a male tabby kitten with blue eyes and a fluffy coat. But don't be surprised if one morning you wake up with a green-eyed, white, short-coated female staring into your window with calm complacency. Somehow she's discovered your house is open, and she's come to fill the bill. You've been chosen.

Sure, you can shoo her away and head off in search of your perfect little tabby. You can rationalize that the stray may require medical attention and might even have picked up a few bad habits in her days abroad. But when you need a cat and one is smart enough to come find you, it would be foolish to turn her away. There's no greater honor than to be chosen by a cat.

Strays can make wonderful pets, especially if they're wise enough to seek you out. But a homeless life—even for a few weeks—does open the door for disease. When you agree to take in a stray, make a veterinary appointment as soon as possible. The cat will almost certainly be in need of vaccinations, worming, and feline leukemia testing even if she seems to feel well. Until you get a clean bill of health, keep her away from your other cats as well as their dishes and litter box.

> Healthy cats have a glowing look, an alert attitude, and a clean, shining coat.

If a stray is obviously ill, she should be caught humanely in a trap—your local animal control office or humane society can loan you a trap and give you instructions—and taken to your veterinarian before you even touch her. In rare cases, unvaccinated wild cats can carry deadly rabies. Don't risk getting bitten if a stray cat seems disoriented or aggressive. Also, if a stray cat dies after you bring her home but before she's checked by your vet, don't just bury her and forget her. Call your veterinarian *immediately* to discuss if you need to have the brain tested for rabies. The test should cost you nothing.

Picking the "Pick of the Litter"

After a little looking, you'll undoubtedly find yourself with several equally adorable cats to choose from. How can you ever pick between the marmalade tom and the calico queen? To get the best-possible companion, you'll need to assess both the physical health and the emotional traits of the candidates. The following sections should help you with these jobs. If two cats score equally well in each category, just listen to your heart. Logic can only take you so far, after all.

Signs of a Healthy Cat

The average veterinarian spends eight years learning the ins and outs of animal health, but you don't need a degree to learn a few basic clues to cat health. You can perform a simple examination that will allow you to avoid adopting obviously unhealthy cats. Remember that this quick check won't replace a thorough veterinary exam.

To start your kitty checkup, stand back and take an overall look from several feet away. What's your first impression? Healthy cats have a glowing look, an alert attitude, and a clean, shining coat. They sit comfortably, walk smoothly, and leap and play with only a little encouragement. The healthy cat should have a lean, muscular body, but he shouldn't look bony. Nor should he be rounded and fat. Avoid a skinny cat with a big, round belly. This combination can indicate serious disease.

While you're watching him, call his name or make a kissing noise. If he's asleep, he should open his eyes quickly and spin his ears toward the sound. He may yawn, stretch, or sit bolt upright, but then he should look at you with

curiosity or pleasure. As he's looking your way, look at his eyes. They should be clear and bright, without any discharge. If you notice a thin membrane covering a noticeable portion of the eye near the nose, it's a clue that he's not feeling very well. While you're gazing at your kitty, observe the skin on his nose. It should look slightly shiny and moist but shouldn't be so wet that it drips. Noses that are crusty and dry or runny indicate sickness.

Now call the cat to you or dangle a toy. He should walk freely and trot briskly, without hesitation or a limp. Healthy kittens generally pounce on a toy almost immediately and perform great acrobatic leaps during play. Older cats may only watch the toy with interest. If they choose to play, the movements should be fluid and free. Beginning to take a swat but wincing and pulling up short suggests the cat is in pain from a muscular or skeletal problem. Keep him playing gently for three or four minutes, watching to make sure he doesn't get seriously short of breath or start coughing. This could indicate heart or lung disease.

Now put your hands on him. The ideal cat will arch and purr at your petting, proving he's not in pain. Feel his coat and skin, making sure there are no bumps, cuts, or scabs. Look inside his ears. You should see smooth, clean skin. Dirty, crusty ears suggest ear infections or ear mites. Open his mouth. A healthy cat has pink gums, white teeth, and almost odorless breath. A kitten's breath may smell milky and sweet. Lift his tail to make sure his bottom is clean and neat, which proves that he doesn't suffer from diarrhea or serious urinary problems and that he's agile enough to clean his own behind.

> A good-tempered cat should begin to relax a bit after five to ten minutes of calm chatting and petting.

Now that you're close to your cat, take a sniff in his general direction. A healthy cat is basically odorless. If you pick up un-

pleasant smells, suspect that he may have an abscess, an ear infection, or another health problem.

If you haven't found anything worrisome by this point, your
adoption candidate is most likely healthy. Confirm this with your
veterinarian before finalizing the adoption or within 48 hours
after taking her home.

Judging Temperament

Clues to a cat's physical health can be seen, smelled, and felt. But
most cats keep their personalities private, especially in front of
strangers or in stressful situations. When the chips are down, cats
withdraw. It's how they protect themselves.

Nothing is more stressed than an adult cat in a shelter. He's
been uprooted from his family, then locked in a bare cage surrounded by loud noises and noxious smells. In such circumstances most cats try to become invisible. He may lie flat at the
back of the cage and watch you with suspicious eyes. He may
even cringe or hiss when you reach in to pet him. None of these
stress reactions mean that he's a
bad cat. Take him home and he
may turn into a belly-up affection
sponge who adores your company.

In many cases the only hint
you'll have of a caged cat's true
temperament is the comments of
someone who knows him well,

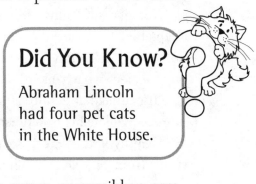

Did You Know?

Abraham Lincoln
had four pet cats
in the White House.

such as a previous owner, a foster owner, or possibly a caretaker at the shelter. If you're contemplating a stressed cat, ask
if you can take him into a private room to spend some time
getting to know him. A good-tempered cat should begin to
relax a bit after five to ten minutes of calm chatting and

Like Father, Like. . .

In 1994 a group of veterinary behaviorists at Cornell University studied the effect of human handling on kittens. Kittens were either handled three times a week for fifteen minutes or not at all, depending on the group they were assigned to. Researchers kept tabs on each kitten's personality features, such as willingness to approach a seated person, acceptance of handling the feet and face, and willingness to be petted, among other things. The results were surprising. Handling the kittens didn't seem to make that much difference in their personality. But parental personalities mattered a lot. In fact, the personalities of the kittens closely matched the personality of the *father*—a creature that these kittens might never have seen. Of course, one study in a laboratory setting doesn't change the fact that years of practical experience in the real world points to the value of early socialization. But it does show that Dad is important, too—maybe more than we ever imagined.

petting. If you get him to purr or nudge you with his head, you've likely found a winner.

Not all adults quiver in fear, of course. Many are outgoing and adaptable. These are the cats who grab your shirt as you walk by, demanding attention. They are good candidates for adoption, but don't expect what you see in the cage to be exactly the cat you get. It can take an adult cat a full six months to settle into a new home and allow his true personality to blossom.

Healthy kittens are basically fearless creatures, so they rarely suffer from cage angst. When assessing kittens, it's important to realize that the prime feline socialization period is between seven to nine weeks of age. Kittens younger than 10 weeks don't have a firmly set personality or a full set of social skills. So the six-week-old fireball might decide that cat napping in laps feels pretty good by the time he's grown. Or peaceful Pearl might learn that she can rise in rank by being a bully.

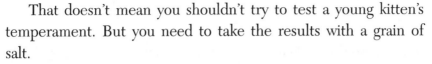

That doesn't mean you shouldn't try to test a young kitten's temperament. But you need to take the results with a grain of salt.

To learn a bit about a kitten's personality, start by watching him play with his family. The ideal adoptee will be playful, pouncing on his littermates as often as he's pounced on. If the kitten bounces up to Mom for a little play and she passes out a few indulgent licks, give him bonus points. He's learned to socialize with adult cats as well as kittens. On the other hand, avoid the wallflower who shuns play. She may either be sick or too timid to make a pleasant pet.

After taking in the family portrait, make a little noise or shuffle your feet. Watch what your kitten does. Ideally she'll stop her play and look at you curiously. If she approaches you at a fearless run, she earns bonus points. Arching and spitting isn't an automatic out, especially if you've made a startling sound. If the kitten runs away, hides, or leaps at you with an angry shriek, look for a different adoptee.

Next extend your hand. A nice kitten will come over curiously to check you out. A real sweetie may brush up against you and arch for a petting, purring all the while. A kitten that dances just out of reach to avoid being touched loses a few points, while one who shrieks, spits, slaps, or bites at you should be marked off your list.

Now pick up your intended. A really sociable kitten will purr and flop in your arms if she's in the mood. Even the best-tempered kittens generally need to wind down before they'll cuddle, so a little squirming to get back to play is perfectly normal. If the kitten bites or scratches in a panic to get free, however, consider her a questionable candidate.

Play Tests

You can use toys to learn a lot about a kitten or an unstressed cat. Both personality and health can be assessed using the following toy tests.

Feather Test

Catch the cat's attention and drop a feather from about two feet high and about one foot in front of the cat. A cat should follow the feather with his eyes and be interested and alert. An outgoing, confident, playful cat or kitten may also pounce on it. If the cat can't keep his eye on the feather, he may not see well. A lack of interest may signal sickness or a dull personality.

Ping-Pong Test

Roll a Ping-Pong ball across the cat's path about one foot in front of her. If she cocks her head and swivels her ears but her eyes don't follow the ball, she's most likely blind. To test her peripheral vision, send the ball parallel to her, again about a foot away.

Traditional homemade hearing tests, such as whistles, stomping your feet, or dropping something loudly on the floor, generate vibrations that even a stone-deaf cat can feel with her paws or whiskers.

Clicker Test

Before you leave home on your kitten quest, tuck a clicker in your pocket. A clicker is a little metal device that makes a sharp sound when you press on it—it can be bought at many pet stores or through dog-training catalogs. The sound isn't too loud, but the pitch is irresistible to cats. Wait until your cat has her back turned, then reach in your pocket and squeeze the clicker once. The cat should quickly turn her head toward you. This is an excellent test for deafness. Traditional homemade hearing tests, such as whistles, stomping your feet, or dropping something loudly on the floor, generate vibrations that even a stone-deaf cat can feel with her paws or whiskers. A clicker can only be heard, not felt.

3

Welcome Home!

In This Chapter

o Preparing for the Homecoming
o Kitty, Come Home!

You've done your preliminaries. After reading about all of the risks and responsibilities of cat ownership, you're convinced that a feline fits your life. Then you scoured shelters, rescues, and neighbors, looking for just the right cat. Finally you found him. He might have come from the most expensive cattery on the East Coast or crawled out of the liquor-store dumpster. It doesn't matter. You've found him, you love him, and now he's yours. It's time to bring him home! Even if you've brought your kitten or cat home, don't skip this chapter. There's a lot of valuable information here, including some important issues you may not have considered.

Preparing for the Homecoming

Once you've found your dream kitten, it's tempting to grab him up and take him straight home. If he's the one for you, then your home is his home, right? Hold on for just a minute. You need to work out a few details to make the homecoming smooth and happy.

A Family Chat

Before a cat sets his paw over the threshold, take time to sit your family down for a little heart-to-heart chat. The new houseguest might be small, but like any addition to the family, a cat can bring big changes. If everyone agrees on cat care basics from the start, your first days together will be much happier.

It's essential that everyone understand who's in charge of each cat care chore. Who fills the food bowl? Who keeps the water sparkling fresh? And who cleans the litter box? Assign these tasks to a responsible adult. Never use Kitty to instill a sense of responsibility in your child. Even a few days of forgetfulness can cause a cat to quit using a litter box or make him sick from starvation. Cat caregiving should be a privilege—something that a kid *gets* to do only when he's proven he's completely reliable.

You'll also need to agree on the basic rules of feline behavior. Do you care if a kitten prowls the countertops? Can he sleep in your bed? Do you expect him to stay out of certain rooms or to leave the plants alone? Set the laws from day one. If you can get everyone to help encourage Kitty to behave, you'll have a mannerly cat in short order.

Two final homecoming tasks—kitten proofing your home and stocking up on feline paraphernalia—require action, not talk. Neither task should be difficult. Read on to make them easier.

Kitten Proofing

You wouldn't dream of turning a toddler loose in your house without making the house safe, and felines need the same consideration. A kitten's incredible curiosity and energy make him especially accident prone. Fortunately, kitten proofing the home requires little more than learning to recognize hazards and a dash of ingenuity.

To assess the hazards lurking in your house, take a kitten's eye view. Get down on your hands and knees and crawl around a little. What looks tempting? That jungle full of philodendron? It's poisonous. That bottle of acetaminophen on the counter? It's deadly. Those curtains? They'll shred under your kitten's claws, and he may choke to death if his collar gets caught in the curtain rods. As you find hazards, take simple steps to make them safe.

> You wouldn't dream of turning a toddler loose in your house without making the house safe, and felines need the same consideration.

Take the philodendron outside. Keep medicines in a bottle with a childproof cap and store them in a cabinet. Consider removing curtains until the kitten is a year old, or at least remove his collar.

While you're looking for dangers, take a close look at your treasures, too. Your antique china and crystal vases may look like cool toss toys to a kitten. You can have your Lenox and display it too, even with the most curious kitten afoot. Just use a bit of double-sided tape or sticky Velcro to attach the treasure to the table. If you're in an earthquake-prone area, a dab of Quake putty works just as well.

Sometimes it takes a little ingenuity to keep Fluffy safe indoors, and the following table should help you eliminate some of the most common household hazards. Problems not on the list can often be solved with infant and toddler safety equipment sold at any hardware or child specialty store. And, of course, your common sense. If you can't solve a cat safety problem, always ask your veterinarian for advice.

Quick Reference to Poisonous Plants

Before letting your cat graze on your greenery, make sure the plants aren't on the following list. All of these plants can be toxic to cats, some mildly so and some fatally. (The worst ones are in bold.) For a more complete list, buy the book titled *Household Plant Reference,* published by the ASPCA National Animal Poison Control Center. It's inexpensive ($15), complete, and accurate.

Almonds (kernel in the pit contains cyanide)

Amaryllis bulb

Anthurium

Apricot pit

Autumn crocus (*Colchicum autumnale*)

Avocado (leaves, seeds, stem, skin)

Azalea

Begonia

Bird-of-paradise

Bittersweet

Bleeding heart

Boxwood

Bracken fern

Buckeye

Buttercup (*Ranunculus*)

Caladium

Calla lily

Castor bean

Cherry pit

Chocolate

Choke cherry (unripe berries)

Chrysanthemum

Clematis

Crocus bulb

Croton (*Codiaeum* sp.)

Cyclamen bulb

Delphinium, larkspur, monkshood

Continued from page 64.

Dumb cane (*Dieffenbachia*)

Elderberry (unripe berries)

English ivy (All *Hedera* species of ivy)

Fig (ficus)

Four-o'clocks (*Mirabilis*)

Foxglove

Garlic

Holly berries

Hyacinth bulbs

Hydrangea

Iris corms

Jack-in-the-pulpit

Jimson weed

Kalanchoe

Lantana

Lily (bulbs of most species)

Lily of the valley

Lupine species

Marijuana or hemp (*Cannabis*)

Milkweed

Mistletoe berries

Mountain laurel

Narcissus, daffodil (*Narcissus*)

Oleander

Onions (raw or spoiled)

Peach (kernel in the pit contains cyanide)

Pencil cactus/plant (*Euphorbia* sp.)

Philodendron (all species)

Poinsettia (many hybrids; avoid them all)

Potato (leaves and stem)

Rhubarb leaves

Rosary pea (*Abrus* sp.)

Schefflera

Shamrock (*Oxalis* sp.)

Spurge (*Euphorbia* sp.)

Tomatoes (leaves and stem)

Yew

KOSHA Guidelines

No doubt you've heard of OSHA, the Occupational Safety and Health Administration, the federal group that oversees workplace safety. Well, when cats lives are at risk, KOSHA, the Kitty Occupational Safety and Health Administration, could come knocking. Don't wait for these fictional prowlers to lay an official paw on you for neglecting kitty safety at home. The following KOSHA check-list will help you fix the most common hazards in your home.

Hazard: Electrical wires.

Why it's dangerous: One bite can stop Kitty's heart or burn a tongue in half.

Quick fix: Run wires out of reach or enclose them in plastic conduit sold at hardware stores. Unplug lamps and appliances when not in use. Cover cords tightly with aluminum foil—the average cat hates the touch of tin on her teeth. Bitter Apple or cayenne pepper may be a deterrent, but some cats ignore these terrible tastes.

Hazard: Human medicines.

Why it's dangerous: Many human (and dog) medicines can kill cats. Even aspirin can kill.

Quick fix: Make sure all medicines have child safety caps and keep medicines in a cabinet out of Kitty's reach

Hazard: Dryers.

Why it's dangerous: A dryer is a warm, dark spot, full of fluffy clothes. What a great place for a nap! Many kittens die tumbling in dryers each year.

Quick fix: Never start a dryer—or washer, for that matter—until you can see your kitten safely outside it. Make sure your kids know this rule, too.

Hazard: Freezers.

Why it's dangerous: Kittens love to dash into cool places. Because of the insulation, you won't hear her calls to get out. Frostbite and death can occur quickly.

Quick fix: Simply locate the kitten before closing the door.

Hazard: Slamming doors.

Why it's dangerous: Cats rarely take tail length into account when adjusting their speed to clear a fast-moving door. Tails are easily broken or the skin may be stripped off the tail, both requiring amputation. If a cat's body is caught in a door, she may die.

Quick fix: Always close doors gently. Adjust the closing mechanisms of screen doors so that the door closes slowly and doesn't slam.

Hazard: Automatic garage doors.

Why it's dangerous: Cats can get trapped under the door as it lowers. Or they may crawl up into the hinges and get pinned—or squished—when the door moves.

Quick fix: Adjust the safety-closing sensor to raise the door if it hits a small object. Because cats are both small and fragile, this may be difficult. Don't let the cat roam in the garage without supervision. Know where your cat is before you open or close the door.

Hazard: Car engines.

Why it's dangerous: Car engines are a favorite outdoor-cat hiding place. Gruesome injuries occur when the motor is started.

Quick fix: Locate your cats before you get ready to leave the house. Thump the car hood in cold weather to frighten off outdoor strays. If there's any doubt, spend an extra second to open the hood and look.

Hazard: Drapery cords.

Why it's dangerous: Kittens can get tangled in a looped cord and strangle to death.

Quick fix: Use childproofing kits to ensure your kitten's safety. Or cut the loop in the cord to make two short, straight cords out of each looped one.

Hazard: Balconies.

Why it's dangerous: Cats and kittens have poor depth perception. They have been known to leap from over a dozen stories high. Obviously, this can be fatal.

Quick fix: If the balcony can't be safely screened in, keep the cats off it!

Hazard: Stairways.

Why it's dangerous: The stairs aren't the hazard; it's the open railings that let Kitty leap into serious trouble.

Quick fix: Install a clear acrylic shield on the inside of the railing to keep your cat in. Netting is less attractive but can work as well.

Hazard: Christmas trees.

Why it's dangerous: Preservatives that you put in Christmas tree water can poison a cat. Needles can perforate an intestine.

Quick fix: Don't add tree preservatives to the water. Simply use clean water, and cover the stand to keep your cat out. Needles aren't attractive to most cats. But if yours gnaws on them, you'll have to lock her away from the tree or else forgo the tree entirely.

Hazard: Recliners and rocking chairs.

Why it's dangerous: When the Laz-E-Boy folds up, Kitty can get squished. Rockers can break bones.

Quick fix: Know where your cat is before you rock or fold.

Hazard: Ceilings, heating ducts.

Why it's dangerous: Small holes look like an adventure. Unfortunately, cats can get lost inside ceilings, walls, and ducts.

Quick fix: Close up holes that lead into your architecture, or lock the cat out of the room until it's repaired.

Hazard: Baby bottle nipples and pacifiers.

Why it's dangerous: These little nubs are made of rubber, plastic, or latex, which can all be tempting chew toys for a cat. If swallowed, they can block the intestine.

Quick fix: Pick up small objects; don't leave them out for your cat to eat.

Hazard: Strings.

Why it's dangerous: Although a favorite cat toy, strings are deadly hazards. Once swallowed, a string can wrap around the back of the tongue or get stuck in the intestines.

Quick fix: Don't let your cat play with long, thin objects, such as string, tinsel, rubber bands, and yarn. If she loves string games, keep your hand on one end and put it away when done.

Hazard: Sewing needles.

Why it's dangerous: These sharp bits of metal can quickly perforate an intestine.

Quick fix: If your cat eats a needle, head directly for your veterinarian. If you get there fast enough, your cat may not need surgery. Your veterinarian may retrieve the needle by inducing vomiting (risky—don't try this at home!) or by using an endoscope and sedation. Once the needle leaves the stomach, however, surgery is required.

Did You Know?

A cat can jump about seven times as high as its tail.

Stocking Up

The average cat needs only a few items to keep her healthy. Following are some tips to help you pick out the best products for your cat.

Dishes

Every cat needs a safe, clean place to eat and drink. Ideally each cat should own two or three bowls. He'll need one for dry food, one for water, and, if you feed canned food, a plate or bowl for this, too.

Although cats are famously finicky about food, they don't tend to be picky about dishes. A shallow bowl to hold a day's allotment of dry kibble is ideal. For wet food, a plate may make it easier to lick the last drops of liquid from a juicy meal.

It's nice to give each cat her own food dish, but don't be surprised to see several cats chowing down together. What we might consider rude behavior at our dinner table—bumping and shouldering for position—is a sign of well-adjusted, emotionally stable cats. Fighting over food dishes means the cats don't like each other very much. Dinnertime squabblers need their own individual dishes as well as a private dining area. Separate rooms work best for these rare cats.

Dishes come in plastic, metal, or ceramic. Plastic is the most popular. Although most cats take to it readily, plastic can cause contact allergies in some cats. If your cat gets a red, itchy, or scabby face or chin, try a different type of bowl. Plastic can also give an off flavor to water, so you may want to use a ceramic bowl for liquids.

Metal dishes can also make water taste bad. Good-quality stainless steel is the least reactive metal. Although it's more expensive, it's generally worth the price in durability and taste appeal. Avoid cheap metal dishes, especially any made with aluminum or covered with zinc—long-term use can cause medical problems.

Most cats love ceramic dishes, especially for water. But some ceramic glazes have a high lead content and can poison a cat with continued use. The riskiest ones are decorative bowls manufactured out of the country. If in doubt, buy an inexpensive lead test kit from a hardware store. Designed to test water pipe solder for lead, the five-minute kit works perfectly on ceramics, too.

Water

Cats can be very finicky about their water. Some like it straight-from-the-well cold; others prefer it as warm as aquarium water. For most, room temperature is fine, as long as it's fresh and clean. Due to their highly delicate sense of taste, it's common for a cat to refuse water the moment it turns stale. Empty and refill water bowls daily and scrub them weekly.

Litter Boxes

Cats are naturally neat with their waste. Most want a safe, clean, peaceful place in which to make their daily deposits. The fact that soiling out of the litter box is the number-one behavior problem in pet cats means that many owners simply don't know how to meet their cat's litter box needs.

From a cat's point of view, the perfect litter box would be large enough for the cat to fit comfortably inside, kept in a quiet, safe location, and filled with an odorless material that is comfortable on the paws. And, of course, it would be perpetually clean. Those standards don't seem too hard to achieve, do they?

You can buy an inexpensive plastic litter box almost anywhere. Despite its simplicity, this is generally the box cats like best. Although the most common sizes fit the average cat just fine, if you own an 18-pound Maine Coon or a

Did You Know?

Americans spend more annually on cat food than on baby food.

two-pound kitten, you'll need to shop for one sized to suit. Small kittens often love a small, shallow Tupperware-type box (or just the lid if a kitten is truly tiny). For the large-sized cat, a plastic dishpan or sweater box will give the depth and width he craves.

Many cats enjoy a covered box. It gives them a sense of security as well as keeping litter neatly inside. It can also give a dedicated sprayer a safe spot to lift his tail. Some cats, however, prefer wide-open spaces. While kittens will usually learn to use whichever suits you, adult cats can have unbreakable opinions of their own. If you don't know what your cat prefers, try one of each.

It's a good idea to place the box somewhere away from noise and confusion. The really shy cat may insist on a room of her own. You can empty out a small closet and prop open the door or install a pet door to make a private privy. You might also turn a large cardboard box upside down, then cut out a small, cat-size entry hole to allow access to a litter box inside. Or you can buy a litter box surround that looks like a cabinet. Privacy boxes are a great way to keep litter boxes away from children or from family dogs that snack on feline feces.

Litter

Even more important than a litter box is the stuff that goes inside. Since Kitty has to dip her precious paws in this several times daily, she'll insist that it meet her strict standards for cleanliness, odor, and paw appeal.

Many cats are turned off by scented litters or by unusual-feeling ones, such as pellets or paper. But a cat comes to prefer certain litters by learning, not by nature. Learned preferences can be extremely strong. So, if you start your little kitten out with pine-scented newspaper litter, you may have to find that exact stuff for the rest of her life. You just have to hope the company stays in business that long.

The best bet is plain, unscented clay in either the finely granular scoopable form or the more coarse standard variety. It's cheap and available, and it's the number-one choice of most cats, anyway. Despite the media hype, not a single medical report has docu-

Litter Box Law

Veterinary behaviorists have a simple law of litter boxes: Always have one box per cat, plus one more. This law allows a cat to have privacy, cleanliness, and a choice of several locations. To keep Kitty using her box, stick to this rule.

mented that scoopable litter causes intestinal impaction, even in kittens. It does tend to give off more dust than the granular form, so if you have a cat with asthma, the regular clay is better.

Outdoor Shelter

When the sun goes behind clouds and the weather turns cold, outdoor cats look for shelter. It's not fair or safe to ask a cat to rely on her wits and good luck to find a safe harbor on her own. If you're keeping a cat out in the elements, even part-time, you need to make sure she has at least one spot in the world where she can go for comfort and safety.

A small doghouse makes an easy shelter. It keeps out wind, rain, and snow, as well as providing shade on a sunny day. One big problem with a doghouse is that it doesn't offer much safety. The entry is so big that small dogs, raccoons, and small children have no trouble reaching a cat hidden inside. You can solve this problem by making an additional hole just big enough for your cat to slip through in the back of the house. This will let her make a hasty exit when a not-so-friendly visitor comes in the front door.

Another option is to install a cat door on an outside entry, garage door, or window to your house. To keep out neighbor's cats and make your own pet safer, you can buy a door that recognizes a chip on your cat's collar.

In wintertime, it's plain cruel to make a cat fend for himself. Yes, cats have survived outdoors with their own wits and heavy coats. But they can and do suffer frostbite and misery. I've seen plenty of cats frozen to death, even in relatively mild Pennsylvania winters. If you can't bring your cat inside when the thermometer hits the freezing mark, make sure he has a warm place to stay.

To make the most of his own body heat, the winter shelter should be just big enough for him to stand, turn around, and lie down comfortably. Extra space won't warm up well, so the more exact the fit, the better. A lot of heat can be lost out of a large doorway. But putting a cover over the door can make a small space overly warm in winter, or it can jam, leaving the cat locked out in the cold. It's best to do without covers. The ideal winter door is the smallest hole your cat will readily enter. Usually that's just a bit bigger than his shoulder circumference, but it varies from cat to cat. When building a cat shelter, start by making a small entrance, then enlarge the hole as needed.

In cold weather, the frozen ground can suck the warmth right out of a cat. To combat this, make sure his house has a thick, solid bottom (wood is best). You'll want to raise it off the ground a little, but don't get it high enough for cold breezes to blow under. A quarter inch of air space is about ideal.

A thick layer of clean blankets or straw will help trap Snowy's body heat and keep the inside of the cathouse warm and cozy.

You'll need to keep this insulation fluffy, because it's the air trapped inside that holds the heat. Don't use heating pads, lightbulbs, or another form of artificial heat. Artificial heat devices are not only a fire hazard but can easily burn cats.

Fine Accommodations

Only the best digs will do for some pampered pussycats. If you want the classiest play yard in town, consider a cat-sized replica of a famous hotel. The Hotel Crescent Court in Dallas, Texas, created a 3,000-square-foot cat-friendly replica of their posh accommodations. The miniature hotel has skylights, murals, a dining room, arched windows, and a fountain that fills in for a water bowl. And you can visit, too—it's big enough for a person to enter. Interested? You'll lay out $2,500 for an unfinished shell or $6,000 for a purrfectly complete hotel.

My favorite winter shelter is built out of a Styrofoam foam ice chest. Choose a size that's just big enough to shelter your kitty comfortably. Tape the top securely on with duct tape, then turn it upside down so the wide top lies on the ground. Use a sharp knife to cut out a small, cat-sized hole in one end and put a layer of fluffy towels on the bottom. Voilà—a very warm winter shelter for less than five dollars. Give each cat one of her own.

Cat Beds

Indoor cats usually prefer to make their own sleeping arrangements rather than use a cat bed. Typically they'll take over an armchair or a lap or cozy up to their favorite person in bed, especially when the weather gets nippy. If you have a few extra dollars, however, there are plenty of cat beds on the market. They range from hammocks to tents, and one is even designed after a human brass bed. There's no guarantee that your cat will accept any of them, but then again, she just might. If you think you understand your cat's tastes, go ahead and pick one out.

Carriers

In the loosest sense of the word, a carrier can be anything that you stuff a cat into to carry her from one place to another. Pet stores sell carriers made of plastic, metal, wood, fabric, or cardboard and in a wide variety of colors and styles. Homemade carriers include pillowcases and heavy-duty cardboard boxes.

Carriers vary widely in quality and comfort for the cat. The worst carrier is a cardboard box, primarily because most cats will shred their way through it in a hurry. Cardboard carriers tend to last just a little longer, but a determined adult cat will rip his way out of these before the trip is over. The best carrier is made of sturdy plastic, has a latching front gate, and is airline approved for safe air travel. The price range between the worst and best is small: from free to about $40. The difference in safety and comfort to the cat is enormous. A good-quality carrier can also be used to house the cat temporarily when you move or if disaster strikes. You can ship her in it by air, train, or car without danger, and you can use it as a crate (see below). A good carrier will last a cat's lifetime, if not longer. Buy one for each cat.

Some owners prefer fabric carriers because they can be slung over the shoulder, like a purse, for easy carrying. They do have one major advantage: they can be slipped under an airline seat so that Kitty can be carry-on luggage instead of shipped in cargo. Make sure to check with the airlines before attempting this trick, however. And don't ever try to ship your cat in a fabric carrier—she could be crushed by shifting cargo around her.

Cat Crates

What's the difference between a crate and a carrier? Mostly the way they're used. A crate is a cat's own private space. It can be his carrier, too, but the main purpose of a crate is to give your cat a comfortable room of his own.

"But my cat owns the whole house," you might say. "Why does he need a crate?" Cats are extremely territorial animals. Even a happy cat marks his territory daily. He'll rub his face and chin on favorite places, such as a door or your couch, turning them into his own personal territory, and he'll deposit his odor from the scent glands in his paws on his scratching post. He'll also leave a trail of territory-claiming pheromones from his paws as he walks his paths in the house.

To a cat, complete rule is more important than territory size. If a cat claims an entire house, she'll feel the need to protect all of it from uncouth behavior and invaders. It can be a stressful job. When she can't control her property, such as when you invite the neighbors over for dinner, adopt a new cat, or rearrange the furniture, she might turn aggressive or very anxious. She might attack, hide, or pace. But most cats react to territory upset by urine spraying. By using urine marks, a cat is both reclaiming contested territory and finding an outlet for anxiety or anger.

You can't do away with a cat's need to own a territory—it's a highly inbred, natural feline feature. What you can do is limit the size of the personal territory, which is where the crate comes in. If a cat can accept a crate as his home territory, he's likely to be a happy cat. The rest of the house will then become shared property, which can be enjoyed rather than defended.

Crates are particularly useful in multicat households, where the overlapping territories of several cats create emotional misery and household havoc. Even in large

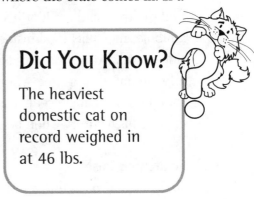

Did You Know?

The heaviest domestic cat on record weighed in at 46 lbs.

populations, crate-trained cats rarely spray in the house. Their own territory is secure, so they don't feel the need.

The best crate is an airline-approved carrier. The portable crate helps ease transitions when you move and can make veterinary visits less frightening. Larger crates are fine, too, and are quite popular with cats. The minimum crate size is big enough for your adult cat to stand up, turn around, and lie down comfortably and to hold water and food bowls.

To crate train a cat, all you have to do is to make it an appealing, private space. You'll want to feed him in the crate and nowhere else. It's also the spot to put his water and comfy bedding. If it's big enough, some cats like to have their litter box here, too. (You'll probably need to step up in size to a cage, rather than the smaller carrier, if you plan to put a litter box inside.) You might even add your cat's favorite toy, a special blanket, and the occasional sprig of catnip.

Kittens can be thoroughly crate trained in just a few days. All you have to do is make sure that the crate is the nicest place in the house. It also helps if he sleeps in it for the first week. Older cats, especially those who currently view a carrier with loathing and suspicion, can take months to become crate trained. To train an older cat, start by putting a tasty treat inside several times a day. Let him find the treat and eat it at his leisure. After he's willing to enter for a nibble, move his food inside. In a few weeks, move his water inside as well. After he's very comfortable, close the door on him for a few minutes at a time when he eats his meals, but don't keep it shut so long that he feels trapped. You'll know he's accepted the crate as his territory when he goes inside just for the fun of it.

Scratching Posts

The clawing routine that can shred couches isn't merely a source of feline fun—it's a physical and emotional necessity. When a cat scratches, he peels away the outer layers of his claws to keep them sharp and healthy. He also lays down a pheromone-rich scent from glands in his toe pads, marking the scratching area as his personal territory. Most declawed cats continue scratching at posts, both for the fun of the motion and to deposit pheromones.

To save your furniture, you'll want to give your cat a scratching post. If you can't afford the fancy sisal and carpet models that sell for hundreds of dollars at the pet store, don't sweat it. I'm sure some cats adore these monstrosities, but I haven't found one that does yet. For maximum success, keep it simple.

The all-time favorite cat scratching post is a two- to three-foot section of bark-covered log. It should be aged enough so that the sap is completely dried. You can nail a sturdy board to the bottom and set it upright or cut it in half and lie it flat on the carpet. Either way, it's a perfect—and natural—way to keep claws trim. Of course, avoid trees that have toxic or irritating sap (you can

> The clawing routine that can shred couches isn't merely a source of feline fun—it's a physical and emotional necessity.

check with your vet or the National Animal Poison Control Center if you aren't sure which local trees might bother your cat) or are twined with poison ivy. Pine has a thick bark and is a feline favorite.

Cats also have a thing for cardboard. They'll scratch on a sturdy box set upright or several layers folded up on the floor. You can buy an excellent corrugated cardboard scratching post at your pet store. For less than $10 you can get the catnip-scented, top-of-the-line cardboard post.

The occasional cat will come up with an oddball scratching post. If the choice is safe and nondestructive, it pays to indulge her desires. One of my most fastidious cats claimed a rubber flip-flop. She would sit on one end of my size-nine beach shoes while she burnished her sabers on the sole. If I took them away, she would turn to the couch, curtains, and even the wallpaper. A pair of three-dollar flip-flops every six months kept her happy—and the house in order.

Kittens take quickly to a scratching post with just a little encouragement. Cats take a little longer, but the training is the same. Show your cat where you want her to scratch by putting her feet on the post, then praising her. Lavish the praise on her (and possibly food treats) when you catch her using her post. At the same time start a strong campaign to stop scratching in other places. If you catch her clawing the couch, startle her with a loud noise. Drop a book on the floor, drop keys, blow a shrill whistle, or shake a can filled with pennies. You can also spritz her with a few shots of plain water from a squirt gun. The key to kitty correction is to make sure she connects the noise or spritz with her actions—not you. Shouting, chasing, and jumping up and down focus your cat's attention on you. If she runs away, it's more likely because she's learned that you're prone to bizarre behavior—*not* because she thinks she did something wrong.

Collar

Very few owners collar their cat. They complain of lost collars and the risk of a collar getting tangled and trapping the cat. Both are  real risks but can be minimized. The risks of a cat's running around unidentified, however, are also real. Public pounds and humane societies often consider noncollared pets as ownerless strays. So if Fluffy bolts out the door one morning, the authorities might euthanize her before you find her.

The only safe collar for a cat is one with a breakaway section or a piece of elastic sewn in. Make sure to test quick-release snaps to make sure they will give way with only a slight tug. Don't ever use a choke chain or sliding collar on a cat. Even solid collars can be a death trap if a cat gets tangled while she's barging through brush or climbing a tree.

Identification and rabies tags often get caught in bushes and on limbs and should not be on an outdoor cat's collar. The safest identification is to write your phone number on the collar in plain view with an indelible pen such as a Sharpie (ask your office supply store if you haven't seen one). It may not be pretty, but it will safely bring your cat home to you.

If your cat loses breakaway collars, consider yourself lucky. You might have lost your cat instead. If your cat loses several collars, you might want to consider keeping him indoors—he's getting in a lot of tight predicaments. If you can't do that, then buy a bunch of cheap breakaways by mail order. At $2 to $3 each, you'll barely notice each loss.

Harness and Leash

Some cats enjoy an afternoon stroll and are quite happy to be on a lead. Even if your cat won't walk with you, a harness and leash may be handy to restrain her on visits to the vet, on carrier-free car rides, or in an emergency situation where you need both secure restraint and identification. Since your cat won't run free in a harness, this is the perfect place to hang those rabies and county license tags you collect each year. You may also want to write your

Did You Know?

All kittens' eyes are blue when they first open.

phone number on the harness with an indelible pen. The only way to keep a cat on a leash is by using a figure-eight harness. This is a simple, continuous strap of nylon or leather that crosses over the shoulder blades and passes under the neck and behind the hind legs. Because it's all one loop, when a cat rolls and pitches in even the most frantic escape attempt, the harness tightens at just the right spot to keep her from slipping free. Obviously, because she can't escape, it can be a death trap if you let her wear it when she runs loose.

The best cat leash is made of lightweight nylon or canvas. It should be between four and six feet long in order to reach the ground and give your cat a little room to walk. It will take some time to get your cat used to being led, but if you let her adjust to it just a few minutes each day, you'll be doing a cat walk together in no time.

Outdoor Enclosures

The ultimate luxury for a cat is an expansive outdoor play yard. It can give an indoor cat a taste of fresh air. And it can be a safe haven for a cat who lives outdoors, too.

If the play yard will be your cat's primary living quarters, plan to build it as large as you can. But it doesn't have to be fancy. If you're handy, you can build a serviceable enclosure in a weekend, using wood and chicken wire. If you want someone else to do the work, a wide range of cat pens can be ordered from pet stores or mail-order companies. Top-of-the-line enclosures include climbing trees, toys, and even air-conditioned rooms where a cat can, literally, go chillin'.

Whether you build your own cat enclosure or buy one, make sure it includes the following for safety and comfort:

❍ Shade;
❍ Protection from the wind and rain;
❍ An easy way to keep cool, clean water available at all times;
❍ An easy, safe entry for your cats that ensures they won't escape when you go to retrieve them;

○ A door big enough for you to enter to simplify cleaning and maintaining the enclosure;

○ Securely attached fencing to avoid cat escapes or injury;

○ No nails or pieces of wire protruding into the enclosure;

○ Sturdy enough construction to withstand the pawing of marauding dogs;

○ A top to keep cats in and to keep out owls, hawks, and other predators that fly or climb.

Toys

Almost all cats and kittens love to play—all they need is an excuse. If you're on a budget, there's no need to spend big bucks stocking up on cat toys. Just break out some paper bags, toss a ball, or pull a string across the floor. Of course, make sure to hold on to the string and that your cat doesn't swallow it! What's fun to play with isn't always safe to eat.

If you'd rather buy cat gadgets, you'll find a huge selection of toys in any pet store, grocery store, or discount center. When you choose your pet's playthings, you'll want to focus on safety. Dangling strings, loose buttons, and sewn-on bells are likely to be chewed off and swallowed. They could all get stuck in your cat's intestines, which requires emergency surgery. If there's anything that's likely to get loose or chewed off by your cat, simply take the scissors, cut it off, and throw it away. In general, the simpler the toy, the better.

> Almost all cats and kittens love to play—all they need is an excuse.

Homemade Toys

Most toys are inexpensive, but some of the best are completely free. Try these wallet-friendly tricks to delight your kitty:

○ Scatter a few paper bags around the house. Your cat will hide inside, peer out, and gallop away, only to start the game all over again seconds later. Two cats have even more fun—the cat in a bag is a sure lure for a full-blown, frolicking cat attack.

○ Put a Ping-Pong ball in an empty bathtub to give your cat hours of delight. Hint: Take it out at nighttime. It can be a noisy game.

○ Tape a tennis ball to an elastic cord and attach the cord to the ceiling or doorway with a nail. This setup will keep kitty bouncing all day long. It's important to keep the ball just out of Kitty's reach and to make sure that the elastic is securely attached to the ceiling. Keep the elastic out of reach—it may cause an intestinal obstruction if eaten.

○ Crumple up a plain piece of paper. Probably 50 percent of cats will happily fetch for you, and the rest will delight in playing paper hockey across the kitchen floor.

○ Fold some long pipe cleaners in half, twist the top third around to form a head, and then separate out the bottom two-thirds so that they look like legs. You'll have a tempting spider that will tease even sedate cats into play. This toy should not be eaten, so make sure to supervise the "tarantula" play.

○ Play peekaboo with a pillowcase. Many cats love to dive inside, wrestle around, and hide underneath.

Four Top Toys

Ace, Zuke, and Baby are my three ordinary cats living in West River, Maryland. Over the last year they've worked hard to check out the cat toys available on the market. Here's a short list of their favorites.

Hoots
Hoot toys are the pick of the house. Filled with catnip, they seem to have tremendous taste appeal to cats. Every time a Hoot hit the floor, my cat test

Continued from page 84.

panel went crazy. Fat Cat, Inc., the manufacturer, says that the secret is simply "super-duper organic catnip." There are several families (or lines) of Hoots, each designed to be fun for the entire family. If you're political, your cat can chew on Newt Gingrich or Bill Clinton. Or you can let Kitty munch on Really Bad Dogs, the Mother-in-law, or (gulp) the Vet. A new generation of Hoots have a crinkly center, which makes a sound sure to delight even the most sedate cat.

Kitty Fishing Toys

A half-dozen toys on the market let you dangle a toy from a stick or metal wire in front of Kitty. My trio of cat testers dance in anticipation whenever a human reaches in the "cat fishin'" closet, where the alluring toys are kept. Baby, the fattest cat, will quickly go aerobic with a fishing toy. Luke is particularly fond of feathered bait, available on some models. Once he catches an imitation avian, he'll lie on it and guard it from all comers with growls. The household favorite fishing toy, the Purr-fect Feather Toy, is sold by Dermapet, Inc., in Potomac, Maryland. You can choose from either feather or fur lures, and the flexible plastic "pole" contains small balls that make a delightfully enticing noise as cats tug and pull.

Catnip Toys

Not all cats enjoy catnip, but my testers loved all the catnip toys they got their paws on. The best: a large, socklike contraption. Ace found it perfect for full-body play, grasping it her mouth and wrapping her front paws around it as she raked it viciously with her hind paws. Simple bags and the classic mouse were also favorites. The best catnip toys had one thing in common: lots of catnip and a simple, sturdy design.

Balls

No high-dollar items here. Cat tester Ace likes the small foam balls best. They roll well, are silent (so they don't disturb you as you work), and apparently have great mouth appeal since all my testers like to carry them around the house.

Although Ace prefers foam, all three cats will play with just about anything that's round and lightweight—Ping-Pong balls, balls with bells inside, even golf balls. If it's round, it's a go.

Kitty, Come Home!

The days of planning, searching, selecting, and preparing are finally at an end. The house is ready, and your heart is open. It's time to bring Kitty home. To make your cat's first night happy and healthy, here are a few tips.

Timing Is (Almost) Everything

If you can, it's best to bring your new cat or kitten home when you have a little leisure time to spend with him. For working people, this usually means a Friday night or Saturday morning, although any time there's a lull in your hectic schedule will be just fine.

A new cat won't demand your attention every moment of the move-in weekend. But you should be within purring distance while your cat begins the hard work of exploring a new home. If you're bringing home a kitten, make sure you keep your eyes and ears open, too. She's sure to test your kitten-proofing technique, so be prepared to run to her rescue if necessary.

Adult cats typically take their time exploring new surroundings. The average cat will find a comfort zone, such as under a bed, and make cautious forays from this zone. As they explore, a cat's foot pads lay down pheromone-filled trails. Within a few days or months, depending on the cat's boldness, she'll mark the house enough to be comfortable throughout.

Mum's the Word

The first night away from mum and sibs can be lonely, cold, and frightening. To help ease a kitten's transition from nest to house, a company in Colorado has come up with a unique idea. ChilsonRoth Company markets a stuffed cat to act as a surrogate mother. She has a heartbeat powered by batteries and reheatable thermal bags that can be stuffed safely inside to provide motherly warmth. She can also be used to help raise orphan kittens. The price? $24.95.

At the same time the cat is exploring, she's beginning to claim territory. To limit the territory and increase a cat's comfort, many experts suggest keeping your cat confined to one room at first, preferably with a crate inside. It's a great idea. Because most cats need a small, safe haven, the crate will be more appealing on the first day home than in all the days following. Let your cat adjust to the crate in a small room. Once she's comfortably eating and drinking inside it, let her explore the rest of the house.

Kittens aren't such cautious creatures. Their exploration is most likely going to be at breakneck speed, with frequent stops for playing, attacking, and stalking. Don't worry if your kitten is fearless, but do keep a close eye on him to keep him out of trouble. And do encourage him to eat, drink, and nap in his crate.

For many kittens, the first night with you is also the first time they've ever slept without their mother and siblings. Don't be surprised if your kitten gets lonely and screams for attention just about the time you're dozing off. If left alone, most kittens will go back to sleep before long. If you want to lend comfort, be aware that you're starting a habit that will outlast the first night. If you don't mind being at your kitten's meow and paw, you can give her some petting or even bring her to bed with you (where she's probably going to sleep just fine, thanks). Be assured she'll expect the same forevermore.

Hey, I'm Not Alone!

If you have other animals, introducing a new cat can rock the boat. Other cats are especially prone to emotional upset, which they can show by stalking, growling, swatting, screaming, hissing, or even attacking the new cat. Or they may simply increase territory marking and take up spraying urine in the house.

To minimize newcomer conflict, put the new cat in his room and close the door. The gap under common wooden doors gives just enough room to exchange smells and greetings without risking a stormy confrontation. In most cases, your cats will be playing patty-cake under the door within the week. Kittens will sometimes become friends within hours. Once play begins, a cautious face-to-face meeting is usually successful. It's safest, however, to confine the cats in carriers or restrain them with a leash and harness just in case the requisite impudent sniffing and sizing up leads to a fight.

When a new cat comes in the house, remember that he's the one expected to do most of the adjusting. Like the furniture and stairs, your other pets are part of the scenery and must be accepted. The best way to help a cat learn his position is to be supportive of the old cats. In other words, if Old Gray hisses, stay out of it. If you run in and protect Newby, he'll think that the other cats don't count, and a serious conflict will almost certainly result. If bodily harm is imminent, separate both cats, but refuse to take the new cat's side. Nine times out of ten, the cats begin to get along the moment *after* the newcomer shows due respect for the old-timer's rank and disposition.

Indoors or Out?

According to a poll by the American Pet Products Manufacturers' Association, 60 percent of cat owners reported keeping their cats strictly indoors. Despite the fact that most veterinarians and humane organizations strongly recommend an indoor life, many cats live outdoors at least part-time.

It's true that outdoor cats have more freedom. They can hunt and roam and have the appearance of liberty. A lot of owners think a cat sleeping in the garden or stalking sheaves of grass makes a pretty picture.

As idyllic as an outdoor life seems, however, the freedom comes with a price. The average life span of the modern indoor cat is approximately 15 years. Outdoor cats, on average, survive about two years. And in those two years they're likely to host fleas and worms, including heartworms. They'll get into fights, be chased by dogs, and face off, for better or worse, with neighborhood kids.

When a cat is left alone, you can count on it to kill birds, use gardens and sandboxes as litter boxes, and leave footprints on clean cars. Many outdoor cats die from ingesting antifreeze, lawn fertilizer, rat poison, and weed killer. Owls and hawks enjoy the occasional snack of fresh cat when they can find it. And raccoons and foxes, both of which carry rabies, won't hesitate to fight a cat.

The average outdoor cat visits the vet five times more frequently than a cat who lives indoors. Car accidents, a bite from a cat carrying feline immunosuppressive virus, or a child's pellet gun can either kill a cat or make for major suffering—as well as major medical bills. If you're going to let your cat outside, set up a medical savings account for him. You'll need it.

On the other hand, safety can be boring. Indoor cats don't get much exercise, so some become lazy and fat. High-energy cats sometimes turn to destructive behaviors—such as couch shredding and curtain climbing—to keep their bodies fit. Bored cats can also become depressed or anxious and might harm themselves by constant licking or taking up noxious habits like sucking wool—a compulsion that can leave your cat sick and your clothes in tatters. A few might turn surly or aggressive to their owners, while many simply lose their sparkle, sitting like a lump for hours and showing little interest in petting or play.

Fortunately, there are ways to enrich an indoor cat's world. Provide plenty of toys. Play with and pet her when you're home. Consider getting a second cat as a companion. You can put a perch on the inside of a closed window to let your cat get a view of the world outside or build her a protected play yard. You might even buy her a feline videotape filled with birds and mice. Even without these aids, the vast majority of cats are quite content to stay inside.

4

Food for Thought

In This Chapter

○ Special Pets with Special Needs
○ Feline Nutrition Primer
○ Feeding for Health

Now that you've brought your kitten home, you'll naturally want to give him a good meal. But literally hundreds of diets line the shelves of pet stores, supermarkets, and veterinary hospitals. You can buy canned, frozen, and dry foods through mail order or on the Internet. Some books even tout home-cooked creations. What's a caring cat owner to do?

Special Pets with Special Needs

When it comes to nutrition, it's natural to treat cats like the creatures we're most familiar with—dogs and people. But the cat, nutritionally speaking, is unique. The tiny tiger in your house is a direct descendant of wild ancestors who fed for millennia on meaty meals of birds, rodents, and insects. Even when cats came to live near humans over 10,000 years ago, they didn't come to share our table. They came to feed on the rodents that we attract.

Scientists call the cat an *obligate carnivore*. This means that cats require meat in order to survive. Because of their nutritional heritage, feline bodies simply cannot meet their basic needs from plants in the same way dogs and people can. Cats are not—and cannot be—vegetarians.

In this chapter we'll take a look at what makes a cat's nutritional needs so different and how to nourish the hunter in your house.

Feline Nutrition Primer

If you're familiar with the basic building blocks of food—protein, carbohydrates, fats, vitamins, minerals, and water—then you've got a good start on understanding feline nutrition. Although these building blocks are the same for all species, cats have very specific needs.

Protein

All animals require protein to grow, build muscle, and make energy. Other species can get plenty of protein from plants, but the best protein source for a cat is meat. Meat protein is rich in feline-required amino acids and micronutrients.

> Other species can get plenty of protein from plants, but the best protein source for a cat is meat.

Essential Amino Acids

Amino acids are the building blocks of proteins. Inside the body, they help build muscle and keep metabolism running smoothly. Although most animals can create their own amino acids from materials found in plants, cat bodies have become so dependent on good-quality meat protein that they have lost the ability to create several of their own amino acids, particularly taurine, arginine, leucine, threonine, and methionine. Taurine and arginine are the most important.

Taurine In the late 1980s veterinarians at the University of California at Davis discovered that a form of serious heart disease in cats could be completely cured by feeding cats a diet rich in taurine. Soon after, the veterinarians found that a type of blindness could be avoided with taurine-rich diets, too. These observations spurred research that proved that felines' need for dietary taurine is much higher than that of any other species.

Most raw meats are very high in taurine, but plants are low. What's more, plant fibers, found in cereal-based foods, can actually bind taurine, making it impossible for the pet to use the taurine in his food. Most animals can make their own taurine by recycling the bile acid inside their own bodies. Cats can't do this very well, so they must eat what they need.

Arginine Cats have a very high need for arginine in their diet. Other animals can make this amino acid from other amino acids, but cats can't. Muscle meat is naturally very high in arginine, and all commercial cat foods are well supplemented, but dog foods are not.

Arginine is used to control the buildup of ammonia, a waste product created during digestion of a meal. Food creates metabolic waste; the cat needs arginine to break the waste down.

When a cat eats a large meal low in arginine—such as a bowl of dog food—her ammonia levels soar. This can cause vomiting, staggering, difficulty breathing, convulsions, and coma—and it can happen within just a few hours. To avoid this ugly scenario, make sure your cat eats food formulated for cats. While a little nibble of dog food isn't dangerous, lunch at the doggie bowl can be deadly.

Fats

Most people think of *fat* as a bad word. In fact, fat plays an extremely important role in health and nutrition. Besides being a very compact form of energy, fats are essential to help certain vitamins, such as D, E, A, and K, enter the body. Fats are also used to create several important hormones. Plus fats contain essential fatty acids, which are required to keep a cat's coat glowing and her immune system strong.

Unlike many animals, cats are excellent at breaking down and using the energy found in fat. Palatability tests show that cats prefer foods that are made up of about 15 percent fat. The fat content of commonly fed commercial food ranges from 8 percent to 23 percent fat. The optimum level for a cat varies. For example, if she's a growing kitten, very active, or nursing a litter of kittens, she'll do best eating the higher-fat diets. On the other paw, if she's older or obese or has pancreatic problems, low fat is the way to go. Since your cat is utterly unique, let your vet advise you on the ideal food for her.

Essential Fatty Acids
Animals need three fatty acids to stay healthy: linoleic acid, linolenic acid, and arachidonic acid. The first two are found in

common foods, but only meat contains high levels of arachidonic acid. Most animals convert linoleic acid into arachidonic acid, but cats, whose body is designed for high meat consumption, can't do this. They must get all three fatty acids from their diet.

Another important type of fatty acids are the omega fatty acids. There are three kinds. Omega-6 fatty acids are found in linoleic acid. Omega-3 fatty acids are hard to find in most plants but are part of flax oil, soybean oil, and many types of marine fish oil. Omega-9 fatty acids are found primarily in olive oil.

Cats need a diet rich in both Omega-6 and omega-3 fatty acids. (Their needs for omega-9 are unknown.) Omega-3 fatty acids help create a rich coat, slow inflammation, and control allergies. Omega-6 fatty acids are needed to keep the coat shiny, but in very large amounts it can increase allergic and inflammatory reactions, potentially making summer itches and some diseases—such as inflammatory bowel disease (IBD) or arthritis—worse.

Nutritionists are working to discover the ideal ratio of omega-6 to omega-3. A 5-to-1 ratio is thought to be ideal for optimal health, although some researchers cite 10 to 1 as acceptable. Veterinarians are using lower ratios (less omega 6 and more omega-3) to help treat severe allergies and certain types of cancer. The average commercial diet in 1998 had a ratio closer to 25 to 1 (much more omega-6 than omega-3). Most cats seem to thrive on commercial

Did You Know?

A cat's tongue consists of small, fleshy "hooks" which come in handy when tearing up food.

diets, but if your cat is plagued by allergies or inflammatory diseases, such as IBD or arthritis, you may want to lower the ratio of omega-6 to omega-3. You can do this by reading labels to find a

Veterinary Nutrition

As if eight years spent hitting the books in undergraduate and graduate courses aren't grueling enough, many veterinarians take their education a step further. They study the science of animal nutrition.

To be certified by the American College of Veterinary Nutrition, a veterinarian must have at least one full year practicing medicine, take a residency program in veterinary nutrition, publish two papers in a scientific journal, and submit three clinical case reports for evaluation to the college. The vet then sits through a three-hour exam in basic veterinary medicine, a three-hour exam in veterinary nutrition, *and* a three-hour exam on ration evaluation, ration formulation, and clinical problem solving.

Sounds tough, right? Absolutely, but these vets really know their calories—and much more. If your cat has a complicated dietary need or if you want to formulate a healthy diet on your own, don't rely on the advice of a pet food salesman. Give the ACVN a call to get a referral to a veterinary nutritionist near you (see the Resources section at the end of the book).

more favorable food or by adding fish oil—an excellent source of omega-3 fatty acids—to your cat's food. You'll want to check with your veterinarian for proper doses for your cat.

Carbohydrates

If you love your pasta and bread, you may be surprised to find that cats don't share our need for starch and sugars. If a cat never saw a potato, slice of bread, or corn kernel, he'd live just fine, say the experts. Feline bodies use relatively little of the carbohydrates found in most commercial cat foods. Cats live best on diets high in both protein and fat, with small amounts of carbohydrate thrown in for a little extra energy.

Pet food manufacturers use a lot of carbo-rich cereal in their diets, primarily for economic reasons—carbohydrates are one of the cheapest ingredients available. Cooking during processing makes the carbos *slightly* easier for a cat to digest than raw cereals, but they're still considered almost totally indigestible. Up to 35 percent of the calories in many commercial cat foods are from carbohydrates. Although cats can eat this without apparent harm, it would be ideal to feed them much less.

Some diets have indigestible fiber, such as cellulose, added to them. Although it doesn't nourish cats, the added fiber can help prevent constipation or make an obese cat feel full faster so he will eat fewer calories. Diabetic cats can also benefit from a diet high in indigestible fibers. These foods are usually marketed as reduced calorie diets.

Vitamins

According to my dictionary, the word *vitamin* comes from the Latin word for *life* combined with *amine*, the scientific term for a certain organic chemical compound that contains nitrogen. In other words, vitamins are nitrogen-containing chemicals that are essential for life. Cats need the same vitamins as other animals, but they do have some unique vitamin needs as well.

Fat-Soluble Vitamins
Fat-soluble vitamins are found naturally in many foods and require some fat in the diet to be absorbed into the body.

Vitamin A   Just like in dogs and people, vitamin A is essential for healthy skin, eyes, and reproduction in cats. Most animals can convert beta-carotene, which is found in many vegetables, into vitamin A. Since cats aren't carrot eaters, they can't make the conversion. Cats must eat fully formed vitamin A, which is found in meat and liver as well as added to commercial cat food.

Despite the importance of this vitamin, you should resist the urge to supplement it in your cat's diet unless your veterinarian specifically instructs you to do so. An overdose of vitamin A can cause crippling bone deformities and severe gingivitis. It's inadvisable to feed your cat liver because it contains a lot of vitamin A, but if you do, limit your cat's consumption to about two ounces a week.

Vitamin D   Vitamin D plays an important role in calcium movement into and out of cells and in maintaining bone strength in both cats and kittens. Too little vitamin D (or an imbalance in the minerals calcium and phosphorus) can cause rickets, a disease characterized by thin, crooked bones.

Kittens have a higher requirement for vitamin D than cats, but the requirement for a healthy grown feline is quite low. Cats easily get enough vitamin D in their diet or by creating their own from the effects of the sun on their skin. As a result, rickets from a vitamin D deficiency are very rare in cats.

Some misinformed people have touted large doses of vitamin D as a "natural" rodent control. Unfortunately, they also suggest that it's safe for cats. Nothing could be further from the truth. Cholecalciferol—the bioactive vitamin D found in Rampage and Quintox— is a potent rat poison that kills by causing a rapid increase in blood calcium. It's as poisonous to a cat as a rat.

Vitamin E   Vitamin E, whose chemical name is alpha-tocopherol, acts as an antioxidant, preventing fats from going rancid. Adequate vitamin E is needed for healthy skin, muscles, and nerves and for normal reproduction.

In 1953 veterinarians reported an alarming condition in cats fed a certain type of canned food. Affected cats became lethargic and extremely sore, then their fat turned lumpy. Some cats died. When investigated by biopsy, the fat often looked dirty and yellow. Today we call this disease steatitis, pansteatitis, or yellow fat disease. It's caused by a cat's eating a diet low in vitamin E but high in tuna, especially the red-meat variety. The tuna oils actually attack the body fat, a process that vitamin E supplementation can stop.

Because vitamin E is found in many common foods, vitamin E deficiency today is rare. Each year a few cats who eat diets extremely high in tuna still develop this deficiency.

Vitamin K   Vitamin K is essential for forming blood clots when a cat is injured or has surgery. Despite its importance, cats don't need to eat it in their diet. The bacteria in a cat's intestines create all of this vitamin the cat needs to stay healthy.

Many of the common rat poisons, such as Rodex, Tomcat, d-Con, and Boot Hill, contain warfarin, diphacinone, brodifacoum, and bromadiolone, which work by preventing bacterial vitamin K from being activated in the liver. Inactive forms don't help clotting, so a cat poisoned by these chemicals can bleed to death. Treatment consists of supplementing with activated vitamin K (a prescription drug) for several weeks.

Water-Soluble Vitamins

Water-soluble vitamins dissolve in water and in the bloodstream. A cat makes many of these herself but requires some fed to her in her diet.

B Vitamins   The B vitamin group contains several vitamins that are essential for a healthy life. Cats need a lot of B vitamins in their diet—about twice as much as dogs. Most commercial cat foods are supplemented with the B vitamin group, so deficiencies are now rare in healthy cats. But when cats refuse to eat or suffer from serious bowel disease, they often can't absorb the B vitamins through their intestines. For these cats veterinarians may choose to supplement the B vitamins with injections or intravenous infusion.

Thiamine (Vitamin B_1)   Thiamine is required for the breakdown of carbohydrates and the proper functioning of the nervous system. Although most commercial cat foods today are well supplemented, thiamine deficiency can still be seen in cats who eat poor-quality cooked diets or large quantities of raw fish. Both cooking and an enzyme in fish called thiaminase destroy the vitamin B_1 in food.

Cats with early signs of thiamine deficiency may look hungry, but they will refuse to eat and often drool. Soon they begin to sway gently when they walk. Over a few days these symptoms soon turn into dizziness, a severely dropped head, and major problems walking. Heart problems can develop. If treated, even severely affected cats usually can return to normal within a day—sometimes within hours.

Riboflavin (Vitamin B_3)   Riboflavin is required for a cat to effectively turn food into energy. It's common in vegetables and meat as well as in commercial cat food, so deficiencies in this vitamin are rare in cats.

Niacin   Most mammals can create niacin, a B vitamin, themselves from tryptophan, an amino acid found in many foods. Cats can't make this conversion and must eat preformed niacin in their diets. Deficiencies in cats fed commercial foods or supplemented foods or eating natural raw-meat diets are rare. Cooked foods might be deficient, so supplementation of home-cooked meals with a balanced multiple B vitamin is wise.

Pyridoxine (Vitamin B₆)   Pyridoxine is found in large amounts in meat and many vegetables. Although cats require this vitamin to make healthy red blood cells and to keep their kidneys healthy, a cat needs a very low amount. Deficiencies are rare but may lead to anemia, calcium oxalate crystals in the urine, which can cause difficult-to-cure bladder stones, and kidney failure.

Pantothenic Acid   Pantothenic acid is very common in most foods, and cats require very small amounts in their diet. This B vitamin helps keep the liver and intestine healthy. Deficiency is not a problem.

Folic Acid   Cats have a low requirement for folic acid. Deficiencies in this vitamin have been created only in the laboratory.

Cyanocobalamin (B₁₂)   Vitamin B_{12} plays important roles in nerve function, maintaining appetite, and red blood cell production. It's absorbed from the small intestine. Gastrointestinal illness, such as diarrhea or inflammatory bowel disease, can cause a deficiency in vitamin B_{12}.

Biotin   Cats use biotin to keep a healthy, sleek coat. A lack of biotin can cause dandruff, dry coat, and miliary dermatitis (pinpoint scabs on the skin). However, almost all foods have adequate supplies of biotin for cats. About the only way a cat can become deficient in bi-

Did You Know?

When a domestic cat chases mice, about one pounce in three results in a catch.

otin is if it's fed raw eggs or dried egg whites. The whites are high in avidin, a substance that destroys biotin.

Choline   Although the requirement for choline, a B vitamin, is extremely low, it may help prevent fatty liver disease. This illness occurs when fat accumulates in the liver, preventing it from functioning properly. Most cats get plenty of choline, but your veterinarian may recommend supplementation if your cat is at risk for fatty liver (this is discussed in Chapter 7, Emergencies and Illness).

Vitamin C   Cats synthesize their own vitamin C and do not need supplements. Despite the current fad of using vitamin C to improve or cure a whole host of problems in man and beast, over-supplementation can cause diarrhea and the formation of calcium oxalate crystals in a cat's urine and kidneys. If you give your cat a vitamin C supplement during times of illness, when vitamin C stores become depressed naturally, use low doses, then stop the supplements as soon as your cat is well. As with any medication, check with your vet for a safe dose.

Minerals

A cat needs many minerals for good health. They are all needed in trace amounts, and most are very easily obtained from both natural and commercial diets.

Although mineral deficiencies are rare, serious problems develop when a well-meaning owner tries to create a natural, all-meat diet for his cat. In nature cats don't eat *just* meat—they also eat the bones of their prey, which are an excellent source of calcium. When a kitten is fed a diet extremely low in calcium, such as all meat, his bones become crooked and painful (rickets). In older cats a calcium-deficient diet can make bones turn brittle so that they break with normal exercise.

Calcium always works in conjunction with phosphorus. Too much of one in the diet results in too little of the other. Don't be tempted to feed a calcium-rich diet or give calcium supplements to your cat without consulting a veterinarian. If you feel the need to supplement, a multiple vitamin-mineral mix marketed for pets is the safest choice.

Water

We don't usually think of water as providing nutrition, but it's the single most important chemical for life. Cats have lived for weeks with little or no food and recovered (don't try this trick at home—starvation is risky for a cat). But it's a rare cat who can live for three days without water.

How much water does your cat need? About one ounce of fresh water per pound of cat each day. For your average 10-pound cat, that means one and a quarter cups a day, while a two-pound kitten needs about one-fourth cup.

> We don't usually think of water as providing nutrition, but it's the single most important chemical for life.

Few cats actually drink quite that much, however. Instead, they fill some of their water requirements by eating canned or moist food or drinking milk and broth. If your cat doesn't seem to be swilling his share but is eating moist foods, you probably don't need to worry. It's essential, however, to keep plenty of clean, fresh water available to your cat at all times.

Feeding Your Feline

Now that you know what nutrients your cat needs, you need to know how to put them all together. There's no one nutrient that's most important. A balanced diet is the key to health.

What Is "Balanced"?

Experts define a balanced diet as one that has the optimal number and proportion of nutrients to give an animal the best-possible health and performance. That sweeping statement sounds simple, but it's pretty hard to nail down those numbers and proportions. Scientists have been studying feline feeds for many decades, yet new discoveries are still being made.

Who Defines "Balanced"?

In the last 10 years a lot of science has focused on cat nutrition. These changes are reflected in the current feline nutrition updating project by the Committee on Animal Nutrition of the National Research Council (NRC), National Academy of Science. This group is *the* authority on canine and feline nutrition, with the most up-to-date facts and figures available worldwide. If you're interested in the facts and figures of feline nutrition, ask for a copy of their latest report (see the Resources section at the end of the book).

The Association of American Feed Control Officials (AAFCO) also defines what constitutes a balanced diet. The AAFCO gets food requirement figures from the NRC and advises pet food manufacturers how to properly balance their rations.

Originally both groups strongly advised testing formulations by feeding trials. In a feeding trial, claims for a food are tested by feeding it to both kittens and cats over a long period and monitoring their health. Unfortunately, in 1985 the AAFCO ended the feed trial requirements, stating that they were too restrictive for manufacturers. Today a pet food can state it's "complete and balanced" if the numbers match one of the AAFCO's formulas. Although most foods based on these calculations will usually meet a cat's nutritional needs, there's no substitute for a feeding trial to ensure that a diet is, in fact, balanced and healthy.

Can I Balance a Diet Myself?

If you can cook for your family, it's logical that you can cook for your cat. That's true, but it can be demanding. The cooking itself isn't hard, but balancing all 43 nutritional requirements of a cat can be difficult to do day after day. If you're willing to do your nutritional homework and can devote the time to creating a diet that suits your cat, not necessarily *your* tastes, home cooking can be healthy and rewarding.

The biggest difficulty in home cooking is developing a balanced diet from ingredients you can easily find. Unless you have a good nutritional computer program designed with cats in mind, it's almost impossible to blend common foods to get proper proportions for all 43 nutrients. If you want to try, order a copy of the NRC guidelines and the book *Bowes & Church's Food Values of Portions Commonly Used*. These publications will give you the tools you need to begin balancing a cat's diet.

Better yet, contact a veterinary nutritionist for advice. She can help you devise a home-cooked program for your cat that meets your personal desires as well as your cat's needs. If you want an all-natural diet, for example, she'll get your

definition of "natural" (there are dozens), then work out your heart's desires. Make sure your nutritionist is a veterinarian who is board certified in nutrition, not a layperson who is a self-proclaimed expert.

Commercial Diets

Because home cooking is tricky, commercial diets are the best answer to most pet owners' needs. They are very easy to feed, are enjoyed by most cats, and are balanced and healthy. The most difficult part of feeding a cat a commercial food is simply choosing one from the thousands available.

Pet food marketing is a $9.4-billion-a-year industry in the United States—and growing, according to the Pet Industry Joint Advisory Council. Most established manufacturers do a good job, but many companies are only chasing a buck, at the cost of your pet's health if necessary. The least reliable companies refuse to do AAFCO trials and may shun frequent chemical analyses of their products simply because of the expense ($10,000 for a feeding trial and $2,000 for an analysis). Their skimping shows up in your pet's health. Avoid diets that aren't AAFCO approved, no matter how appealing the sales pitch.

When I talk to veterinary nutritionists about how to choose cat foods, they keep emphasizing that in today's market the rule is "buyer beware." Although most foods tested in AAFCO trials are excellent, even those trials aren't an absolute guarantee of quality. When choosing cat foods, make sure to ask your veterinarian his opinion of the product. He sees the physical results of all the common cat diets in your area and can tell you which ones to avoid.

Feeding Forms: Canned, Dried, Semi-moist

Most cat owners feed dry food as the main food. It's a good choice. The dry kibble provides some exercise to the jaw and helps scrape the teeth clean. Because it's crunchy and contains some fiber, dry food helps cats to feel full, so they are less likely to get too fat.

Canned foods are tasty for snacks, but few are labeled as complete and balanced, which is necessary for a main diet. Canned foods more often cause diarrhea and foul-smelling stool. They are rich in calories and highly flavorful, so cats who eat a lot of canned foods may tend to get fatter quicker than their kibble-crunching companions. On the positive side, canned foods provide a lot more water and so are easier to eat than dry foods. They are excellent foods for cats who drink only small amounts of water or can't chew well.

Semi-moist foods were the rage just a few years ago, but few are on the shelf today. Semi-moist foods are highly processed and are high in sodium, sugar, and preservatives. Worse, many semi-moist foods were preserved with propylene glycol, a chemical that can cause serious anemia in cats. In 1996 the Food and Drug Administration (FDA) officially stated that this chemical is no longer "generally recognized as safe" in cats. Since then, semi-moist diets have nearly disappeared from the shelves. What remains are semi-moist snacks, which cats adore. They're fine if used as occasional treats but aren't recommended as a steady diet.

People Food

Snacking is an American pastime. We love our candy bars and cookies so much that we think our pets must enjoy snacks, too. And cats don't do much to convince us otherwise. When you crinkle a Frito bag or open some tuna, Tiger is likely to twine around your leg, screaming for his share.

Despite the caterwauling, snacks are no healthier for your cat than they are for you. Chocolate is always a no-no—some cats love the taste, but it's toxic in large doses. Chips are high in fats and carbohydrates and add waist-expanding calories. Even tuna and steak—high-protein, healthy foods—are poor snack items because they tend to be so tasty that your cat will chow down on them and skip his healthier, balanced meals.

If a snack-free world sounds dull, take heart. You *can* give your cat a little nibble here and there without totally ruining her diet or her waist. Pick a low-fat snack that your cat craves—a bit of popcorn, a sliver of turkey, or even a chunk of cantaloupe can drive cats wild. If you keep snacks healthy and infrequent—I recommend they make up no more than 10 percent of a cat's total daily calories—you can share without endangering Tiger's health.

Premium Foods and Grocery Store Foods—Is There a Difference?

To most shoppers, the major difference between generic cat food, national brands bought at a grocery store, and the premium foods sold through veterinarians and pet stores is the price. Generic foods are the cheapest and look surprisingly similar to national and premium brands.

The difference between the cheapest foods and the premiums is very much like the difference between straw and hay. They look alike, and the cost difference is huge. But anyone who has fed a horse straw knows that it's not very nourishing. If you just fed straw, your horse would eat tons of it but not look or feel very good. Just like cats who eat generic foods.

The Cost of Eating

When I was in veterinary school and on a tight budget, I compared the actual cost of a "super-premium" food to that of a good-quality, nutritionally complete nationally named brand bought from the grocery store. When I fed the grocery food to my cats, they ate nearly twice as much, pooped three times as much, and had scurfy coats. When I fed the premium food, my cats nibbled like ladies and had one firm stool each per day, and within the month their coats glowed.

Although the grocery store food cost half as much, the cost of cat food per month was nearly the same because I bought so much more of the cheaper food. On top of that, I bought more litter. And I figured that the healthy glow probably meant at least one less veterinary visit a year. The more expensive brand turned out to be the bargain.

The *actual* cost of a cat food isn't what you pay for it on the shelf. In order to make money on low-priced diets, manufacturers have to substitute inexpensive fillers such as carbohydrates for more expensive, more digestible foods such as meat. The resulting formulas may look good on paper, but your cat may not agree. Your cat will have more stool as she rids her body of the indigestible fillers. Inexpensive foods rarely contain highly digestible nutrients, so you'll have to buy more of it more frequently to make your cat feel full. Because excellent nutrition is the cornerstone to good health, cutting corners is likely to make your cat sick—and raise veterinary bills.

That doesn't mean extravagance will buy you health. Some of the most expensive foods are tiny tins of succulent morsels that are not nutritionally complete. A steady diet of only those little cans will not only break the bank but can ruin a cat's health.

To get the most bang from your buck, pick a diet that your veterinarian likes and whose labeling shows it to be complete, balanced, AAFCO tested, and, preferably, high in meat protein. If your cat doesn't positively glow with health in about two months, switch to another, comparable diet. With a little "feeding trial" of your own, you'll find the perfect diet at the best price.

How to Feed

Almost as important as the food you choose for your cat is how you feed. Although cats can adapt to many schedules, they are creatures of habit. If you can choose a feeding method and stick to it, your cat will thank you.

Free Feeding and Planned Meals—What's Best?

Left to his own whims, a cat will eat frequently—and that may mean 12 to 20 times a day. He's not being a pig; he's just satisfying the needs of his metabolism, which is designed for fre-

quent, small meals the size of a grasshopper or a mouse. Given a cat's metabolic preferences, it's best to simply let him graze. Put out a bowl of dry food once or twice a day, and let him nibble.

Of course, some cats don't handle temptation well. Free feeding can sometimes lead to obesity. If that's the case with your cat, you'll need to measure his daily caloric intake, then divide it into two to four meals each day.

How Many Calories Does My Cat Need?

When you ask your veterinarian how much food your cat needs, be prepared for a little hemming and hawing. He's not being difficult; it's just that each cat is metabolically unique. The calories that turn Tabby into Tubby might barely be enough to keep muscle on your Abyssinian. Your cat's caloric needs depend on her own body's efficiency in breaking down food, her activity level, and her stage of life.

Although the *precise* amount of food your cat needs is unique, scientists have formulas that will give you a close estimate based on the resting energy requirements (RER) of an average cat. From the average RER, you add calories based on activity, life stage, and illness to come up with a good estimate of your cat's daily calorie count.

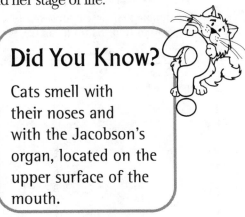

Did You Know?

Cats smell with their noses and with the Jacobson's organ, located on the upper surface of the mouth.

If you loathe calculations, look at the food label. It should offer recommended food portions for an average cat or kitten. These are usually listed in cups or half cups. Be sure to use a measuring cup meant for dry ingredients, not Aunt Nellie's teacup or a Big Gulp cup from the corner minimart. Even when accurately measured, the bag recommendations are usually a little high. If there's food left over at the end of the day, feed a bit less the next day.

Your cat is your final guide to calorie needs. If he's thin and ravenous, he needs more food. If increasing the meal size doesn't satisfy him, then he'll need a veterinary visit to make sure he doesn't have an overactive thyroid gland or other illness. On the other hand, if a cat begins to gain weight, simply cut back his food by 10 percent. With a little fine-tuning you'll soon find the exact proportions that are perfect for your cat.

Kitty Calorie Chart

Calculating a daily calorie count may look difficult—especially if math isn't your best subject. But with the following table, it's really pretty easy. A cat's resting energy requirement (RER) is the amount of calories he uses per day when all he does is lie around. Since most cats are active, the true calorie requirements (the maintenance energy requirements, or MER) are figured by adding numbers based on a cat's activity, age, weight, and hormonal factors.

To make calorie counting simple, locate your cat's weight in the left column below and then the matching RER on the right. At the bottom of the chart find the description that best matches your cat. Then simply use the formula next to the description to find the total calories your cat needs each day.

Cat's weight (pounds)	RER (calories per day)
1	39
2	65
3	88
4	110
5	130
6	149
7	167
8	184
9	201
10	218
11	234
12	250
13	265
14	280
15	295
16	310
17	324
18	339
19	353
20	366

To calculate MER or calories needed each day:
Growing kittens: RER × 2.5
Normal neutered adult cat: RER × 1.2
Intact adult cat: RER × 1.4
Geriatric cat: RER × 1.1
Obesity-prone cat: RER × 1.0
Weight loss: RER × 0.8

Example: A 10-pound cat has an RER of 218 calories a day. If he's a normal neutered cat, he should eat 261.6 calories each day. If he's obese, you may need to *slowly* decrease his calorie intake to 174.4 calories each day. (Consult with a veterinarian before reducing a fat cat below this level.)

Should I Give My Cat Supplements?

If your cat is eating a good-quality commercial food, the answer is "no." There's just no benefit to spending your money to add expensive vitamins and minerals. The manufacturer has already added them.

But if you're home cooking or the food isn't AAFCO labeled, then a balanced vitamin and mineral supplement is probably a good idea. Also, when a cat is sick, her body may have special needs. Your veterinarian can help decide if supplements are wise. Megadosing vitamins, popular in human alternative medicine circles, can be harmful for cats.

Feeding for Health

The Most Common Nutritional Disease

Of all the things that can go wrong with a cat's complex diet, one nutritional disease is epidemic: obesity. Overnutrition resulting in a fat cat is more common than all other nutritional diseases *combined.*

Some people think a fat cat is cute, but in fact he's on the road to physical ruin. Obese cats are at risk for diabetes, heart disease, arthritis, and breathing problems, to name a few. Not only that, but carrying around a thick layer of fat robs a cat of his athletic heritage. A sleek, muscular feline feels much better than the tubby heap that sleeps all day long.

> Some people think a fat cat is cute, but in fact he's on the road to physical ruin.

Growing a Cat

The underlying equation is simple: Ounces are laid down when a cat takes in more calories than he burns off. But the reasons behind obesity can be complex. For example, a cat may have a slow metabolism naturally, or he may be too bored to exercise. If he's suffering from joint problems, he's likely to refuse to romp. Veterinarians have discovered that a few cats may actually develop obsessive-compulsive disorders. These cats can become fixated on food and will go to great lengths to eat endlessly. Medication can help stop their compulsion.

Of course, the major cause of obesity is simply lifestyle. Our little hunters no longer hunt—they just walk a few feet to the dining bowl. As a colleague said to me not long ago, "Hey, if I had gourmet food brought to me daily and all I had to do was walk from the couch to the table, I'd be fat, too."

Losing Weight

Once a cat has become obese, it can be a long battle to retrieve his figure. The direct approach—a severe cut in calories—is more likely to cause liver failure than weight loss. Of course, calories have to be cut, but the trick is to do it very slowly. The ideal weight loss is about 1 percent of body weight a week. That translates to two-tenths of a pound for a 20-pound cat—an amount not measurable on your bathroom scales.

To reduce the weight at the right rate, it's important to start by knowing how many calories go into your cat. Start feeding him in measured cups and note how much he eats. Add up all snacks, too, including the late-night popcorn he shares with you. After a

Feline Body Condition Score

Is that cat fat or thin? Svelte may be in for fashion models, but some people just love a pudgy puss. Although fat facts can be hard to face, cats who are either too fat or too thin are often unhealthy—or become that way quickly. The following table is widely used by veterinarians to assess a cat's weight condition.

Score	Classification	Characteristics
1	Very thin	The ribs and the points of the hips are felt easily. They feel hard and bonelike. The belly is tucked up, with a marked waist when seen from above.
2	Underweight	The ribs and points of the hips are easily felt, with a very minimal fat cover. An obvious waist can be seen from above.
3	Ideal	The ribs can be felt easily but do not feel extremely hard. There is a slight, soft fat layer over them. The points of the hips can be felt but are well padded. A small waist can be seen from above and there is a minimal pad of fat between the hind legs.
4	Overweight	The ribs are hard to feel distinctly but can be recognized with a little prodding. There is little or no waist. The stomach is round, and there is a noticeable pad of fat between the hind legs.
5	Obese	The ribs area is very difficult to feel. The chest is soft and covered with fat. There is no waist, and the belly is rounded. There is a prominent fat pad between the legs and there may be soft, fatty deposits on the back, face, and legs.

Calorie Content of Favorite Foods

The following table is hardly complete but offers a quick rundown of the calorie count of some of the most popular dry food brands. If you don't see your kitty's favorite kibble listed or to get calorie counts for canned food, check with the manufacturer. Their phone number should be on the label, and most are happy to give out calorie counts over the phone. Note: *Kilocalorie* (kcal) is the scientifically correct term for the energy found in food. When people talk about diets, *calorie* is the popularly used shorthand term for kilocalorie.

Regular Diets

Purina Cat Chow	345 kcal/cup
Meow Mix	360
Kit and Kaboodle	372
Purina One Special Formula	360
Friskies Beef and Liver	343
Friskies Gourmet	338
Chef's Blend	330
Alpo Gourmet	303
Science Diet Savory Recipe Original	503
Healthblend Feline Adult	489
Nutro Max Cat	420

Light and Senior Formulas

(Some companies market their senior or mature cat diets as low-calorie foods.)

Cat Chow Mature	323 kcal/cup
Friskies Senior	308
Science Diet Light Formula	243
Healthblend Feline Geriatric	292
Nutro Max Cat Senior	380
Nutro Max Cat Lite	329

Veterinary Weight Loss Diets

Purina Veterinary Diet OM-Formula Feline	283 kcal/ cup
Hill's r/d	226
Hill's w/d	246
Waltham Calorie Control Cat	228

Ten Tips to Keep Tabby Trim

1. Keep him from getting pudgy in the first place. If the scales start to tip, cut back *before* he gets fat.

2. Feed a good-quality cat food. It will ensure he's getting the nutrients he needs and will help him feel full.

3. Don't overfeed. Check out the charts in this book to estimate what he needs each day, then stick to it.

4. Encourage exercise. Play with him for at least 10 minutes twice a day.

5. Hold the snacks—or at least substitute. Offer puffed rice instead of cheese twists, for example, or cantaloupe instead of chips.

6. Add up the calorie count of any snacks given, and figure them into the cat's daily intake.

7. Keep Kitty out of the kitchen when you prepare food—it increases her appetite and encourages snacking.

8. Feed her several small meals instead of one or two big ones—she'll be less hungry and less likely to overeat.

9. Keep an eye on her physique. Use the charts to estimate the body-conditioning score (BCS) and keep a record of BCS as well as weight.

10. If her appetite can't be satisfied, take her to the vet. She may be sick or have an obsessive-compulsive disorder. Either way, she can be treated.

week of calorie counting, reduce his intake by 10 percent. You can do this by using low-calorie food, feeding less of his ordinary diet, or cutting out snacks.

At the same time, add some exercise to the daily routine. You can dangle a toy in front of him or toss a wad of paper in a game of fetch. A simple calorie-cutting exercise is to place part of each day's kibble in several paper bags, then scatter them around the house. This trick also banishes boredom by turning Tabby back into a hunter. A similar trick is to put half of a meal at the bottom of the steps and half at the top.

If your cat shows no appreciable weight loss in four weeks, you can cut her intake back by another 10 percent. But when the calories begin to fall below your cat's resting energy requirement based on her current weight, it's safest to monitor her progress with your veterinarian.

Diets to Fight Disease

What a cat eats affects her entire body. Not only can feeding the wrong food make a cat ill but feeding the right food can actually fight disease. If your cat is suffering from such diseases as diabetes, allergies, kidney failure, lower urinary tract disease, or liver disease, her health can be improved with the proper diet. Ask your veterinarian for suggestions. He might offer a prescription diet, direct you to products on the store shelf, or suggest home cooking.

If your cat has kidney disease, you may be tempted to pick up one of the diets that bill themselves as promoting urinary tract health. That's a common mistake. These diets treat or prevent feline *lower* urinary tract disease, which is the formation of stones or crystals in the urine. They actually can be harmful for a cat with *kidney* disease. If you're tempted to use a diet that carries health-promoting claims, ask your veterinarian if it's appropriate for your cat's medical problems before you open the bag.

Feeding Multiple Cats

Tabby's tubby, Callie's a kitten, and Randy is an old cat with well-controlled kidney dis-

Nutritional Diseases of Cats

Veterinarians recognize a host of problems caused by nutritional deficiencies. They also suspect many more diseases can be brought on or worsened by improper nutrition.

Nutritional Deficiencies Causing Serious Disease

Arginine   Taurine
B vitamins   Vitamin E
Potassium

Suspected Nutritional Diseases

Hyperthyroidism
Pancreatitis
Renal disease

Diseases Treated by Dietary Modification

Cancer	Liver failure
Diabetes	Lower urinary tract disease
Diarrhea	Obesity
Food allergies	Pancreatitis
Heart disease	Steatitis
Inflammatory bowel disease	Vomiting
Kidney disease	

ease. They each have special dietary needs. To paraphrase a cliché, there's more than one way to feed a cat, so it's entirely possible to manage all three perfectly well. All it takes is a little ingenuity.

Randy's diet is the most important—kitten chow or diet food just won't do. He needs to have the right food and have it out at all times to encourage his waning appetite. Put a bowl of his prescription diet down inside an empty kitchen or bathroom cabinet. Prop the door open with a wedge of plastic foam, then narrow

Natural Foods

It only makes sense: A cat should eat the food that his body is *meant* to eat. For a cat, whose metabolism is tightly bound to a high-meat diet, a natural diet is particularly appealing.

But what, exactly, is *natural?* The word means "of nature," so in its purist form a natural diet would imitate what a cat eats in nature. For a cat that means mice, rats, birds, and insects. Not a very appealing mix, especially if we allow our little hunters to eat them raw, the way nature intended.

Even if we could tolerate all this gore in our house, a raw "natural" diet is risky. Mice and rats can carry hanta virus, bacteria, and other diseases. Birds harbor salmonella, which can cause a severe intestinal illness. Even substituting human meats doesn't help much. Unless the meats are cooked, beef, pork, fish, and chicken carry disease, too. In nature, natural doesn't always mean healthy.

On the whole, today's cat foods are much safer than a cat's ancestral natural diet of rodents, bugs, and birds. The average life span of a domesticated cat today hovers around 15 years, with many cats living to be over 20 years of age. Feral cats, who eat a wild diet, have an average life span of two years. Good-quality commercial diets aren't ruinous to health.

The ideal food would be complete, balanced, and easy to feed and meet a cat's nutritional needs without risking disease—or requiring the feeding of live victims. Modern commercial foods meet these criteria.

But commercial foods should be improved. To be closer to a cat's traditional food, the ideal pet food would have fewer carbohydrates and more meat than is currently popular. Pet food would also use only ingredients that are wholesome before processing, avoiding rendered meat products, which often come from sick animals. It also makes sense to avoid synthetic chemical concoctions that are not part of a cat's natural diet, such as the propylene glycol that causes illness in cats eating semi-moist food. In some circles, these changes would constitute "natural." In fact, the current AAFCO definition of the word focuses on the lack of synthetic chemicals, not the closeness to the bird, bug, and rodent diet.

the opening by tying a string from the handle to the inner latch. Until Tubby gets thin, she can't get in, but Randy can eat at will.

Of course, Callie will get in, too, but the kidney diet won't hurt her. It doesn't have enough calories, however, so you'll want to supplement with a couple of meals of kitten food each day. Set her down in the bathroom with a bowl of kitten chow mixed with a little canned food. Close the door for fifteen minutes and voilà—a well-nourished kitten.

To get Tubby to eat only low-cal chow, you have several choices. You can be at her beck and paw, feeding her four to 10 private meals a day to fill her up. (Randy shouldn't eat more than a few bites of this food.) Or you can buy an automatic feeder. Keep the meals small and frequent, and soon Tubby will be awaiting the moment when the feeder opens up. Or purchase a pet door with an identity sensor. Only the cat wearing the ID tag can get through and eat the diet food.

5

Keeping Kitty Well

In This Chapter

- ○ Meet Your Veterinarian
- ○ The Well-Kitten Visit
- ○ The Inside Scoop on Preventive Health

Now that Kitty's nestled into your home and nibbled a few good meals, it's time to visit the vet. Ideally, you should schedule your cat's first visit within a week of adoption. At this visit you'll meet your cat care team, Kitty will get a thorough exam, and you'll learn how to help your cat lead a long and healthy life.

Meet Your Veterinarian

Besides you, your veterinarian is the most important person in your cat's life. She will strive to keep him healthy but also will guide him through the bumps and bruises that come with living. She'll be his internist, dentist, radiologist, surgeon, nutritionist, and behaviorist—to name a few of her skills. She can also help ease suffering when the end of life comes. A caring, competent veterinarian can make a huge difference in the length and quality of a cat's life.

How to Choose the Best Vet

Most people choose a vet for two superficial reasons: price and convenience. For some, the closest clinic is the first choice. Other people are willing to drive across town in search of the cheapest vaccination. Although convenience and low cost are nice, the most important features of a veterinarian are harder to measure: caring, compassion, and competence.

Because caring, compassion, and competence are hidden assets, it may take several visits before you completely size up your veterinarian's skills. But you can get a few clues before you even shake hands with the man (or woman) in the white coat. You'll want to make sure to size up his staff, too, since cat care is a team event.

Caring

It's possible to find a terrific veterinarian hiding inside a dumpy office, but it's unusual. Cleanliness inside and out reflects a caring attitude. A veterinarian may not own his own building, so he may have no control over the paint peeling outside. But he does have control over what goes on inside. At minimum the hospital should have clean windows, neat curtains, and scrubbed floors.

When entering a clinic, take a deep sniff. If the air smells fresh, it's a very good sign. On the other hand, the smell of medicines and tomcat urine can be almost impossible to hide, so a slight off smell should probably be ignored. If the hospital is running an ozone machine—an air cleaner that cleans by energizing oxygen—leave immediately. (Ozone machines are usually small boxes that look like stereo speakers.) The doctor either doesn't care much about the health of you or your cat or is ignorant of medical facts. Ozone is a strong free radical and can damage the respiratory lining, especially in old or asthmatic cats. These machines can remove odors but should be turned on *only* when the hospital is empty.

Caring hospitals are concerned about safety. Electrical plugs will be covered if they are within the reach of children or pets. Emergency exits will be clearly marked. You should also see evidence of an active fire safety program, such as sprinklers overhead. Not only does ignoring safety mark the hospital as uncaring, it also should be taken as a warning—it may not be a safe place to leave a pet overnight.

Clues to caring can be found in the exam room, too. The instruments the veterinarian uses on your pet—the otoscope (to examine your pet's ear) and thermometer, for example—should be clean and sanitary. Also, be sure to check the dates on any medications that are left sitting out. If they're out of date, you know you've found a hospital that cares more about the cost of replacing old goods than your pet's health.

Compassion

Compassion begins with the front staff. In the best hospitals, the receptionist will greet you courteously and quickly. It's a particularly good sign if she knows your name—and your cat's—by the second visit. In very large hospitals, however, such neighborliness

can be hard to come by, so courteous efficiency may be the best you'll come by in even the best megadoctor office.

When your animal is truly ill, the staff of the compassionate hospital will help ease the difficult time. They may share with you their wishes for your cat's recovery or express sympathy about your situation. When you call with a question or to check on your hospitalized cat, the compassionate staff won't say, "I don't know; call back later." Instead they'll say, "Let me check on that for you."

Of course, the most important element in the compassion puzzle is the veterinarian. Not only will a compassionate vet treat you with respect, but he'll respect your *cat,* too. He'll show this by using gentle words and calm movements and giving your cat the occasional pet. Of course, if Kitty is Lucifer reincarnate and lunges for the throat, your vet will have to move quickly. But a compassionate cat doc won't indulge in retaliation—he'll simply go about his business as calmly as possible, even if he must wear thick leather gloves to protect himself from Lucifer's fangs.

> Not only will a compassionate vet treat you with respect, but he'll respect your *cat,* too.

Competence

A competent veterinarian is skilled at what she does, keeps up-to-date with new innovations, and thinks through health issues that affect your cat. Competence is *not* the ability to tell jokes and stories or be otherwise personable. Although it's great to have a vet who treats you as a friend, it really reflects nothing about medical skills.

You'll find a few clues to a veterinarian's competence. One visible clue is the medical library. If the shelves are stocked with fairly new books on medical issues and a couple of medical jour-

A Special Kind of Veterinarian

Feline medicine is a relatively new specialty. Less than 30 years ago veterinary curricula centered on farm animals, with a little dog medicine thrown in. Other than spaying, neutering, vaccinating, and worming, cats were pretty much ignored. Today the world of feline medicine is booming.

The American Association of Feline Practitioners was formed in the feline dark ages, about 28 years ago. The organization's prime goal was to expand the medical knowledge and care of the cat. Through their untiring efforts the American Board of Veterinary Practitioners—a group that certifies high achievement in specialty skills—recently recognized feline practice as a bona fide specialty. Veterinarians certified by this board have undergone rigorous training and testing and earned the title of feline specialist.

Although many general practitioners do a terrific job, feline specialists and AAFP members concentrate their skills on cats. Not every town has a cat-only hospital, but if one is nearby, consider checking it out. Also, if your regular vet has trouble diagnosing your cat's problem, insist on a referral to a cat specialist.

nals, you probably have a winner. If, however, the shelves bulge with books on practice management and investments, you can bet the hospital priority is the dollar sign. If there's no library at all, it doesn't bode well for medical competence. Even the most brilliant mind can't store the sum of veterinary knowledge.

The state licensing board can give you another clue. Although the exact name varies, all 50 states have a legal body that enforces the state veterinary practice act and issues veterinary licenses. These boards are created to protect the consumer, not the veterinarian. They should readily tell you if there have been any formal actions or complaints against a veterinarian. The American Veterinary Medical Association can give you the phone number of your state board (see the Resources section at the end of the book).

You can also get a clue to a vet's competence by asking questions. One of the best questions is to ask how he decides what vaccines to give a cat. Nonthinking vets vaccinate by rote: every animal gets the same vaccines on a set schedule, and usually a lot of them. The thinking veterinarian, on the other hand, has a flexible schedule depending on a cat's needs. If your veterinarian offers a schedule based on your cat's disease risks and can explain those risks, then you've found a competent veterinarian.

The Cat Care Team

Feline health is a team game, and it takes at least three to play: you, your cat, and your veterinarian. Your veterinarian is highly skilled and is an expert in medicine and cat care. He's essential for your cat's health. Your intuition, skills, and love are also vital for getting and keeping your cat well. A good veterinarian doesn't work for you; he works *with* you.

In the ideal team your veterinarian designs preventative care to keep your cat well, makes diagnoses, performs difficult medical care, and forms a treatment plan. You decide if you can work with the treatment plan, then perform home medications and therapy and keep up a line of communication with the doctor. You work together in the best interest of your cat. If your cat is cooperative, it makes the job easier for everyone. But her basic job is simply to get well.

During your first visits, see if your veterinarian is willing to be a real team player. Can you call for simple advice, or do you have to make an appointment every time you have a question? Does he talk to you and respect your role in decision making or just pop your cat full of injections, with no explanations given? To do

Questions to Ask Your Vet

Ask questions such as those listed below to help you get to know your prospective vet better.

○ What are your clinic's hours and where are you located?

○ How many vets work at the clinic? Can I request to see the same vet each time I visit or will I see whomever is available?

○ What type of equipment do you have on-hand at the clinic? If you do not have certain equipment, where would you send my cat to receive treatment? What is that facility's reputation?

○ Do you have a lab on-site or do you send out for test results? How quickly are results available?

○ Do you offer any add-on services, such as boarding or grooming?

○ What are the average fees for check-ups, spaying/neutering, vaccinations, etc.? Do you offer a wellness program or a multi-pet discount?

○ Are you a member of the American Association of Feline Practitioners (AAFP) or board certified in Feline Medicine by the American Board of Feline Practitioners?

the best for your cat, you have to be fully informed, so don't settle for information blackout. If one doctor downplays your part on the team, there's another one close by who will treat you better.

Emergency Services

When accidents happen in the middle of the night, it's essential to have emergency care close at hand. Veterinarians used to not only work 10 to 12 hours each day but answered all the emergency calls

Questions Your Vet May Ask You

○ Is this your first cat?

○ What are your feelings on spaying/neutering? (Cats who are pets and are not going to be bred should be spayed or neutered. This helps prevent over-population and also is healthier for your cat.)

○ Is your cat going to live indoors, outdoors, or a little of both?

○ What do you feed your cat?

○ What types of toys does your cat play with? How do you play with your cat? (Remember, never use your hands to roughhouse with a kitten or cat.)

○ Are you crate-training your cat?

○ Do you have any questions concerning disease prevention, nutrition, etc.?

themselves. This personal service sounds nice—until you consider that a doctor who doesn't sleep can't perform her best during the day, when her skills are most on the line.

If your veterinarian doesn't take emergencies, don't hold it against her—as long as a good emergency hospital is close by. In small communities without an emergency hospital, several veterinarians generally rotate on-call nights. If this is the case in your town, make sure you get a doctor who participates with the group. It's not necessary that your own veterinarian see your animal in an emergency, but she must provide clear instructions as to who will.

The best vets, however, generally make exceptions to the "no emergency" rules. You'll want to be able to reach your own doctor if your cat is under intensive therapy for a serious condition, such as diabetes or cancer. The hospital should also provide rou-

tine treatments on weekends for short-term therapies that require medical expertise, such as infusing subcutaneous solutions
for cats in kidney failure. If the veterinarian will make arrangements for personal care on a case-by-case basis, she's a real team
player. Keep her.

The Cost of Medicine

After a visit to the veterinarian, your cat may feel better, but your
own wallet will be a bit thinner. There's no doubt that it costs
money to care for your cat. But compared to human medicine,
cat care is a real bargain.

Recently I sat in my dentist's chair. As he sized up the thousands of dollars he'd be earning in the next couple of months, he
started chatting. "Man, you vets have it made!" he said. "It cost
my friend $200 just to get his cat's teeth cleaned the other day."
When we listed the work, it turned out that the cat had preoperative lab tests, an hour of general anesthesia, heart monitoring,
three extractions, ultrasonic scaling, and fluoride treatment.
Turns out that my dentist would have charged over $2,000 to do
the same work on a person. And he would have substituted local
anesthesia for general.

Veterinarians are the lowest-paid health care professionals. According to the American Veterinary Medical Association, the average starting salary of a veterinarian in 1998 was $36,000. Only
about 80 percent get any type of benefits, including vacation, and
fewer than 70 percent are offered health insurance. Only 40 percent had sick leave. At the same time, the average indebtedness at
time of graduation from veterinary college was over $60,000.

Practice owners do a bit better, but it takes time. A hospital
owner rarely draws a salary for the first three to four years of
business. He lives in debt until the practice begins to pay for

itself. Even in a very efficient, established practice, the average owner is lucky to take home 17 percent of his gross income. That translates to about $2.50 on each $15 vaccination—or about what you'd tip a waitress for a good meal. The rest goes to cover operating expenses, buy medications, and pay his support staff.

Veterinarians don't like to talk about how little they make or how hard they work. They figure it just comes with the job. But the next time you think your veterinarian is getting rich, take the time to compare his services with a human hospital's. Equal work doesn't translate into equal pay.

Veterinarians go through rigorous schooling similar to that of human doctors. You are paying for the expertise of a highly skilled and knowledgeable professional. The vet must also cover the overhead costs of running a clinic, including rent or a mortgage for the building itself, employees' wages, equipment, supplies, insurance, and utilities. These costs add up and are reflected in the price you pay for your veterinarian's services.

What if an emergency happens and you don't think you can afford your vet's bills? By all means, be up-front about your situation. Some clinics accept credit cards, while others may set up payment plans in dire situations. However, do not take advantage of your vet's kindness. You should be prepared to pay for lifelong medical expenses before you buy a cat. Distress over the expense of veterinary services does not provide a legitimate reason for not paying your bill. Your vet may not offer payment options because of this potential for abuse.

Paying the Price

Although veterinary fees are a great bargain compared to human medical costs, it may not seem like it when you see the bill. If you're like most people, a visit to your physician rarely costs more than a $10 or $15 co-payment since your insurance picks up most of the tab. But those dollar signs on your veterinarian's bill come straight out of your own wallet. There are several ways you can minimize sticker shock at the vet hospital.

Ask for an Estimate   Except in a dire emergency, there's always time to talk about money before treatment is performed. Even in the ER, while the vet is absorbed with stabilizing your injured cat, an office manager will give you a quick assessment of expected costs and give you an opportunity to set spending limits. And once the crisis is over, you'll be given another estimate for any other treatments that will help your cat heal.

Hospital Savings Plans   Some hospitals offer pay-ahead plans for your cat's medical needs. You mail a check as often as you wish, and they enter the amount onto your medical record. In a short time, if you make regular payments, you'll have substantial credit on account. These plans are very convenient, especially if you have plenty of pets and don't want to keep a bank account for each or if you have an erratic income and are rich one month, poor the next. However, the hospital doesn't pay interest as a bank would, so you end up losing money over time. Nonetheless, many owners like the security of paying ahead.

Some of the larger hospitals offer well-pet plans where, for a fixed fee, you get well pet care for the year. While this is convenient, it's usually not a great bargain. By slightly discounting the regular service for a lump-sum payment up front, the hospital insures that they will get paid for an entire year's services. If for some reason you wish to take your cat to another hospital, the money is not refundable. Read these contracts carefully to make sure the terms really are favorable before you sign up.

10 Questions to Ask Every Provider

Before choosing a pet insurance or membership plan, be sure to get straight-forward answers to all your questions. If it makes you more comfortable, get the answers in writing.

1. Does your policy follow fee/benefits schedules? If so, please send me your detailed coverage limits. In the meantime, please give me examples of coverage limits for three common feline procedures so I can compare them to my current veterinary charges.

2. Does your policy cover basic wellness care, or does it cover only accidents and illnesses? Do you offer a wellness care endorsement that I can purchase on top of my basic plan for an additional fee? What other endorsements do you offer, and how much do they cost?

3. Under your policy's rules, can I continue taking my cat to its current veterinarian, or do I need to switch to another veterinarian?

4. Does your policy cover hereditary conditions, congenital conditions or pre-existing conditions? Please explain each coverage or exclusion as it pertains specifically to my cat. Is there a feature where pre-existing conditions will be covered if my cat's pre-existing condition requires no treatment after a specified period? What is that period?

5. What happens to my premium and to my cat's policy if your company goes out of business? What guarantees do I have that I won't be throwing my money away?

6. How quickly do you pay claims?

7. What is your policy's deductible? Does the deductible apply per incident or annually? How does the deductible differ per plan?

8. Does the policy have payment limits over a year's period or during my pet's lifetime? How do the payment limits differ per plan?

9. What is the A.M. Best Co. rating of your insurance underwriter, and what does that rating mean?

10. Is there a cancellation period after I receive my policy or membership? How long do I have to review all my materials once I receive them, and what is the cancellation procedure?

©1999 Solveig Fredrickson

Pet Insurance   There are currently several companies offering health insurance for pets. Some are reputable and have records of serving clients well. Others have very limited service for large up-front fees. Many are quite new, with no track record to allow judgement on their service.

While health insurance is a great comfort for the owner and may allow expensive treatment in an emergency, it's not always a great financial bargain. You may find that tucking money away in a savings account will save money in the long run. However, if you're not much of a saver, a health insurance policy might be the answer for you and your pet.

The Well-Kitten Visit

A kitten's first visit to the veterinarian is designed to give her the best-possible start in life.

Starting Off on the Right Paw

Vaccinations and feline leukemia testing normally start when your kitten is about nine weeks old. However, even a young kitten should be examined within the first week you bring her home.

The well kitten needs to visit a veterinarian three to five times in her first year. She'll need a series of vaccinations, a test for feline leukemia, and surgical sterilization.

The well cat needs one veterinary visit a year. The exception is the new-to-you adult cat who may never have been vaccinated before. He'll need at least two vis-

> A young kitten should be examined within the first week you bring her home.

its to get his vaccines up-to-date and also testing for feline leukemia and feline immunosuppressive virus.

The First Visit

The well cat or kitten should get a head-to-tail exam. Your veterinarian should look at her eyes, ears, nose, mouth, and tail. He should run his hands over her body, feeling for lumps, bumps, and pain. He'll also use his hands to estimate the size of her internal organs, particularly the kidneys, liver, and spleen. Expect him to put a stethoscope to her chest to listen for heart or lung disease.

Taking a temperature is a good idea but isn't always done if the cat passes the rest of the physical. Cats strongly dislike thermometers placed in their rectum, so many veterinarians prefer to avoid temperature taking unless they feel there's a chance that the cat is sick.

It is, however, very important to keep track of a cat's weight, so expect your feline to see the scale. For kittens, gaining weight at the expected rate over several visits will help show they're on the right track. But weight loss in older cats is often the first sign of disease.

If this is your feline's first visit, your veterinarian should request a test for both feline leukemia virus (FeLV) and (in older cats) feline immunosuppressive virus (FIV). He may also suggest testing for feline infectious peritonitis (FIP) if your cat is at particular risk for the disease (if he comes from a commercial cattery or if he appears ill).

Testing for these diseases requires drawing a small amount of blood from the vein of your cat. Many cats don't mind giving a bit of blood, but some will yowl and hiss during the procedure. They are *not* in pain—a blood draw is no more painful than an injection—but they *are* furious at being re-strained. When a needle is in a cat's vein, it's essential that he sit perfectly still, so he must be held firmly in position. A cat may combat such an indignity with wails of protest.

A parasite check is a quick but important part of the first exam. Your veterinarian may use a comb or her fingers to check the coat for fleas, ticks, and mites. The parasites that live inside, however, can be found only by examining a stool sample under the microscope. If you haven't brought in a fresh sample of your kitten's stool, expect your veterinarian to ask you to drop one off at your next opportunity. You can collect a fresh stool from the litter box by turning a zip-lock Baggie inside out and putting your hand inside. Use your protected fingers to pick up a small sample, invert the bag, seal it, and deliver it to your vet within four hours.

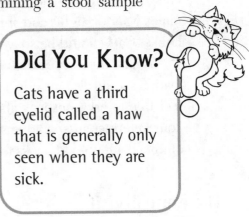

Did You Know?

Cats have a third eyelid called a haw that is generally only seen when they are sick.

Heartworm is an internal parasite that lives in the blood-stream, and it cannot be diagnosed by examination of stool. If your cat is over six months old and you live in a region with a lot of heartworm, your veterinarian may need to draw a blood sam-ple to check for this parasite. Not every cat needs heartworm testing or prevention—it depends solely on the likelihood of dis-ease from her lifestyle (indoor or out) and the region of the coun-try where you live (see Chapter 6, What Bugs Your Pet?, for a more detailed discussion of parasite control).

One important part of the first visit is the creation of a vaccina-tion schedule. For most cats this will include vaccination against feline panleukopenia (feline distemper), rhinotracheitis, and calicivirus. All cats also need a rabies vaccine—whether they live indoors or out. Other vaccines that are available but should be used only in certain situations are for feline leukemia, ringworm, feline infectious peritonitis, and bordetella.

At the cat's first visit, your veterinarian should also discuss spaying or neutering your cat. There are very few reasons to add kittens to a world where hundreds of thousands of unwanted cats are killed each year. On top of that, intact cats usually make lousy pets. The females can stay in nearly constant heat, and the males wander, fight, and spray strong-smelling urine all over the house. Cats should be spayed or neutered by six months of age.

As if all this isn't enough for one office visit, a well-kitten examination should also include a few minutes of discussion. You should feel free to ask questions about your kitten's health and behavior. Your veterinarian should answer your questions, and he may recommend a few good books for fun and informative reading.

The Annual Visit

Once your new cat has been examined, wormed, vaccinated, and spayed or neutered, he's finished with the veterinarian until next year. The next visit—the annual exam—is extremely important for your pet's health.

Cats hide illness very well, even from the most observant owners. A veterinarian can catch obscure signs, such as a mild change in breath odor or a slight shrinking of kidney size, during a routine office exam. Catching serious disease early—before the cat *looks* sick—can make treatment much easier and less expensive. Many times early detection can save your cat's life.

Owners used to be drawn to the office once a year, primarily for their cats' booster vaccinations. The veterinarian performed an exam at this time, of course, but the emphasis was on boosters, not the benefits of the extremely important vet check. Currently

A Tale of Two Kitties

Disease is much easier—and cheaper—to prevent than to cure. Take for example Buster and Scooter, two four-month-old kittens who visit the hospital where I work. Buster has had a feline leukemia test, two wormings, two FVRCP (a combination that includes rhinotracheitis, and panleukopenia) vaccinations, and one rabies vaccination. He'll be neutered soon, and he's feeling fine. He's already cost his owner about $120, but he's protected against four major diseases.

Scooter's owner, on the other hand, heard what it cost to protect Buster and opted to spend the money on pizza and sodas for the family. Now Buster is running a fever, has a runny nose, and looks miserable. I'm pretty certain he has a moderate case of a common upper respiratory infection, which would have been prevented by vaccination. We'll treat him conservatively and don't need tests at this time. His bill for an office exam, one injection, and take-home medication costs $65. But he still has worms, isn't protected against rabies or panleukopenia, and is likely to harbor the upper respiratory virus for life, even if he makes a rapid recovery.

Five days later Scooter comes back. He's not feeling any better. We take blood for an FeLV and FIV test, because those diseases can make it difficult to fight minor diseases. We take x rays to make sure he hasn't gotten pneumonia, and we send out a complete blood work to see if the usually minor disease is taking over his body. While we're waiting for these results, he'll go home on stronger—and more expensive—antibiotics. His family will spend around $200 on him today. And if he's gets sicker, he'll end up in the hospital with intensive treatments of injectable antibiotics and fluids, which cost somewhere around $100 a day. Although the initial costs are higher, Buster's owner ends up with a lot more pizza money—and a healthier cat.

veterinarians are beginning to stretch out the optimal time between boosters, and soon most cats may be vaccinated only once every two to three years. Although vaccination recommendations may change, the need for an annual well-cat checkup does not. Make sure to visit your veterinarian once a year.

The Inside Scoop on Preventive Health

Thinking owners want to know why vaccinations, surgery, and parasite control help your cat stay healthy. Just following a simple schedule isn't enough. In this section I'll discuss the whys and wherefores of vaccinations and surgery. Parasite control is a little more detailed—it gets a chapter of its own.

Vaccinations

What Is a Vaccination?

A vaccination is immune system training—a college course in body protection. A vaccine is made of small fragments of virus or bacteria or sometimes whole but weakened bacteria. When your veterinarian injects this under the skin or into a muscle, your cat's immune system sniffs it out and sends cells to learn about the strange substance. A few cells stay at the site, but others circulate throughout the body, sharing their newfound knowledge with the rest of the immune system.

Once the immune system recognizes the disease, the body produces a new generation of cells born with the skills to fight off the virus or bacteria. If the "real" disease ever infects the body, the immune system makes a fast attack, and the cat stays feeling fine.

If the body never sees any hint of the disease again, the immune system will eventually lose its memory. Newer generations

of immune cells are born without any knowledge of the vaccine or the disease. At this time, if your cat is exposed to the disease, she'll get sick. If she's given a booster vaccine, however, the immune cells take a quick refresher course and stay ready to protect your cat.

The Downside of Vaccination

Vaccination schedules must be designed to get the very best immune system response but without causing illness. When the immune system is overloaded or overworked, it can become exhausted and fail to fight the real disease. Or it can become overstimulated and, like a swarm of angry bees, may attack anything in its path—including a cat's own body. This is why autoimmune diseases may start or worsen after vaccination.

Cats have a particularly sensitive immune system. When anything repeatedly irritates a cat's skin—sunburn, constant scratching, constant irritation from trauma—the immune system can cause intense local inflammation. After a time a small percentage of cats develop can-

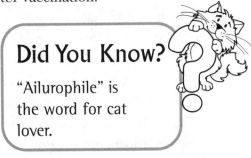

Did You Know?

"Ailurophile" is the word for cat lover.

cerous tumors at the irritated site. Some vaccines are created with an adjuvant, which is a local irritant designed to increase both local and whole-body immune system response. Although this is safe in people and dogs, recently it's been discovered that cats can overreact to seemingly harmless adjuvants. Within the last few years vaccines with adjuvant (rabies and feline leukemia) have been linked to the formation of a vaccine-site cancer in about one in 10,000 cats.

Scheduling Vaccines

Because vaccines aren't completely harmless, veterinarians must balance protection from deadly disease against potentially harmful side effects. Because of the rare but real risk of cancer, feline veterinarians in particular are questioning the wisdom of the traditional once-a-year vaccine booster schedule.

An annual vaccination schedule was originally adopted for two reasons: (1) the manufacturer tested the vaccine duration for only one year, so no data existed on how long the vaccines actually lasted, and (2) yearly boosters not only ensure a good immune system memory but also allow for the all-important annual examination.

Studies are currently under way to determine how long immunity lasts in a vaccinated cat. Preliminary data suggest that upper respiratory vaccines give reasonable protection for three years, whereas panleukopenia vaccination may last seven years or longer. For that reason, many veterinarians are now vaccinating every two to three years. Others are waiting for more studies before they reduce vaccination intervals.

In short, creating a vaccine schedule is an art. The proper schedule ensures a cat won't catch a serious disease. At the same time it minimizes the possibility of negative side effects. New information is flowing into your veterinarian's hands every day. Insist on a vaccine schedule that meets your cat's needs and that keeps up with the recommendations made by the American Association of Feline Practitioners.

Why Vaccinate?

As the media hypes vaccine side effects, fear runs through the hearts of many cat owners. But negative side effects are rare—vaccines still save lives. They are extremely important, and every cat should get them.

When I first began to practice in 1987, we lost dozens of kittens each year to panleukopenia. The victims were almost always young, unvaccinated kittens. They suddenly became sick with terrible diarrhea. Despite treatment, they generally died.

The most memorable was a little gray fluffball who was about 12 weeks old. She was thin and nearly comatose when brought in. I took her home and personally nursed her day and night for a week, giving her fluids and trying anything I could think of to

Hold That Needle!

Although vaccines are vital to keep a cat free from serious disease, in some cases they can make a cat sick. Experts suggest avoiding vaccinating in the following cases:

○ Cats who are undergoing chemotherapy for cancer;

○ Cats who have had organ transplants;

○ Cats with an autoimmune disease;

○ A cat with a positive test for feline immunosuppressive virus;

○ A cat with a previous serious vaccine reaction.

combat her disease. She was a real fighter. She would rally a little one day, then get worse the next. She finally gave up and died, exhausted by her battle with the virus. I was exhausted too—and frustrated. She didn't have to die or even get sick. With a vaccine, she would have lived a full life.

I haven't seen a single case of panleukopenia in a good 10 years. But the disease hasn't gone away; it's routinely reported in strays and in unvaccinated cats. In owned cats, however, the disease is completely prevented by a simple and safe injection. Because I now practice in an area where cat owners care enough to vaccinate their cats, I won't spend another sleepless night fighting this disease.

Preventable Diseases

There are many feline vaccines on the market and more being created all the time. The following is a discussion of the preventable diseases and the wisdom of vaccinating—or not—against each.

Feline Panleukopenia (Feline Distemper)

The feline panleukopenia virus attacks the lining of the intestine. It's a parvovirus—a family of viruses that has members causing disease in every species, including people and dogs. Feline panleukopenia is very similar to the disease called parvo in dogs. When the virus goes to work, the result is bloody, foul-smelling diarrhea, vomiting, and often death. Young kittens are most at risk for catching and dying from the disease.

The virus can live for months to years in the environment. Microscopic traces of virus can be found in tiny bits of feces in yards, on bowls, on cages, in litter boxes, or even on human hands. In unborn cat fetuses or newborn kittens, the virus (or the modified live vaccine) may cause brain damage.

All kittens should receive a foundation series of vaccinations, then a booster one year later. Annual booster vaccination is recommended by the manufacturer. Because a recent study demonstrated that many vaccinated cats keep a low level of immune system response to panleukopenia for up to six years, the American Association of Feline Practitioners (AAFP) panel currently recommends extending boosters to once every three years.

Feline Herpesvirus/Feline Calicivirus

Eighty to 90 percent of upper respiratory diseases in cats ("cat flu") is caused by the feline herpesvirus and calicivirus. In adult

cats the "flu" is usually mild. But the virus can make a permanent home in a cat's body, causing repeated illness over many years.

The disease can be spread either through the secretions of a sick cat's eyes and nose or through coughed-up phlegm. Calici can also be shed in the stool. The viruses pass from cat to cat by contact, from sneezing, or from contaminated hands, feeding bowls, or other objects. Vaccination may not prevent disease completely, but the vaccine reduces illness and makes it less likely that a cat can pass the disease on to other cats.

All kittens should receive a foundation series of vaccinations, followed by a booster one year later. Annual booster vaccination is recommended by the manufacturers. Currently the AAFP recommends three-year boosters based on studies but suggests that veterinarians vaccinate more frequently if the cat is at high risk of exposure. Ask your veterinarian what booster schedule he recommends for your own cat.

Chlamydia

Chlamydia is blamed for 5 percent or less of all upper respiratory infections in cats in the United States but seems to occur more frequently in the United Kingdom. Infected cats often have runny red eyes, may sneeze, and may have a nasal discharge. The disease is usually minor and can be treated with antibiotics if necessary.

Vaccination reduces the symptoms of the disease but doesn't eliminate it. The AAFP has stated that because chlamydia vaccines have greater side effects than other common vaccines and the incidence of the disease is low, chlamydia vaccines should be given only to cats at risk of exposure.

Rabies

Rabies is a deadly disease of pets and people. It's transmitted through direct contact—usually bite wounds—from an infected animal. An unprotected cat bitten by a rabid animal will most likely die from the disease. While he's sick, he can infect his owner, too.

The risk of contracting rabies is highest in an outdoor cat, but even an indoor cat is at risk. An infected bat can enter the house or your cat can slip outside accidentally. For the safety of both your cat and your family, rabies vaccination is essential. It's also mandated by law.

The vaccination schedule for rabies is set by state or local law. Usually one vaccine is given before 16 weeks, then repeated one year later. Boosters may be given at one- to three-year intervals.

Feline Infectious Peritonitis

Feline infectious peritonitis (FIP) is caused by a corona virus. The exact way the virus causes disease is unknown, but it's a complex interaction between the virus and the individual cat's immune system. Some infected cats become ill quickly, while others linger for years before any real damage is done. Other cats will never get sick. The current tests can tell only if a cat has become infected with a corona virus, not if a cat will develop FIP.

There are two forms of the disease. The "wet" form is most common in kittens. It causes the belly to fill with fluid, causing a huge potbellied look. Kittens and cats with this form usually die within months of the first signs. The "dry" form causes lesions to form on internal organs, interfering with their function. Death occurs only when the liver or kidneys finally begin to fail. There is no cure for FIP.

Feline infectious peritonitis is thought to spread from the fecal matter of infected cats to the mouth or nose of uninfected cats. Cats less than a year old are at the greatest risk of infection. Certain breeds, such as Persians, and certain lines within breeds are also at increased risk, possibly because their immune system overreacts to the virus—but no one really knows why. No truly effective treatment exists.

Vaccination against FIP is controversial. Some studies seem to demonstrate that the vaccine will prevent disease, whereas others suggest that in some cases vaccination makes the disease worse. Until more is known about the disease itself and the way the virus works in the body, it's probably wise to vaccinate only if there's a real health risk to the cat, such as sharing a house with a cat sick with FIP.

Feline Leukemia Virus (FeLV)

Feline leukemia virus is caused by a retrovirus that is similar to (but not the same as) the immune-system-crushing virus responsible for human AIDS. Infected cats can develop anemia, cancer, or immune system disease, although some live well for years while carrying the disease. The virus becomes a part of an infected cat's cells, and most infections are for life. It's possible for healthy-looking cats to be infected, and these cats can infect other cats. Humans do *not* catch AIDS (or FeLV) from cats.

Kittens less than 16 weeks old are at the highest risk for contracting and becoming sick with feline leukemia. Older kittens and cats seem to be able to fight off infection a little bit better. Cats catch FeLV by close contact with infected cats, through bite wounds, through saliva, in the womb, or by milk transmission from mother to kitten.

Feline leukemia vaccine is recommended only for cats that live at-risk lives: any indoor-outdoor cats, outdoor cats, strays, feral cats, multicat households without an FeLV testing program, or households with an FeLV-positive cat in residence. Currently vaccination is suggested for all at-risk cats. Annual boosters are also recommended.

Ringworm

Ringworm is caused by infection with a fungus. The disease can show up as a widespread skin infection, which usually isn't itchy,

Did You Know?

Most white cats are born with a "grease spot"—a fluff of black fur on top of their heads—which usually disappears by the age of six months.

but many cats never show any signs when infected. Any infected cat can pass on the highly infectious fungus via contact with skin, infected bedding, or—rarely—through contaminated air-handling systems to other cats and occasionally to people. Ringworm in people is usually quite mild and responds quickly to medical treatment.

Ringworm in cats can be treated by pills, bathing with medicated shampoo, or both. Cure rates are high in single cats but more difficult in large households. To get rid of all the fungus, you may have to treat all contact animals plus clean and disinfect the house. It's also a good idea to replace the filters in your air conditioner.

A vaccine has been approved for the treatment and prevention of ringworm, but it's not known if the vaccine prevents or eliminates infection or just eliminates the signs of the disease. Because it's unproven and usually unnecessary, the vaccine isn't recommended for the average cat but can be useful in helping control ringworm in a crowded house or cattery.

Bordetella

Bordetella—the agent of canine kennel cough—can also make cats sneeze and cough. This bacteria may be a problem in cats who visit shows, stay in kennels, or are housed in large groups. It's thought to be uncommon in ordinary pet cats.

A vaccine was released in 1998 but has not yet gained wide acceptance for use in the average cat. Some experts state it's "a vaccine in search of a disease," whereas others find bordetella vaccination quite helpful in the occasional disease outbreak.

Because bordetella in cats can be easily treated, vaccination of the average cat is not suggested at this time. Veterinarians may elect to vaccinate cats at high risk of exposure, with the vaccination schedule determined by the manufacturer's recommendation.

Healthy Surgeries

No one likes to go "under the knife"—or to put their cats through surgery, either. But modern surgeries in healthy animals are safe and rapid. One surgery—sterilization—should be a matter of course for almost all cats. Another elective surgery is declawing.

Why Spay or Neuter?

Unless your cat is an excellent specimen of a pure breed, it should not be allowed to make kittens. Overpopulation is a tragic disease, claiming more feline lives than any other disease. Simple surgical sterilization can avoid this tragedy.

> Spays and neuters are very safe for healthy cats and kittens.

Safety First

In the modern world, spays and neuters are very safe for healthy cats and kittens. The safety comes from a careful health examination before surgery and from proper anesthesia. The health exam should include a thorough physical exam by a veterinarian. It's also a good idea to run a preoperative blood test to check for subtle signs of disease. If a cat is found to have medical problems, the sterilization should be delayed until he's treated.

The safest anesthesia for a spay begins with a short-acting injection to allow placement of a tube into a cat's trachea (windpipe). This tube keeps anesthetic gas flowing into the lungs to keep your cat safely asleep while surgery is performed. The surgery is done with the cat asleep under the effects of a gas. Although many veterinarians—especially spay-neuter clinics—use injectable anesthetics alone to cut costs, they don't provide the safe, long-lasting, deep surgical sleep that can be achieved with gas.

Neuters are very fast surgeries, so injectable anesthesia without gas is still routinely used. The exception is when a tom is getting declawed along with the neuter. Proper declaw procedure makes for a lengthier surgery, and gas anesthesia should be used.

The Spay

If a cat were a woman, an ovariohysterectomy would be considered very serious surgery. She would have a four- to six-week recovery period and a bill upward of $7,000. Your cat, on the other hand, will be her old self within three or four days. You can expect a bill in the $150 range, including the physical exam and preoperative blood work.

In the standard spay, the surgeon removes both ovaries and the uterus through an incision in the abdomen. If the ovaries are left behind, the cat will still come into full-blown heat from time to time. She won't be able to get pregnant, but she won't be a very happy pet. If the surgeon doesn't remove all of the uterus, on the other hand, the cat won't cycle but she'll be at high risk of uterine infection later in life. Both of these techniques are sometimes used in other countries but are considered substandard practice in the United States.

The Neuter

A male cat is sterilized by neutering. In this procedure the testicles are completely removed through incisions on the scrotum. This description may make men cringe, but it sounds worse than it is. The surgery is done quickly while the cat is deeply asleep. Most cats are up and playing just hours after the surgery.

Declawing

No one feline surgery causes more debate than the declaw. People hate to live with shredded furniture, but they don't want to do their cats harm, either.

It's true that a cat's claws are part of his natural heritage. He enjoys clawing with them. When he claws, he also uses scent glands on his pads to mark territory. In an ideal world, a cat would be allowed to keep his claws. Even in the *real* world, if a cat can be trained to use his claws only on accepted scratching areas and if you can keep up with clipping them, then it's best to leave claws in place.

But claws can be remarkably destructive. The claws of a frightened cat can leave painful tracks on an owner's lap or arms. And a cat's claw-sharpening routine can quickly ruin furniture, shred curtains, and enrage even a patient owner. When living with a cat becomes an armed standoff, no one wins. Cats hate to be yelled at or punished, and owners hate to have their homes ruined or their skin injured, no matter how unintentionally. The end result is often a cat who keeps her claws but loses her home. And perhaps her life.

If a cat has a choice between a healthy, safe, secure indoor life without claws or being dumped, abandoned, or euthanized because her claws are a problem, I believe there would be no contest. Cats can be quite happy without claws.

In my own house, the clawless part of the clan enjoy the scratching post just as much as their clawed compatriots. The clawless ones, however, enjoy clawing the couch, the bed—even on my legs—when they want to play. They can use their imaginary claws to leave pheromones from their paw-pad scent glands anywhere they want, and I don't care.

My clawed cats, on the other hand, don't have it so easy. They are very polite, but their permitted scratching posts are few. My

The Eight Rules of Declawing

If you're considering declawing your cat, these rules are for you:

1. Declaw only the front. Cats need their rear claws for defense and climbing.

2. If you're certain that you must declaw, do it early. Younger cats recover much more quickly than older cats.

3. Don't declaw simply because the cat is scratching a child. This most likely means the cat is defending herself. The child must first be taught to be kind to the cat, lest the cat be forced to bite in self-defense.

4. Keep declawed cats indoors. Although a cornered cat, clawed or not, is a fearsome fighter, clawless cats are definitely at a disadvantage in paw-to-paw combat. They also have trouble fleeing up trees.

5. Cats who are easily trained to a scratching post and who will allow frequent claw clips should be allowed to keep their natural set of claws.

6. Pick a good surgeon who will do the declaw properly. Laser surgery offers advantages over removing with a scalpel.

7. Avoid surgeons who lop off parts of the pad. This is extremely painful and should be considered cruelty.

8. If you think you must declaw, don't feel guilty. Your cat will mind it much less than you think.

old lady, Ace, sometimes gores me when she leaps on my lap, so she can't keep me company as often as she'd like. Her claws grow quickly, so it's quite a chore—and one that Ace hates—to keep them short. But when her claws get a little long, she snags in the carpet. It can be painful to get her free.

Front-paw declawing can improve the life of a cat. It can even allow a cat that would otherwise be unwanted to live peacefully in a loving home. While many people can live with clawed cats, some cannot. If you wish to declaw your cat, put your mind at rest. It might not be politically correct, and you might catch heat from animal rights activists, but you are probably doing your cat a favor.

Declawing Alternatives

There are ways to avoid declawing. If your cat is pretty good about scratching the post but still goes after a few pieces of furniture, she's probably a candidate for training. To discourage off-limit scratching, you can apply a *small* amount of eucalyptus oil or citronella oil on the forbidden fabric. Don't put much down—either one can be toxic if eaten. For a less fragrant approach, turn a plastic carpet runner pointy-side up directly underneath the no-scratch zone. If her hind feet aren't comfy, a cat won't scratch.

Another alternative is to purchase nail caps from your veterinarian or pet store to cover your cat's claws. These are little pieces of soft latex that fit neatly over your cat's nails. A drop of sterile glue keeps them in place.

Nail caps are ideal for short-term solutions, such as visits from grandchildren or to protect the eyes of a new puppy. Long term, however, they don't work very well. When used constantly, the claws can become soft and misshapen. They often become infected, too. The nails must still be trimmed regularly and a new cap applied at each trimming.

Alternative Surgery

Tenectomy　For people who want to keep the furniture in shape plus keep a cat's claws, veterinarians offer a procedure called the tenectomy. Instead of removing the claws, the tendon that allows the cats to extend the claws is clipped.

Surgeons love this—it's very fast, especially when compared to the more complicated and time-consuming declaw. The cats have very little pain after surgery, often walking normally the next day.

Unfortunately, the tenectomy has some significant downsides. The nails are in place but useless, so a cat can't enjoy clawing. Unlike a declawed cat, she can't even go through the motions for enjoyment or to mark her territory. Also, her nails still must be trimmed. Because the cat can't help keep them groomed, they actually require more care than the natural cat's nails. If the nails aren't trimmed, they will continue to grow and eventually puncture the tender pad, causing infection and intense pain. A cat with a tenectomy is absolutely dependent on you for nail care for the rest of his life.

American Association of Feline Practitioners Panel

In the late 1980s veterinarians discovered that in rare cases, cancerous tumors form at the site of vaccinations in cats. When the link was first established, the American Association of Feline Practitioners created a group to study the situation and to come up with recommendations for a more reasonable, safer vaccination protocol.

The group's formal name is the Advisory Panel on Feline Vaccines of the American Association of Feline Practitioners and the Academy of Feline Medicine, or the AAFP Panel, for short. In 1997 the AAFP Panel published guidelines that recommended less frequent vaccinations, creating a storm of controversy. Several veterinary colleges embraced the guidelines, but they met with sharp criticism from other colleges and many practitioners. To read the report for yourself, contact the AAFP (see the Resources section at the end of the book).

Nosodes

In the realm of alternative medicine, *nosodes* replace vaccination as a means of preventing disease. A nosode is made by taking a tiny piece of diseased tissue, then diluting it greatly. After each dilution the solution is "energized" by succussion, or shaking, for an exact number of times. At the end of the process there is no measurable disease agent left in the nosode. The energized water is given to the cat by mouth. The energy of the nosode and the energy of the pet are said to resonate, making him healthier and better able to fight off the disease.

No one has found any measurable effects of nosodes on a cat's body. Cats don't make antibodies to the disease as a result of nosode treatment, and there's no evidence that the disease-fighting capabilities of the immune system are enhanced. A scientific study in which nosode-protected animals are challenged with natural disease to see if the nosodes work has never been done. Why? Because, believers say, such a study would be against the paradigm of the vital life force. Energetic effects are, in essence, unmeasurable.

Despite the lack of facts, many holistic and alternative practitioners say they have luck with nosodes. But there may be reasons for this. Most nosodes are given after the initial series of kitten vaccinations. New studies show immunity from these vaccinations may last six years or more. Nosodes aren't protecting these cats; the vaccines are.

Nosodes will also seem highly effective as long as most cats in the area are vaccinated. The protected animals prevent the spread of the disease, keeping nonvaccinated pets safe. As soon as the nonvaccinated population becomes large enough to allow spread, outbreaks can be expected.

For one veterinarian, the luck with her nosodes program ran out dramatically. In January 1999 Dr. Celeste Yarnall, a respected holistic practitioner, reported that 29 cats under her care died of panleukopenia, a deadly disease that is rare in vaccinated cats. Twenty-eight of those cats had been "protected" only by nosodes, and only one had received a conventional vaccine. The editor of the *Journal of the American Holistic Veterinary Medical Association* reported that Dr. Yarnall "feels she was ill-served by the advice not to vaccinate her cats."

At this time nosodes are not recommended as the sole protection against disease. If you're holistically minded, you should vaccinate on a minimal schedule and use homeopathic remedies (such as nosodes) *along with* traditional preventative medicine.

Laser Surgery   One of the newest tools in your veterinarian's office is the laser. It can help a surgeon perform delicate procedures much more easily than with a blade. The laser does less tissue damage and stops blood flow more quickly than a scalpel, too. This makes it a perfect tool for claw removal. Surgeons who are skilled with the laser report that their cats recover much more quickly than from traditional surgery, with almost no bleeding.

Laser surgery isn't available in every veterinary office yet. But if you can find an experienced surgeon in your area who has a unit of his own, consider using his services if you decide a declaw is necessary.

6

What Bugs Your Pet?

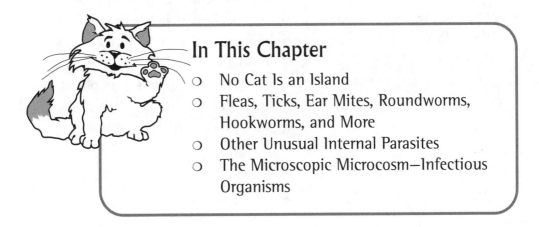

In This Chapter

- ○ No Cat Is an Island
- ○ Fleas, Ticks, Ear Mites, Roundworms, Hookworms, and More
- ○ Other Unusual Internal Parasites
- ○ The Microscopic Microcosm—Infectious Organisms

You love your pet, and you can't imagine living without her. A whole host of other creatures would love to get to know her, too. Insects, internal parasites, bacteria, and various viruses all long to make your cat their home.

No Cat Is an Island

Your cat lives her life as a colony. Even a healthy cat serves as a home to many microscopic creatures. Her skin and intestinal tract harbor dozens of different types of bacteria and yeast. Most of these live quietly without bothering your cat, and some actually *help* your pet. For example, a normal intestinal bacteria called lactobacillus can slow the growth of over 10 types of disease-causing bacteria. It helps keep the bad actors at bay and your cat feeling fine.

Unfortunately, many of the creatures that live in and on your cat aren't so benign. Several intestinal bacteria can make your cat quite sick, and so can a whole host of other critters. To keep her healthy, it helps to have an understanding of nature's nasty creatures.

> The most bothersome bug on the block isn't a bacterium, worm, or virus. It's the common flea.

First, let's take a look at these hangers-on and itch mongers—the external parasites.

Fleas

The most bothersome bug on the block isn't a bacterium, worm, or virus. It's a six-legged insect with a bristly body, a dagger-like mouth, and an insatiable hunger for blood—the common flea.

Fleas live just about everywhere. Worldwide there are about 2,400 species waiting to feast on a feline—or any animal. In North America the fleas that commonly bug our cats (and our ankles) go by the name of the cat flea, the dog flea, and the human flea. Their formal names are *Ctenocephalides felis*, *Ctenocephalides canis*, and *Pulex irritans*, respectively. They aren't picky about where they get their blood—any of these will feed on a cat.

Whatever the species, a flea is built for two purposes: to reproduce and to suck blood. They are relentless feeders and will continue to eat even after they are full. The extra meals are passed as stool, which veterinarians call "flea dirt." This looks like black grains of sand, but it's really protein-rich food for newly hatched flea larvae.

> Vacuuming provides enough heat and motion to cause pupae to hatch. Because most chemicals kill adults, not pupae, you can improve the efficiency of household sprays by vacuuming a couple of hours *before* you spray.

When feeding, fleas literally drain the blood out of a cat. A heavy infestation can make healthy adult cats extremely ill, but it only takes a few fleas to kill a kitten.

Fleas create more mischief than simply stealing your cat's blood. The saliva of fleas is a strong allergen, and many pets exposed to it will develop an allergic reaction. Once a cat becomes allergic to fleas, only one bite from a flea can cause excruciating itching. The cat may rip out her hair and tear at her skin to stop the itch—even after the flea has gone away.

As if that's not enough trouble, fleas carry a little extra present—tapeworms. Fleas can become infected with tapeworms by eating tapeworm eggs in the feces of cats. When cats manage to catch and eat the flea, the tapeworm hatches and attaches to the lining of the cat's intestine. It hangs there, irritating the gut and robbing her of nutrients.

In addition, researchers have recently discovered that fleas carry *Bartonella*—the agent that causes cat scratch fever. Although *Bartonella* doesn't make the cat sick, it's thought that an infected cat can pass it on to a human from a bite or scratch. The disease is easily treatable in humans, but good flea control can help avoid it altogether.

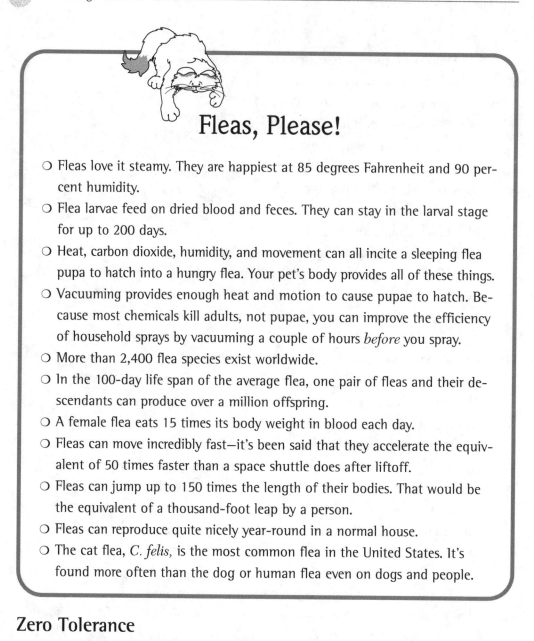

Fleas, Please!

○ Fleas love it steamy. They are happiest at 85 degrees Fahrenheit and 90 percent humidity.

○ Flea larvae feed on dried blood and feces. They can stay in the larval stage for up to 200 days.

○ Heat, carbon dioxide, humidity, and movement can all incite a sleeping flea pupa to hatch into a hungry flea. Your pet's body provides all of these things.

○ Vacuuming provides enough heat and motion to cause pupae to hatch. Because most chemicals kill adults, not pupae, you can improve the efficiency of household sprays by vacuuming a couple of hours *before* you spray.

○ More than 2,400 flea species exist worldwide.

○ In the 100-day life span of the average flea, one pair of fleas and their descendants can produce over a million offspring.

○ A female flea eats 15 times its body weight in blood each day.

○ Fleas can move incredibly fast—it's been said that they accelerate the equivalent of 50 times faster than a space shuttle does after liftoff.

○ Fleas can jump up to 150 times the length of their bodies. That would be the equivalent of a thousand-foot leap by a person.

○ Fleas can reproduce quite nicely year-round in a normal house.

○ The cat flea, *C. felis*, is the most common flea in the United States. It's found more often than the dog or human flea even on dogs and people.

Zero Tolerance

From the cat's perspective, there's no such thing as a good flea. Nature designed these creatures to breed swiftly and eat heavily. They do no discernible good other than to control the population of mammals by killing the young from anemia or—in the presence of infected rats—by bringing scourges such as black death (bubonic plague) to humans from time to time.

Spotting even a single flea spells trouble. They don't travel alone, so when you see one, you can bet there are at least a hundred more lurking in the house or yard. Even a lone flea won't stay lonely for long. A female can lay up to 50 eggs each day.

Controlling Fleas

No one wants a house full of fleas, but until recently flea control was a full-time job. The flea fight used to be heroic: weekly baths and dips of all the animals, sprays in the yard, plus bombs and sprays in the home. This was so labor intensive and toxic that it's no wonder many people simply threw up their hands, declaring, "Fleas are forever!" Today, however, effective flea control is easy.

Modern Weapons for Flea Control

In the last few years three companies have put new products on the market that are not only extremely effective but are much less toxic than the old-fashioned sprays, bombs, and dips. They're extremely convenient, too. Two are applied to the skin on the back of the neck, and one is a pill given by mouth. With these drugs flea control is now a once-a-month endeavor.

Here's the rundown on the newest drugs:

○ Advantage: The active ingredient in Advantage is imidocloprid, a drug used as a crop insecticide in several countries. It comes packaged in individually dosed, cat-sized vials and can be used on kittens older than 10 weeks. When placed on the fur over the shoulders of a cat, it covers the coat, providing flea protection for at least a month.

The drug works by interfering with an insect's nicotinic receptors, found in the nervous system. Cats do have these same receptors, so it's theoretically possible to get an overdose. Manufacturer's tests show Advantage to be safe at five times the recommended dose, at least in dogs. Insects have a huge number of nicotinic receptors, so they die at tiny doses, much less than what would affect a cat. The drug is also very bitter tasting, so cats don't want to lick it. Once it dries, Advantage is very stable and won't come off the cat, so it won't rub off on you.

○ **Frontline Top Spot:** Frontline Top Spot is a liquid that comes in single-dose vials. The active ingredient is fipronil, which kills both ticks and fleas. It's used monthly for ticks but can be used once every *three* months for fleas. It mixes with the cat's skin oils and follicles, so it won't rub off the animal once dry. It doesn't wash off easily, even with soap and water. Frontline also comes in a spray, but the Top Spot product is much easier to use.

Fipronil kills by poisoning a bug's nervous system. It does this by stopping calcium from flowing through what are called GABA channels, which are numerous in an insect's nervous system. Cats, on the other hand, have extremely few GABA channels, so the drug is quite safe in the average cat. It can be used on kittens at least 12 weeks old.

○ **Program:** Lufenuron is the active ingredient in the tablet called Program. This drug works by stopping the synthesis of chitin, which makes up the exoskeleton, or outside skeleton, of the flea. Because mammals don't have chitin, the drug has little or no effect on a cat's body. Although Program is quite safe, it doesn't kill adult fleas. It works by preventing the next generation. After a female drinks Program-rich cat blood, few eggs hatch and the flea larvae can't grow into adults.

Program can be used in kittens as young as six weeks. An injectable form has been approved for cats, but since there's a link between skin irritation and cancer in cats, it's wise to avoid injecting any potential irritant into your cat. The pill form works well, so there's no need to turn to the needle.

Natural Flea Control

When Mother Nature made the flea, she created a tough, resilient little bug. She must have liked fleas, because she didn't make many things that controlled them—at least very few that are safe for animals, too. Because fleas are so annoying and dangerous, even organically minded cat owners should consider the new, safer products described above. A touch of nonnatural methods can actually be healthier than either living with the pests or dousing the cat in more toxic herbals or oils.

It's always wise to minimize the amount of chemicals you use, however. The good news is that there *are* a couple of effective, totally nonchemical flea control methods.

Get Your Combs Ready!   My favorite nonchemical way of controlling fleas in indoor cats is to use a fine-toothed flea comb. The teeth of the comb are placed very close together—so close that even the narrow body of the tiniest flea can't squeeze through. Comb your cat carefully, especially around her neck, under her chin, and on her back near her tail, snagging fleas as you go. Dump them into a jar containing alcohol or flea spray to kill them.

By using the flea comb daily until no fleas are found—not a single one—for a month, it's possible to eradicate an infestation. I know because I've done it more than once in my decades of living with cats! It's labor intensive and slow. If your cats are old, ill, very

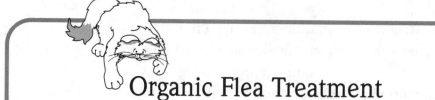

Organic Flea Treatment

Flo is a tabby with a flea allergy. Each summer her skin turns scabby, and she wastes so much time and energy licking and scratching herself that she gets thin. Her owner, Mary, has been fighting fleas for years. Bathing, dipping, spraying, bombing the house—it's been an endless battle. And she's tired of it.

This year Flo showed up at the vet's for her early spring checkup. She still looked fine, and Mary told me about her new plan to fight fleas. "I'm sick of all these chemicals. They can't be healthy," Mary says. "I'm going organic." Her regime would include filling Flo with garlic and brewer's yeast, putting citronella oil on her bed full of cedar chips, and using ultrasonic flea repellers to keep the fleas out of the house.

Mary was proud of her plan, especially since it was natural and wouldn't harm the environment. But there were a few holes in it. "Mary, we need to think this through," I began. Then we discussed the fact that to a flea, feeding on a cat is a totally natural and organic experience. Their urge to feed is so great that they aren't easily repelled. A hungry flea, if living, will find a way around almost all natural treatments in order to eat.

On the other hand, garlic and brewer's yeast aren't part of a cat's natural diet. Garlic can actually harm a cat's red blood cells and can make a cat sick. Brewer's yeast won't hurt a cat but doesn't stop fleas, either. Citronella, with its pungent smell, does repel fleas and can even kill them. But strong odors such as citronella and cedar are offensive to the highly sensitive nose of a cat. What's more, citronella can be quite toxic.

The ultrasonic repellant is a bad idea, too. Just like those of bugs and rodents, a cat's super-sensitive ears are tuned to ultrasonic ranges. Ultrasound is silent to you but sounds something like an air raid siren to your cat. Although these devices annoy cats, they won't stop a hungry flea from eating.

Unfortunately, most cat parasites are playing out the role given to them by nature. They don't mean to make a cat sick; that's just a side effect. And it's one that nature intended, too. In the natural state cats live for only a few years, just long enough to put a few litters on the ground but not so many that the gene pool is flooded with one cat's offspring. These parasites are doing their job, and nature favors their survival.

Of course, we don't raise our cats to fill all of their natural roles—especially ones that make them sick. While going organic and natural is a great idea in theory, few natural remedies work very well against these evildoers. Using chemicals to help control parasites and other nasty microorganisms isn't wrong. It's essential, however, to use such powerful tools carefully and wisely.

young, or flea allergic, then flea combing isn't for you—the cats will still suffer while you're working on the infestation. Also, allowing a cat outdoors will destroy your comb-eradication program. He'll bring in far more than you can comb away.

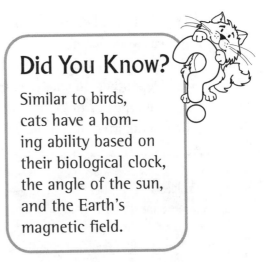

Did You Know?

Similar to birds, cats have a homing ability based on their biological clock, the angle of the sun, and the Earth's magnetic field.

Would You Consider . . . Moving?
If you want to escape fleas naturally, there's one surefire chemical-free way to exterminate the pests: move. Sure, it's a radical solution and probably not practical. But if you're like me, it's nice to know that there *are* havens safe from fleas. Fleas hate dry, thin air, so for year-round relief, the place to live is an area with both low moisture and low oxygen content. This means altitudes of 5,000 feet or greater, such as parts of the Rocky Mountain range in the western United States. For seasonal respite, move to areas with freezing winter weather. Because fleas flourish in warm air, a winter frost will kill adults and keep the eggs from hatching.

If moving isn't practical and you find combing can't keep up with your flea hatching, then chemical controls will be more effective than most alternative natural remedies. The new products mentioned above are all safer than many natural methods currently used, such as botanicals, garlic, and essential oils. These substances are natural, but they can make cats very ill.

Ticks

Although ticks drink blood and feed on felines, these eight-legged creatures are more closely related to spiders than to the six-legged flea. Unlike a flea, a tick takes one large meal and then drops off the cat when its hunger is eased. The meals, however, are large. A tick may suck a half teaspoon of blood before it becomes full.

Depending on where you live, your cat may play host to one of several types of ticks. The most common ones are the deer tick, brown dog tick, and American dog tick. Many people call any tiny tick a "deer tick" or "Lyme tick" (*Ixodes* species), but in fact, the juvenile nymphs of any of the species can be quite small. If you want to learn which tick is which, ignore size and look at a couple of more reliable physical characteristics.

> Unlike a flea, a tick takes one large meal and then drops off the cat when its hunger is eased. A tick may suck a half teaspoon of blood before it becomes full.

○ *Ixodes* (deer tick): Solid color, often small, with long, pointed head
○ *Rhipicephalus* (brown dog tick): Solid color, variable size, rectangular head
○ *Dermacentor* (American dog tick): Body has white markings on a brown background, square head

Although ticks feed on cats less often than on people or dogs, they can still cause serious problems when they latch onto your cat. They can spread infectious diseases such as Lyme, *Ehrlichia*, and *Babesia*. A tick can pick up any of these microscopic organisms when it bites a sick animal and then injects it into a cat when it begins to suck its blood. All three diseases work differently inside the cat, but all can make her run a fever, feel sluggish or lame, and might cause anemia.

Parasitologists describe most of the ticks that feed on your cat as three-host ticks. That means that instead of living full-time on one cat, they also spend part of their life on other creatures, such

How Do You *Really* Remove a Tick?

When you find a tick on your cat, the best thing you can do is get it off as quickly as possible. If it's not yet imbedded in the skin, all you have to do is work up the courage to pick it up. There's no risk that the tick will harm you—it takes them hours to position themselves and bite. You can put the tick in a small jar of alcohol or flea spray to kill it.

Ticks that have already dug into your cat are a little more difficult to remove, but it's easy enough with a pair of tweezers. Simply lay the tweezers firmly against your cat's skin, with the imbedded head between the blades. Push down on the skin as you tighten your grip on the tick so you grab the head as close to the skin as possible. Then give a sharp jerk to pull the tick free. You're likely to pull a tiny tab of skin off your cat, too, but the cat will barely notice.

Don't be overly concerned about leaving the head in the skin—it's rare to have an infection. If you see swelling or inflammation at the site, ask your vet to take a look.

The biggest trick to removing ticks safely is to avoid harming them during removal. If you irritate a tick by burning it, painting it with nail polish, or dousing it with oil, the tick is more likely to release the disease organisms it may be carrying into your cat. Fast, direct removal is best.

as mice or deer. Hungry ticks love to lurk in tall grass and shrubbery, just waiting for a cat to pass. Then they drop onto the cat's coat or climb up from the ground.

When ticks feed, they swell with blood. After about two days they become fully engorged, then drop to the ground. The female finds a cozy crevice and lays from 2,000 to 6,000 eggs. Newly hatched ticks, called "seed ticks," molt three times before they become adults. They need one blood meal before each molt and one before laying eggs.

Ticks are notoriously difficult to control. They are resistant to a lot of chemicals and can breed just about anywhere—including inside a house. Keeping your grass trimmed short will decrease the tick population, and keeping a cat indoors will limit the chances she'll become a tick meal ticket. I have never found a truly effective tick spray or collar for use on a cat. However, Frontline Top Spot is safe, effective, and easy to use as a once-a-month treatment during the tick breeding times in your area (usually spring and fall).

Ear Mites

A cat's ear canal is the perfect home for mites. These eight-legged bugs thrive in warm, humid, sebum-rich places. They love to munch on the flaking skin and other natural debris found in the ear.

The most common ear mite is called *Otodectes cyanotes*. This is the culprit that usually causes the coffee-ground-looking debris inside the ears of young cats. These little pests cause a tremendous amount of itching. The irritation they cause can set up the ear for infections from either bacteria or yeast. If mites are left untreated, the eardrum can rupture, leading to middle and inner ear infections and sometimes even death.

Ear mites are passed from one infected cat to another or sometimes from dog to cat. In rare cases, they can even be passed from an animal to a human although they find our short, straight ear canals distasteful places to live.

You can buy over-the-counter treatments for ear mites, but starting treatment without a microscopic exam of the ear debris isn't wise. With a simple ear swab your veterinarian can quickly tell if your cat is suffering from an ear mite infestation, an infestation with a less common mite, or a bacterial or yeast infection. Each requires different treatment.

Of the several types of treatment for ear mites, most veterinarians prefer a product called Tresaderm or another drop-in-the-ear medication. Because it takes about three weeks for a newly laid egg to hatch into an adult that can be killed by treatment, medicine has to be instilled on a strict schedule for weeks or sometimes longer. A quicker treatment is an injectable form of ivermectin, a common anti-parasite drug. However, it can be toxic to kittens and cats if given in too high a dose, so it's generally used only as a last resort.

Cheyletiella, a.k.a. "Walking Dandruff"

This mite not only has a big name; it's a big bug. *Cheyletiella* can often be seen with the naked eye as they wander along the fur of a cat. If you think your cat's dandruff is actually moving, chances are he's picked up this bug.

Cats infected with this mite can get a little itchy and occasionally will get a thickened skin, but usually signs of the infestation are mild. *Cheyletiella* walk easily to a cat from infested premises or another cat. Although it's unusual, they sometimes try to live on people, too. Humans usually develop a red, itchy patch of skin when the mite moves in.

Your cat is quick to lick at itchy things, and she may catch the mite when grooming. Once swallowed, it passes through the stool unharmed. To diagnose an infestation, your veterinarian may look at samples of hair, dander, or stool under the microscope.

Treatment isn't particularly difficult—the mites are usually killed by a bath in any common cat flea shampoo. But the mite can live a long time when it's off

> If you think your cat's dandruff is actually moving, chances are he's picked up this bug: Cheyletiella.

the cat, so repeat treatments may be needed. In some cases, the house may need to be treated with a premise spray as well.

Lice

Lice live just about everywhere: on birds, cats, dogs, pigs, and even people (and that's just to name a few hosts!). Fortunately, most lice are host specific. In other words, they only live and breed on their favorite animal. Although they may hitch a ride on another species, they don't live on them for long. This means that you can't catch your cat's lice, and he can't catch yours. Which should make a cat happy, since humans get lice much more often than cats do.

The cat louse has the scientific name of *Felicola subrostratus* and can be passed from cat to cat by direct contact or from brushes, blankets, or combs. Lice spend their entire life attached to the hair of the cat, chewing on dander, hair, and skin. They lay characteristic eggs, called nits, on the hair shaft.

Lice are extremely itchy, and cats will scratch and bite to ease the itch. Lice often carry the common tapeworm, and cats become infested with the worm when they catch and eat the slow-moving lice.

The one good thing about lice is that they are easily treated with almost any cat-safe insecticidal shampoo. Besides a bath, care should be taken to wash all bedding and grooming tools in hot, soapy water to kill any lice that have strayed off the cat.

Cuterebra (Rabbit Botfly)

Cuterebra is one of the ugliest parasites you'll ever see. The adults aren't so bad. They are flies that look almost exactly like a small bumblebee. The fly lays her eggs around rabbit or rat holes. When a curious cat pokes her nose in the hole, the larvae don't realize it's the wrong animal. The eggs hatch, and the larvae burrow into the cat's skin and proceed to grow—and grow. The larvae (technically a maggot) can grow to a half inch long. They are ghastly white and covered with black spines.

The larvae take a full month to mature, and during this time the cat develops a wound that looks very much like an abscess. A small hole in the center serves as a breathing hole for the *Cuterebra*. The cat isn't terribly uncomfortable, but the hole can become infected. In some cases the larvae will set up shop in the nose or even the brain, causing serious disease or even death.

Your veterinarian can provide a quick cure if he can capture and extract the *Cuterebra* through the small breathing hole in the cat's skin. Although the extraction is pretty easy for those with practice (and a strong stomach), it's a touchy procedure and shouldn't be tried at home. Injuring or killing the larvae inside the pet may cause it to release stress chemicals, causing a serious and sometimes fatal reaction in the cat.

Now, let's take a look at the bloodsuckers and nutrient stealers that live inside your pet.

Roundworms

The roundworm is a very common parasite. These big, long, spaghetti-like worms live in the intestine of a cat. They tend to coil up like a bracelet when passed in stool or vomited up on the rug—which is how they got their common name. The scientific name of the most common feline roundworm is *Toxocara cati*.

Kittens usually get roundworms from their mother's milk or from soil contaminated with stool from an infected cat. Older cats occasionally catch roundworm from eating infected mice. Cats often tolerate a few *Toxocara* without problems, but they can make kittens quite sick. Badly infested felines often get potbellies, become weak, and get a scruffy-looking coat. These worms can also cause a cough or obstruct the intestines.

> Kittens usually get roundworms from their mother's milk or from soil contaminated with stool from an infected cat. Older cats occasionally catch roundworm from eating infected mice.

Recently the Centers for Disease Control in Atlanta, Georgia, has promoted worming all kittens starting at about two weeks of age to protect children. Although people don't get intestinal roundworm, the larvae can—very rarely—migrate through the body of a child. This is called *visceral larval migrans*. Children usually recover completely, but even the possibility of such a problem points to the need for good parasite control and good personal hygiene. Simply washing the hands after contacting larvae-contaminated soil protects most children.

Since roundworms are so common in kittens, your veterinarian may elect to begin a deworming schedule as young as two weeks of age. The wormings are then repeated every two to three weeks until the end of vaccinations. Afterward routine fecal examinations can show if your cat has roundworms.

Hookworms

Hookworms are tiny, thin worms that hook onto the intestinal lining and suck blood. The two most common species in cats are *Ancylostoma* and *Uncinaria*. The adult worms prefer to live in the small intestine, but sometimes the larvae migrate through the circulatory system, heart, and lungs. The larvae can also infect humans, causing "plumber's itch," an itchy, red skin condition in people who lie on infected ground.

Cats usually catch the worm by licking their feet after walking on hookworm-infected soil, but they can also catch it by eating mice, or the larvae can penetrate skin. Very young kittens can become infected in utero or by drinking their mother's milk. Besides coughs and illness caused by larval migration, adult hookworms can attach to the intestine and are heavy feeders. Their voracious bloodsucking can quickly make both kittens and cats very anemic and weak.

Although a hookworm-infested cat may look unthrifty—thin with a dry, scruffy coat—or become suddenly weak, you'll need your veterinarian's help to diagnose hookworm. He'll float a sample of your cat's stool in a special solution that brings the eggs to the top. Then he'll check the upper layer under a microscope.

Did You Know?

The cheetah is the only cat in the world that can't retract its claws.

Once discovered, hookworms are easily treated with oral worming solutions available from your veterinarian.

Whipworms

Whipworms are an important parasite of dogs but almost never bother cats. Cats do have a species of whipworm all their own, *Trichuris campanula,* but kitties in the United States can breathe easy—they are rare here. Even if you had the rare cat with a whipworm infestation, you'd probably never know it. Unlike the

What Worm Isn't a Worm?

Cats can catch an ugly skin condition called ringworm. It can cause rings of lost hair, a thin and patchy coat, or a coat full of dander and scabs. But some infected cats look and feel just fine. Any infected cat, no matter how bad or good he looks, can pass the problem on to other cats—and even to people.

Although the name conjures up images of wiggly worms crawling through your pet's skin, ringworm isn't a worm. It's actually caused by a fungus that normally grows in soil or on other pets. It's a treatable condition and usually not too severe. But it's not a parasite.

dog variety, *Trichuris* is a peaceful parasite in cats and rarely causes any problems.

Tapeworm

Tapeworms are long, flattened creatures made up of many segments. If you can imagine a cloth measuring tape, soft and mobile, with marks visible at regular intervals, you can imagine the tapeworm—and how it got its common name. The most common tapeworms in cats are *Dipylidium* and *Taenia*. Their head has both hooks and suckers, so it's a perfect tool to grasp onto the lining of a cat's intestine. Tapeworms primarily get their nourishment from food in the intestinal tract.

Fleas become infested with *Dipylidium* by eating the eggs that pass from a cat's stool. Mice or rabbits can become infested with *Taenia*, again through a cat's stool. The fleas and mice are known as *intermediate hosts*. They pass the infection back to the cat who dares to dine on them, and the life cycle is complete.

One type of tapeworm, *Echinococcus multilocularis,* can be a hazard to humans. Theoretically it can be passed from cats (or dogs, wolves, coyotes, and foxes) to humans through contaminated soil. Fortunately, this worm is very rare in most of the United States and the chance of your cat or you catching it is almost nonexistent. Only one person has been reported with the disease in the United States. But in Alaska, the Dakotas, Minnesota, Nebraska, Illinois, and Iowa, where the worm lives, it's important to wash your hands whenever you handle soil or fruit and to control all tapeworms in cats and dogs.

Tapeworms rarely cause serious disease in cats. Because they steal nutrients, a cat with a heavy infestation can be unthrifty and weak. The only clue you're likely to see is small, rice-like particles clinging to the area under your cat's tail. These are egg-filled segments of tapeworm. Tapeworms are killed easily with the proper medication, such as praziquantel (Droncit). Most effective tapeworm medications are available only through your veterinarian.

Heartworm

Heartworm was first diagnosed in cats in 1920 but considered rare for many years. Recently, however, cats seem to be infested more often. In some areas 5 to 10 percent of all cats have one or more of these worms living in their heart.

The scientific name of heartworm is *Dirofilaria immitis,* and it lives in the heart and arteries of either dogs or cats. Because the worm can grow to 11 inches long and a cat's heart is about the size of a large strawberry, big problems can occur when a cat is infested by even a single worm. There's just no way the heart can work well.

Cats with heartworm may cough, vomit, or go into heart failure. Sometimes the first sign of the problem is simply sudden death. Many veterinarians think there's a link between heartworm and feline asthma in some cats.

Heartworm is transmitted by mosquitoes. When a mosquito bites an infected cat (or, more commonly, an infected dog), it sucks up baby worms, called microfilariae, that circulate through the blood. These grow inside the mosquito and within two weeks are ready to take up residence when injected into a cat during normal mosquito feeding. Within four months these worms have reached the heart. In dogs *Dirofilaria* then reproduce, sending microfilariae into the bloodstream once again. A cat's immune system, however, keeps the worms in check and rarely lets them reproduce.

> Heartworm was first diagnosed in cats in 1920 but considered rare for many years. Recently, however, cats seem to be infested more often.

Your veterinarian can diagnose heartworm disease by testing your cat's blood and from x-rays of her chest. Ultrasound may also be used to examine her heart. Currently there's no safe treatment that will kill the worm lodged inside your cat, but veterinarians can treat the symptoms and keep your cat well until the worm dies a natural death. Better yet, a monthly preventative is now available to avoid the problem altogether.

Toxoplasmosis

Toxoplasma gondii, a one-celled protozoan, is designed by nature to live in cats. When a cat eats a mouse (or any raw meat) infected with *Toxoplasma gondii* (toxo for short), she seldom gets

Heartworm Preventive

Heartworm disease is becoming more common in cats, and it can be very dangerous. There is no safe, effective treatment to clear a cat of heartworm once she's infested. Your veterinarian will only treat her symptoms.

A heartworm preventive has been approved for use in cats. Taken monthly, this chewable tablet can keep a cat's heart beating free of disease. The pill helps control roundworms and hookworms, too.

Whether or not cats should be on this preventive is a matter of debate. In most areas of the country heartworm is still a relatively rare disease in cats. Since the preventive is somewhat costly, it may not make sense to give it when the risk is so low. On the other hand, if your cat contracts heartworm, there's a real risk of her dying of the disease. When prevention is so easy, why not give it—even in areas of little risk?

There's no answer that's right for every cat or cat owner. If you live in a hotbed of canine heartworm and your cat roams outdoors, then the preventive is a great idea. If your home is in a heartworm-free zone, you'll probably want to skip the added expense. For middle-risk areas and even for indoor cats in heartworm zones, the answers aren't at all clear. When you set up a preventative health plan for your cat, ask your veterinarian to help assess the risks of infestation versus the cost of treatment in your particular area.

very sick. She may develop a little diarrhea and, rarely, a few more serious signs, such as a cough.

Inside the cat, toxo sets up house in the intestines and begins to reproduce. For a few days the cat will pass cysts in her stool. These cysts will become ready to invade the next host in about 48 hours. If the next host is a human, problems can result. (See Chapter 10, Your Cat—Part of Your Family, for more about people and toxoplasmosis.) If the next host is a mouse or other rodent, however, the organism wanders through the muscles. Once it's clear that there's no friendly feline intestine around, toxo forms cysts—microscopic, hard-shelled homes—inside the muscles. The organism rests in these cysts until the mouse is eaten by a cat, then the cysts hatch and the toxo happily begins its life-cycle in her intestine. Cats normally catch toxo from eating infected rodents.

Other Unusual Internal Parasites

Capillaria

Capillaria are very small worms that can live in the bladder, small intestine, or lungs of your cat. Although three species of *Capillaria* seek out a cat for shelter, none seem to cause serious disease. Occasionally a cat may get a bladder infection or bronchitis from these worms, but it's rare.

The eggs are usually found by accident when your veterinarian is checking a stool or urine sample. It's good that *Capillaria* rarely cause problems, because they can be difficult to treat. Currently most veterinarians carefully dose affected cats with ivermectin. Since large doses of this drug can make a cat ill, don't try treating your cat with it at home.

Physaloptera

The "stomach worm" of dogs and cats, *Physaloptera* has an interesting life cycle. Cats can catch the worm from eating beetles, cockroaches, or crickets. Once eaten, the worm nips and burrows into the lining of the cat's stomach, where it lives and reproduces. Although this worm is very uncommon in cats, it can cause ulcers, lack of appetite, or vomiting. Occasionally adult worms will show up in vomit, although the common way of diagnosis is through a fecal check under a microscope. Treatment isn't difficult, but *Physaloptera* doesn't respond to over-the-counter medications—your cat will have to see the vet.

Strongyloides

If you're a horse person, you're familiar with strongyles, a common worm of horses. Although cats can't catch horse parasites, they do have a *Strongyloides* species of their own. The cat strongyle lives in the cat's large intestine and can cause chronic, usually mild intestinal problems, including diarrhea. This parasite is rare in most of the United States.

Lungworm (Aelurostrongylus)

The cat lungworm can be found in the southern United States It lives in a cat's lungs, where it can cause coughing, sneezing, and bronchial disease. Fortunately, most infected cats don't get sick.

Lungworm has a complicated life cycle. An infected cat will cough up lungworm larvae and swallow them. These larvae then pass in her stool, where they must be eaten by a snail or slug. Then the snails or slugs are eaten by a rodent, frog, lizard, or bird. When a cat eats any of these (from snails to birds), she can become infected.

Lungworms are typically diagnosed by x-ray or stool sample. Your veterinarian can treat them, but they can be difficult to cure.

Lung Fluke (Paragonimus)

Paragonimus is another worm that can live in a cat's lungs. It's not considered common, although it's often been reported in the Ozarks and other parts of Missouri. When a cat eats a crayfish infected with these flukes or drinks water in which sick or dying crayfish live, the young flukes first go to the stomach and intestine, then burrow through the abdomen to

the lungs. Cats can suffer from peritonitis, muscle pain, or even hemorrhage caused by migrating flukes, and adult flukes can cause pneumonia. Rarely, a fluke will migrate to the brain.

Your veterinarian can diagnose a lung fluke infection with a microscopic stool check, x-rays, or a blood test. Fortunately, the flukes are fairly easily treated. The best treatment, however, is simply to keep your cat away from crayfish.

Platynosomum (Cat Liver Fluke)

The cat liver fluke rarely causes serious disease in cats, but it can occasionally make a cat quite sick by blocking the gallbladder's bile duct. The fluke lives in small numbers in Hawaii, Florida, and some of the other southern states.

An infected cat will pass liver fluke eggs in his stool. They will die unless they are eaten by a very specific type of snail. The snail then passes an infective stage, which is eaten by certain reptiles and amphibians—most commonly a lizard. When cats munch on an infected reptile or amphibian, they contract the flukes, which head for the gallbladder and its bile duct.

Cats who get a few flukes generally only lose their appetite briefly, but when the infestation is heavy, cats can get diarrhea, may vomit, and may even experience liver failure. Your vet can diagnose the fluke by finding its eggs in your cat's stool and will treat the parasite with medicine. You can also prevent the problem entirely by keeping Kitty indoors and away from snail-eating reptiles and amphibians.

Cytauxzoon

If you've never heard of *Cytauxzoon*, consider yourself lucky. This parasite isn't a problem for most of the country but has been reported in Missouri, Oklahoma, Mississippi, Arkansas, Florida, and Texas. It's a particularly dangerous parasite that attacks cats' red blood cells and the lining of blood vessels. Infected cats run very high fevers (106 degrees or greater) and usually die in just a few days. Treatment is generally useless. Because the protozoan parasite is passed only by infected ticks, the trick to keeping your cat safe is good tick control.

The Microscopic Microcosm—
Infectious Organisms

Infectious organisms are rarely thought of as parasites, but they do fit the definition. A parasite is an organism that is, at some point in its life, dependent on another animal (the host). Infectious diseases are certainly that. They set up a home inside your cat to serve their own purposes, which are to thrive and reproduce as rapidly as possible. The fact that the cat gets sick is just a side effect, not the aim, of the organism.

Did You Know?

Black cats are considered lucky in England and in parts of Asia.

A successful disease organism is one that can live quietly inside your pet. Because it depends on the cat for its own life, a disease organism only harms itself if it kills the cat. This is why even the most deadly diseases grow milder over the course of several years. They adapt to keep their host alive.

Bacteria

Many bacteria fulfill the role of parasite very well. Hundreds of them live in and on your cat, doing no real harm. Some actually help the cat—the host and the parasite adapt to become commensal (mutually beneficial) organisms.

But many bacteria are extremely harmful to cats. They can cause system-wide disease, illness, and sometimes death. Some of the most important feline bacteria have familiar names—*Escherichia coli, Salmonella,* Lyme, *Ehrlichia,* and *Staphylococcus,* to name just a few. Entire thick textbooks are dedicated to the description and classification of the many diseases that bacteria cause.

Most bacteria affect a cat's body in similar ways. Once they invade the body, the cat usually responds by running a fever. Her body will also usually pour large numbers of white blood cells into her bloodstream, where they circulate, searching for the bacteria. Depending on the bacteria, she'll show different signs of illness. For example, a cat with Lyme disease would be expected to have joint pain and limp, whereas salmonella normally cause profuse diarrhea.

Because there are so many bacterial diseases, your veterinarian will use his years of study and clinical practice to help narrow down the likely candidates for your cat's problems. Then he may ask for tests to pin down the culprit exactly so he can treat it appropriately. If a fever starts shortly after a tick bite, for example, your veterinarian may take a sample of your cat's blood and submit it for testing for common tick-borne diseases such as Lyme and ehrlichia.

Bacteria are normally brought under control by both the cat's own natural defenses and antibiotics. In some cases, such as a cat with an abscess, it's not necessary to know exactly which bacteria are causing the problem to cure it—a round of broad-spectrum antibiotics will almost always do the trick. In other cases, however, such as a cat with *sepsis*—the spread of disease-causing bacteria into the bloodstream—knowing exactly which bacteria are causing the disease can be critical for proper treatment. For those cases your veterinarian can take a culture. She will collect a small sample of blood or tissue, then send it to a laboratory where they will grow the bacteria until there are enough to be harvested and identified. At the same time the bacteria can be tested against several antibiotics to help identify which drug stands the best chance of curing your cat.

To know more about bacteria and your cat, see the Resources section at the end of this book.

Viruses

Viruses aren't exactly living, and they aren't made up of cells, but they can certainly bug your cat. These "creatures"—if anything only bordering on life can be called that—are made up of a string or two of nucleic acid (genetic material) surrounded by a capsule.

There are two major types of viruses—those that attack with a wallop, such as feline panleukopenia, and those that work by stealth. Retroviruses, such as feline leukemia and feline immunosuppressive virus, are good examples of stealthy viruses. These viruses can actually become part of a cat's cells, living quietly for a while, then causing disease when a trigger such as stress or malnutrition causes massive viral reproduction. Some viruses, such as feline leukemia, have even been associated with cancer formation.

Many bacteria fulfill the role of parasite very well. Hundreds of them live in and on your cat, doing no real harm. Some actually help the cat.

When a virus attacks a cat's body, his temperature will probably rise. Unlike in a bacterial infection, his white blood cell count often actually drops. Instead of flowing into the circulation, the white blood cells often follow the virus deep into the body part that's affected, so fewer are in the bloodstream.

Despite intense study, no good cures for viruses exist. In humans some of the newer antiviral agents such as Acyclovir help slow down outbreaks of viral disease. But in cats these agents are proving fairly toxic and relatively ineffective. Your veterinarian isn't completely helpless—some drugs and supplements can be used to slow down many viruses—but his weaponry is very limited.

> There are two major types of viruses–those that attack with a wallop, such as feline panleukopenia, and those that work by stealth such as leukemia and feline immunosuppressive virus.

But scientists have much better luck vaccinating against viruses than bacteria. Vaccines exist for the major upper respiratory viruses, panleukopenia, and feline leukemia, and other vaccines are in the works.

Veterinarians can diagnose viruses based on clinical signs, complete blood cell counts, blood chemistry profiles which can suggest infection that settles into major organs such as the kidneys or liver, and special testing for specific viruses. Feline leukemia, for example, can be diagnosed from a small blood sample in only minutes at your veterinarian's office.

Prions

Recently the prion, which causes a rare type of diseases called spongiform encephalopathies, was discovered. These diseases melt holes in the brain, so that microscopically it looks like a sponge. The most common of these diseases is Bovine Spongiform Encephalopathy (BSE) or mad cow disease. Other, similar diseases exist in sheep, goats, humans, and minks. In Britain, Norway, and Italy, spongiform encephalopathy has even been seen in cats. It's rare and hasn't been found in the United States.

Before the discovery of the prion, this agent of brain destruction was thought to be a tiny virus that became part of the body. Such viruses were called "slow viruses" because an animal typically harbored the disease for years before exhibiting the first sign of illness.

Basically, a prion is a small piece of protein. It can react with the body's own proteins, causing them to lose shape or melt into an amorphous little blob. There's no cure for prions, and prevention could be difficult because these nonliving pieces of proteins are extremely difficult to destroy. They have even remained deadly high-temperature surgical sterilization procedures.

Fortunately, the disease seems to be difficult to pass from animal to animal. Outbreaks have almost always involved feeding tissue from the brain or nervous system to a healthy animal, who then becomes sick several years later.

Affected cats in Europe suffer from nervous system disease. It can progress quickly but more often develops slowly. Although no cure exists for this disease, there's no evidence that it spreads from cat to cat. Right now, prion disease isn't a concern in the United States.

Did You Know?

Sleeping cats are still alert to incoming stimuli. If you touch the ears of a sleeping cat, they will twitch even though the cat will likely stay asleep.

7

Emergencies and Illness

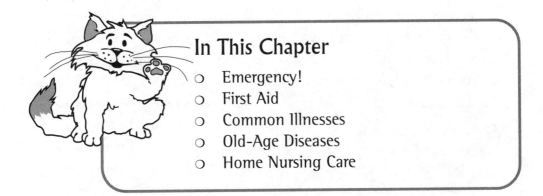

In This Chapter

- Emergency!
- First Aid
- Common Illnesses
- Old-Age Diseases
- Home Nursing Care

There's a lot to know about your feline friend. Although you'd need a medical degree to truly understand the feline body inside and out, every cat owner can learn the basic facts pretty quickly. Armed with an introduction to emergencies and common illnesses, you'll be better able to understand what happens when things go wrong inside your cat and how best to help her.

> Armed with an introduction to emergencies and common illnesses, you'll be better able to understand what happens when things go wrong inside your cat and how best to help her.

Emergency!

You're all alone and your cat needs a hand—fast. Do you know the signs of a medical emergency?

Signs of a Medical Emergency

Cats are small creatures, and they instinctively know that showing weakness can mark them as a victim to a prowling dog or hungry owl. So cats try to hide illness. For this reason, whenever your cat isn't acting normally, call your vet. If your cat is very obviously ill—staggering, repetitively vomiting, bleeding, crying at the litter box, hanging his head over a water bowl, lying limply, or having trouble breathing—you can bet it's an emergency.

> Cats are small creatures, and they instinctively know that showing weakness can mark them as a victim to a prowling dog or hungry owl. So cats try to hide illness.

Sometimes emergencies aren't so obvious. Learning to look for clues, such as color of your cat's gums, her response to the press test, her body temperature, and the way she breathes, will help you know when your cat needs help.

Gum Color

The color of a cat's gums reflects the workings of her circulatory system. Normal gum color is medium to bubble-gum pink and means the blood is flowing well. Pale gums are a sign of a serious problem—your cat may be anemic or in shock, a life-threatening response to grave illness. In shock the blood flow slows to the gums and limbs, making the extremities cool and the gums pale. Blue- or gray-colored gums mean that your cat's blood flow is fine, but her blood lacks oxygen. Bright, brick red gums may be a sign of poisoning or severe infection. Any change in gum color should be considered an emergency.

Press Test

Another way to assess your cat's circulation is with what's called the press test, or capillary refill time. Raise your cat's upper lip a little so you can see her gums. Use your index finger to press firmly on the gum, then release as you count, "One thousand one, one thousand two..." In a healthy cat the white finger mark you left on the pink gum should completely disappear within two seconds (before you begin to say, "One thousand three"). If it takes three seconds or more, your cat's circulation is poor and you should call your vet immediately.

Taking a Temperature

Cats loathe thermometers, but body temperature is such a vital clue to kitty illness that every owner should—ideally—be handy at the temperature-taking game. You'll need a thermometer, a little lubricating ointment, and a friend to help you hold the cat.

Digital thermometers are the best. The tip is small, they read the temperature rapidly, and they beep to tell you when the ordeal is over. The lubricating ointment should be either Vaseline, a bland, pure petroleum jelly, or K-Y jelly, a water-based lubricating gel. Your friend should be cat savvy and capable of helping you calm and distract your cat while you insert the thermometer.

The act itself is pretty simple. Put a little lubricant on the thermometer tip and have your friend grip the scruff of your cat's neck as he talks to her. Lift your cat's tail and insert the thermometer gently into her rectum. It's not important to sink the thermometer its full length—just make sure the metal

tip disappears from sight. If you feel resistance or your cat seems extremely uncomfortable, don't fight. Let your vet check out what's wrong.

A cat's normal temperature is 101.5 degrees, give or take a degree and a half. A reading of 103 or higher generally means a fever and that your cat needs attention. Temperatures above 105 or below 100 degrees mean an emergency.

A cat's normal temperature is 101.5 degrees, give or take a degree and a half. A reading of 103 or higher generally means a fever and that your cat needs attention.

Breath Check

Your dog may pant with his mouth open every day. It's part of his normal cooling mechanism, not a reflection on his heath. Healthy cats, however, pant only during severe stress (such as a car ride) or after extremely strenuous exercise. Even then they rarely pant more than just a few breaths. If your cat pants like a dog, it's a sign of breathing trouble and needs immediate attention.

Healthy cats don't cough. They make a hacking sound as a prelude to a hair ball, sure, but you'll notice they're hunched over, with their neck extended. And the hacking ends with a gooey little mass appearing on your floor. If you hear a coughing sound when your cat is sitting upright, walking, or lying down or if it doesn't end with vomiting, it's not a hair ball. Your cat may have asthma or a heart condition and needs help.

If you watch when your cat breathes, you'll see that the breaths of a healthy cat are effortless, with an easy, smooth rhythm. If her breaths become fast and shallow, your cat may be telling you that she's in pain or has problems with her lungs. If her breaths slow down and her chest rises and falls markedly with each effort, she most likely has fluid in her chest or badly con-

It's an Emergency!

The following signs or events mean an immediate trip to the veterinarian or emergency hospital. Delay could cause serious complications.

Pale gums
Bleeding
Hit by car
Bitten by dog
Shot with BB gun
Bone sticking through skin
Coughing
Difficulty breathing
Won't play or move easily
Staggering
Seizuring
Has bitten an electric cord

Has eaten a poisonous plant, medication, or other poison
Sitting on litter box frequently
Crying when attempting to urinate
Can't urinate
Violent, repeated vomiting or vomiting that continues longer than 24 hours
Profuse diarrhea, especially if bloody or if cat vomits as well
Frantic pawing at face
Any burn

gested lungs. Check out her nostrils, too. If they flare out at the corners as your cat inhales, she can't breathe right. Any of these changes indicate an emergency—put your cat in a crate, keep her as quiet as possible, and get her to your veterinarian without delay.

First Aid

When your cat is hurt, your first instinct is to do something—anything—to help her feel better. In an emergency, the best thing you can do is to get her to professional care as quickly as possible. But sometimes you can lend a helpful hand in the minutes before you leave for the veterinary hospital.

Kitty Emergency Kit

When your cat is in trouble, you can't waste precious minutes searching for supplies. A good emergency kit not only contains the things you need for emergency treatment but also prepares you to transport your cat to the vet, pronto.

1. Sturdy cat carrier

2. Digital thermometer

3. Diluted povidone iodine (Betadine) antiseptic for cleaning minor cuts—it should be ready to use, not concentrated

4. For bandages:
   - ◯ 2-inch gauze
   - ◯ 2 × 2 telfa-type pad
   - ◯ 1-inch adhesive tape

5. Scissors (preferably blunt tipped)

6. 1 or 2 thick bath towels to use for restraint or for warmth

7. Tweezers

8. Saline in a squirt bottle (eyewash) for rinsing wounds before bandaging

9. Activated charcoal—buy small pills (pediatric) at the pharmacy to use under direction of your vet if your cat swallows something poisonous

10. Extra set of all medicines your cat routinely uses

11. Copy of current vaccination records, especially rabies certificate

12. Copy of your cat's medical records

13. Credit card with at least a couple of hundred dollars' available credit

14. Emergency phone numbers of your veterinary hospital, the closest emergency hospital, and the National Animal Poison Control Center

15. A good pet first aid book

Car Accidents

When cat meets car, the cat is usually a big loser. It may sound rough, but roadside first aid is rarely helpful. Without proper equipment and emergency drugs, even a trained veterinarian may not be able to stabilize a cat roadside. The best place for a critically injured cat is at the hospital.

In the seconds following the accident, do a quick assessment of emergency signs (see above) and check your cat's heartbeat by putting a finger and thumb on each side of her chest, at the spot where her elbows normally rest. If you can't feel a heartbeat or your cat isn't breathing, try CPR.

Ideally, you'll keep your cat still as you transport her to your vet hospital. If possible, slide a board or piece of rigid plastic under your cat, then wrap a towel over her body to keep her from moving and to keep her warm. But don't waste a lot of time looking for the right equipment. Be as gentle as possible to avoid making broken bones or internal bleeding worse, but do get her transported to your vet immediately.

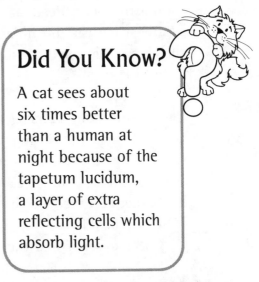

Did You Know?

A cat sees about six times better than a human at night because of the tapetum lucidum, a layer of extra reflecting cells which absorb light.

Once your cat is at the veterinary hospital, where she has the benefits of emergency drugs, oxygen therapy, and intravenous fluids, her chances of survival—and complete recovery—improve dramatically. Focus on this fact, breathe deeply, and stay as calm as you can.

CPR

Cardiopulmonary resuscitation (CPR) consists of two parts: *rescue breathing,* which fills your cat's lungs with life-sustaining oxygen, and *chest compressions,* which push blood through her body.

Before you begin, make sure your cat actually needs help. Don't attempt CPR on a conscious animal. You'll both get hurt.

Watch closely for any signs of breathing. Then touch your pet to try to awaken her. Finally, check for a heartbeat: lay a thumb and finger on either side of your cat's chest, just behind her elbows. Feel several spots near that location before deciding that she has no heartbeat.

If your cat doesn't have a heartbeat and isn't breathing, perform both rescue breathing and chest compressions. If she has a heartbeat but isn't breathing, perform only rescue breathing. If she's breathing, you can assume she has a heartbeat, so don't perform CPR.

Rescue Breathing   First clear the airway. Extend your cat's head and neck, then pull her tongue forward. Sweep your finger inside the pet's throat to remove vomit or foreign objects that might obstruct breathing. Normal cats have a smooth, skin-covered, bone-like structure called the hyoid apparatus deep in their throat. Don't pull on this.

Check to see if your cat will start breathing on her own once

the airway is clear. Watch for her chest to rise and fall and listen for breath sounds. If she shows no sign of breathing by the count of 10, breathe for her.

Cover your cat's nose and mouth with your mouth. Hold the cat's upper lip down over the corners of her mouth and breathe forcefully into her nose. Watch for the chest to rise. When it does, take your mouth away. Don't try to keep the chest expanded—you could injure the lungs.

Give five breaths about three seconds apart. Then stop to see if she has begun to breathe on her own. If not, push down gently on the stomach area to push out gas that may have entered it when you breathed for her. Also, check again for a heartbeat. If you don't find a heartbeat, begin chest compressions.

Chest Compressions   Place your hands around your cat's chest, with your palms resting just behind her elbows, locking your fingers under her chest. Squeeze the palms of your hands firmly down, compressing the rib cage about half an inch. Give 12 quick compressions, less than one second apart, then breathe for your cat again.

Give a set of chest compressions after every two breaths. Continue CPR until:

○ You become too tired to continue
○ You get to a veterinary hospital
○ You feel a pulse or heartbeat (stop cardiac compression)
○ Your cat begins to breathe on her own (stop rescue breathing)

Seizures

A seizure is set off by random electrical signals dashing around in the brain, much like a short circuit. As the brain waves become scrambled, the body convulses. In most seizures the cat will fall to the ground, thrash his legs, and chomp his teeth and may urinate or defecate. He won't be conscious or respond to his master's voice or being touched. Less commonly a seizure may involve just one set of muscles, resulting in uncontrollable twitching of a leg or another body part.

The seizure itself generally isn't harmful to your cat. Most episodes will stop on their own within a minute or two. Seizures that continue without stopping for five minutes or more, however, can be very dangerous. They drive your cat's body temperature up, potentially damaging the brain, and may even kill him. This kind of unrelenting seizure is called status epilepticus and can be stopped only with intravenous drug therapy.

Because you can't do anything to bring your cat out of a seizure, the best first aid is simply to keep him from harming himself. You can put him inside a crate to prevent him from slamming himself into walls or rolling down a flight of stairs. Just make sure he doesn't jam his head into one of the crate's corners and suffocate. Some owners prefer to wrap their cat in a heavy towel so they can hold him until he recovers. But this is risky—you may get injured by your cat's violent and unconscious thrashing. Do *not* reach into the mouth of a seizuring cat. He won't choke on his tongue, but he *will* bite your fingers.

> **B**ecause you can't do anything to bring your cat out of a seizure, the best first aid is simply to keep him from harming himself.

If a full minute passes and your cat continues to convulse, it's best to make a quick phone call to your vet and follow her directions. Most vets will want to see the cat immediately for treatment.

If your cat has already been diagnosed as an epileptic and is undergoing therapy, you'll simply want to note the date and duration of this episode. If this is your cat's first seizure, however, it's important to visit your vet as soon as possible—ideally within an hour. The faster your vet can examine your cat, the more clues she can get about the cause of the seizure and the faster treatment, if needed, can begin.

Choking

If your cat begins to paw frantically at her face, acting as if she's trying to dislodge something from her throat, she may be choking. Although an obstructed airway can be life threatening, it's often hard for an owner to help. Even if a toy or twig is lodged nicely within finger reach, a choking cat will most likely bite you if you reach in to get it. She's not being mean; she's simply panicking.

If your cat's gums are still pink, she's getting enough oxygen. In that case, whisk her off to your vet's office. He can remove the object safely, although he may have to sedate your cat to reach inside her mouth.

If your cat's gums are blue, try to look in her throat for an obvious blockage. If you see something, you can—cautiously and quickly—reach in and try to pull it out.

If you can't see an obstruction, don't risk your fingers. Instead try a modified Heimlich maneuver. Stand behind your cat, cup your hands, and lay them on your cat's sides so that your thumbs are over her last ribs and your palms lie just behind the ribs. Give a firm, quick thrust with both hands, depressing each side about a half inch. If you're lucky, the air pressure will shoot the object out of her airway. You may repeat the maneuver several times.

If nothing comes out, nothing may be lodged in her throat. Cats often act as if they're choking when they're suffering from a severe bout of feline asthma or from anaphylaxis—a sudden, severe, life-threatening allergic reaction. Both of these conditions

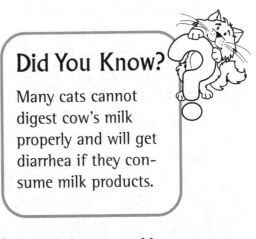

Did You Know?

Many cats cannot digest cow's milk properly and will get diarrhea if they consume milk products.

can be treated by your veterinarian, but like choking, they are extreme emergencies.

Dog Bite

A dog's teeth are sharp and can easily pierce the skin of a cat, causing ugly, dangerous wounds. But even more damage can be done by the strength of a dog's jaws. The same jaws that can crunch a soup bone into shards and slivers can easily do the same to your cat's bones. The powerful crunching action can also rupture a cat's liver or bruise his lungs, sometimes without leaving a mark on the skin. Because internal injuries are so common—and so hard to detect—a cat's run-in with canine teeth always warrants a quick check with your vet.

Broken Bones

Cats are pretty tough creatures, but given enough force, bones can break. The most common fractures occur on any of the four legs, although the pelvis can be broken in a fall, by a hard kick, or when a cat is hit by a car. It's also common for a cat to break his lower jaw when he takes a nosedive off a porch.

Broken legs are usually pretty obvious—the cat won't want to put weight on her leg, and it may dangle when she moves. A cat with

a broken pelvis won't be able to use either hind leg well and will usually drag his rear along the ground. A cat with a broken jaw is likely to hold his mouth partially open and drool. If the break is really severe, you may actually see the bone puncture the skin. This type of break, called a compound fracture, demands immediate emergency attention to prevent serious infection.

Although broken bones are quite painful, they aren't usually life-threatening emergencies in and of themselves. But a cat who has taken a blow hard enough to break a bone may have internal injuries that *are* life threatening. So any suspected bone injury should be a signal to see the veterinarian immediately.

The best first aid for a broken bone is to keep your cat quiet and leave the broken bone alone until you arrive at the hospital. Splinting a break can cause excruciating pain and is likely to do more harm than good. If you suspect a broken bone, put your cat in a small crate to keep her quiet. Then—you guessed it—head to the vet.

> The best first aid for a broken bone is to keep your cat quiet and leave the broken bone alone until you arrive at the hospital.

Screaming in Pain (Estrus)

It happened again yesterday—I got a phone call from a panicky owner, describing his cat's peculiar emergency. Apparently the cat suddenly became wildly vocal, screaming and yowling in what seemed to be horrible pain. She was even rolling around and dragging her belly across the floor. She couldn't walk normally, so the owner thought her back might be broken.

No stranger to this alarming scenario, I calmly asked, "Is your cat about six months old and a female?"

"Yes," he said, sounding frantic.

"And I bet she's never been spayed," I went on.

"No, not yet," he replied.

"Tell me, if you rub her along the back, what does she do?" I asked.

"Hold on." The owner dropped the phone, and I heard yowling in the background, then the owner's bewildered voice. "She screams in pain, then lifts her tail straight up in the air."

Aha! Diagnosis confirmed! The cat is experiencing her first heat cycle.

A cat's estrus, or standing heat, is dramatic and loud. Many owners are sure that their cat is injured or seizuring. But she's not. She's senseless with desire. If you leave her alone, she'll get well on her own in a week or so. But she'll do the same thing her next heat—which can come as quickly as every three to four weeks.

Most owners like to get at least some sleep every night, which can be impossible with the caterwauling of an estrual queen. Besides screaming and rolling, a female in heat may start spraying urine all over the house. And the habit may not stop when she comes out of heat, either.

The best first aid possible for an in-heat cat is to bring her in to be spayed. Although the blood vessels to the uterus are slightly larger when a cat is in heat, the surgery is still quite safe. And spaying is the only permanent cure for this alarming nonemergency.

Bleeding

Many different kinds of accidents can cause a cat to bleed. Cuts, scrapes, and punctures all make the blood flow. A little blood isn't a bad thing. It washes bacteria away from the wound and brings infection-fighting cells to the wound. Of course, losing too much blood can hurt—or kill—a cat.

Pressure is the best treatment for bleeding. Direct pressure right on the wound works the best. You can use your clean hands, a clean piece of fabric or gauze, or even a sanitary napkin on the wound. Just press down firmly for two to three minutes, then remove your fingers and see if the blood flows again. If you're using a covering, be aware that a clot will form on it. Don't pull it away, or you'll freshen the wound and start it bleeding again.

When blood pumps out of a wound or bleeding continues despite direct pressure, you may have to take more serious steps. In addition to direct pressure, try placing the flat of your hand on the pet's limb between the wound and the trunk of her body, then press down firmly into the flesh. You can even wrap your hand all the way around her limb and squeeze. Watch to see if the blood flow slows down. If it does, continue holding for two to three minutes and release. If blood flows heavily again, press back down, releasing briefly every few minutes until you arrive at your vet's. If the wound is on the trunk of the body, not a limb, just keep pressure on the wound and the surrounding area as you head to your vet's office.

Burns

Cats don't willingly burn themselves, but an adventurous nature has caused more than one cat to go pitty-pat across a hot stove, charring his pads in the process. Besides heat—which is known as a thermal burn—your cat can also be burned by electricity or caustic chemicals.

Thermal burns often look mild at first but can become large, painful, and infected within a day or two. Burns to the paw pads are particularly painful and difficult to cure. If you cat sustains a thermal burn, even a small one, douse the area in cool water, then let your vet help you treat it.

Electrical burns are potentially deadly. They not only char skin; electricity can cause a deadly

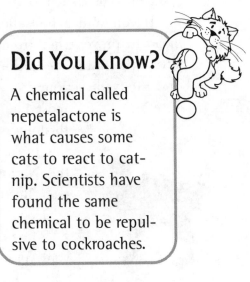

Did You Know?

A chemical called nepetalactone is what causes some cats to react to catnip. Scientists have found the same chemical to be repulsive to cockroaches.

shock. It can kill a cat in a second, or it may cause an irregular heartbeat. Even if she looks fine at first, the kitten who chewed an electric cord may find her lungs filling up with fluid from the shock or the burns on her mouth deepening dangerously in the first 48 hours.

If you find your kitten unconscious, electric cord in mouth, resist the impulse to grab him. Make sure that you unplug the cord or shut off the power to the cord, or you may be shocked, too. If you can't turn off the power, use a wooden or plastic stick (or broom) to pull him free of the live electricity.

Once the current is broken, it's safe to touch your kitten. If he isn't breathing and doesn't have a heartbeat, begin CPR. If he's conscious and looks all right, consider him lucky. But he may not have escaped completely. Get him immediately to his vet, who will do a thorough exam and institute therapy to ward off potential complications.

Chemical burns, fortunately, are rare. If a chemical is strong enough to burn the skin, it can also do severe damage to the cat's tongue, mouth, and digestive tract when she licks the burn. And, of course, she'll try to lick it to get herself clean.

If you spill a household chemical on your cat, hold her head to prevent her from licking. Then try to get it off her coat—the faster the better. If the chemical has a label, follow the safety directions for removing it from human skin. For most chemicals, such as bleach, this means flushing with water. But water can make certain burns worse. If you can't find a label, call the National Animal Poison Control Center (see Resources) or your vet for immediate advice.

After following the label instructions, let your vet see your cat. Chemical burns can get worse over several days, but rapid treatment can minimize damage. Some chemicals can also leach through skin, damaging a cat's kidneys or liver or even poisoning her. Consider any chemical burn a true emergency and seek rapid professional help.

Eye Injury

Most eye injuries are very painful, so your cat will give you clear clues when his eye is hurt. He'll most likely keep his eyelids squeezed shut and may paw at his face. You may notice tears or blood around his eyelids.

If you're lucky enough to see a splinter or piece of hair fall into your cat's eye, you may be able to help him by gently flooding the eye with sterile saline eyewash. This will wash away debris and dust and is harmless even in more serious eye injuries.

If your cat continues to squint after the wash, if you see blood around his eyelids, or if you think he's taken a blow to the eye, then head directly to your veterinarian's office for treatment.

Common Illnesses

Cats tend to be pretty healthy, but every once in a while your cat may have a run-in with one of the following common cat illnesses. Infections are common, too, and are discussed in Chapters 5 and 6.

Abscess

An abscess is a painful swelling that is filled with bacteria and pus. It's very common, especially in outdoor cats. When an outdoor cat fights with other cats, a deep scratch or, more often, a bite can inject thousands of bacteria deep inside the skin. The initial wound may look minor and heal in a day or two, but the bacteria will continue to grow under the skin. Soon the area is badly infected, and your cat feels terrible, too.

Untreated abscesses will eventually burst, causing an obnoxious, smelly, sometimes bloody mess. Without proper care, the abscess is very likely to form again. Abscesses can spread widely, destroying a lot of skin—and sometimes kill the cat, too.

> Untreated abscesses will eventually burst, causing an obnoxious, smelly, sometimes bloody mess. Without proper care, the abscess is very likely to form again.

If you notice a bite wound on your cat, treating him with antibiotics immediately may avoid an abscess completely. Once the area swells, however, it should be lanced and cleaned by your vet. Your cat will need antibiotics, and you'll be instructed to keep the wound clean and open for several days. In almost all cases, this simple treatment provides a rapid and complete cure.

Asthma

Like humans, cats can develop asthma, a condition in which the airways constrict, causing mild to severe problems breathing. In cats, asthma may be triggered by allergies or lung irritation from many causes, such as ozone (from air purifiers or air pollution), smoke, or perfumes. Just as in people, there may be a genetic link—certain cats may be born with sensitive airways, easily triggered to spasm by any number of causes. Siamese cats seem especially predisposed to asthma.

The first sign of asthma may be just a soft cough. Your cat may sit up or stand when he coughs, or he may hunch over as if throwing up a hair ball. As the condition gets worse, your cat will have more trouble breathing. His nostrils may flare when he breathes, and his chest may move a bit more than normal. When things get really bad, your cat may rattle, wheeze, and breathe with an open mouth. His gums may turn blue, and he may become frantic—pawing at his face, running, scratching, and biting in a panic because he can't breathe. When things get this bad, it's a dire emergency.

Most cats respond well to medical treatment. In an asthmatic crisis, your vet will give your cat oxygen and several drugs, usually by intravenous injection, to help him breathe better. Don't wait until your cat is blue and frantic to bring him in, though. Any abnormal breathing should be addressed immediately. The earlier you get treatment, the easier it will be.

Asthma is a very serious disease, and treatments are improving rapidly. Modern vets still use prednisone and bronchodilators to control most cases of asthma, but many vets are now also using certain human drugs, such as Accolate, and nutritional therapy, such as omega-3 fatty acids, to improve control. If you think your cat may have asthma, work closely with your vet to help keep your cat breathing easy.

> **Did You Know?**
>
> Napoleon was terrified of cats.

Diabetes

Most people think of diabetes as a disease caused by too much blood sugar. In fact, it's really caused by a deficiency of insulin, the hormone that regulates the flow of blood sugar into cells. Diabetic cats either make no insulin of their own (type I), or their bodies can't use the insulin that they do make (type II). Either way, the sugar— or raw energy—derived from food can't get into the body's cells. Instead the sugar circulates in the blood while the body literally starves.

Diabetic cats are typically very hungry, but they lose weight, no matter how much they eat. They also tend to drink and to urinate a lot. Untreated, diabetes is fatal.

Most diabetic cats are type I (insulin dependent), which means that their pancreas isn't making enough insulin. These cats will require insulin injections for the rest of their life, either once or twice a day. Type II (non-insulin-dependent) cats can usually avoid daily injections or may need insulin only for short periods. The classic type II cat is obese. He produces insulin, but the fat keeps it from being useful. If the cat's diet is corrected and he loses weight, he can become perfectly normal again. Type II diabetics may be treated by temporary insulin injections, diet changes, or oral medication.

> **D**iabetic cats are typically very hungry, but they lose weight, no matter how much they eat. They also tend to drink and to urinate a lot. Untreated, diabetes is fatal.

Diarrhea

Veterinarians recognize two major forms of diarrhea: acute and chronic. Acute diarrhea comes on suddenly, may be intense, and often goes away very quickly—sometimes within a day. The most common causes of acute diarrhea are a sudden change of food, overeating, drinking milk if the cat can't digest milk sugar, minor infections, and intestinal parasites. Poisons, allergic reactions, and serious diseases such as pancreatic disease can also cause bouts of acute diarrhea.

As long as your cat feels well and has less than four episodes in a day, acute diarrhea isn't an emergency. If you see blood in the stool, if your cat has more than six episodes in 24 hours, or if she's listless, depressed, or just plain looks like she feels bad, she needs medical help right away.

Chronic diarrhea, by definition, is any change in consistency, frequency, or volume of the feces that lasts longer than three weeks. Chronic diarrhea usually points to a more serious problem than the acute form. In some cases, the cause may be as simple as untreated parasites or a poor diet. But chronic diarrhea can also be a clue that your cat has an intestinal obstruction, a persistent infection, or even a serious systemic disease, such as kidney failure.

Because stool changes can signify so many different problems, expect your veterinarian to do a careful physical examination. Sometimes the cause will be obvious on exam—tapeworm segments on the tail, a toy that can be felt inside a loop of bowel, or kidneys that feel abnormally small. Most of the time, however, your vet will need to do some sleuthing to get to the bottom of your cat's problem. He may examine a stool sample for parasites, take blood to check organ function and look for signs of infection, and take x-rays to check for tumors or foreign objects. Sometimes special tests, such as blood tests for FIP or stool cultures for salmonella, may be helpful, too.

Usually the treatment for diarrhea is simple: a food change, worming your cat, or keeping her away from the milk bowl. In other cases treatment may include antibiotics, fluid therapy, or even surgery to retrieve a toy from your cat's bowels.

Feline Lower Urinary Tract Disease

Feline lower urinary tract disease (FLUTD) is painful urination resulting from bladder inflammation or infection. The inflammation is most commonly caused by formation of crystals or stones inside the bladder. Why

these form is still not known, but food plays an important role in both cause and treatment.

When a cat urinates, stones and crystals move out of his body along with the urine, passing through the urethra. The urethra of the female cat is short and straight, but in a male cat it twists upward, then narrows as it passes through the penis. Females get FLUTD as often as males, but the stones pass easily. Even the smallest stone can get stuck in the twisting urethra of the male, blocking all urine from passing and creating a dire emergency.

When a cat can't urinate, he'll die a miserable and painful death within 48 hours unless he's unblocked. This requires anesthesia, and he'll have to be hospitalized for several days afterward. If you can catch the problem while your cat is still urinating freely, treatment is much easier—usually a change in diet will suffice, although some cats will need antibiotics or other medication.

The signs of FLUTD are numerous, but they all center around abnormal urination. The first sign is often simply urinating outside the litter box. This is followed by crying out when urinating, squatting often, or licking his penis (or her vulva). Don't ignore the first signs—male cats can block very quickly. If you see your cat squat and nothing comes out, he must be treated by a vet *immediately*.

The best diets to manage FLUTD are sold through your veterinarian's office. Some pet food manufacturers, however, now market "special care" or "urinary tract health" diets. It's important to understand that these diets are good for preventing or controlling stones and crystals. But they *aren't* good for cats with kidney disease, and they may not be good for growing kittens, either. Make sure to ask your vet for advice before feeding these special diets.

Killer Hair Balls

Most hair balls are small—from a few wisps of hair to a small tube about an inch long. But some veterinarians have seen hair balls "the size of a small banana"—about six inches long and an inch wide. In 1994 a cat choked to death on such a monstrosity. It caught in his throat and shut off his air supply when he tried to throw it up. Obviously, cats can't pass such huge masses—but a surgeon can quickly relieve your cat of such a burden.

Hair Ball

If you haven't been awakened in the middle of the night to the dramatic sound of a cat heaving a hair ball, you probably don't live with a cat. The piles of hair and vomit are disgusting and distressing to both you and your cat, so hair balls do need to be treated. But they rarely cause a severe problem.

The best way to prevent hair balls is good grooming. A brush a day normally keeps the hair ball away, simply because there's little hair left to swallow. Other remedies include feeding a high-fiber food, such as the new Hill's Science Diet Hairball Control, or giving a small amount of a hair ball preventative, such as Laxatone, daily. Not all hair ball remedies are equally safe to use day after day, and some can cause vitamin deficiencies if used in excess. Ask your vet for his advice.

Although hair balls are considered almost normal in a cat, they can be easily controlled by brushing, diet, and/or hairball remedies. If your cat throws up despite treatment, she most likely has something other than hair balls bothering her.

Heart Disease

The heart of an average cat beats over a quarter of a million times each day, day after day, for 15 years or more. It can't rest—just a few skipped beats and the whole body shuts down. Fortunately, most of the time a cat's heart works continuously, without a single hitch.

Sometimes cat hearts do get sick. Heart disease can be caused by low taurine levels in a cat's food (see Chapter 4, Food for Thought) or by heartworm disease (see Chapter 6, What Bugs Your Pet?). Or the muscle or the valves of the heart may get worn down with age or disease.

A cat with heart problems may act weak or tired. He may have trouble breathing, especially when he tries to exercise, or he may cough. Occasionally a cat with heart disease will faint. Your veterinarian can often detect heart problems early, before your cat gives you a clue, by simply listening to your cat's heart at the annual exam.

If you suspect all is not well with your cat's heart, don't hesitate to get to your vet's office. The chances of improving the condition are good. For the most advanced treatment, ask for a referral to a veterinary cardiologist—a vet who has special training in diagnosing and managing heart disease.

Hepatic Lipidosis

The common name for hepatic lipidosis is "fatty liver disease." Just as the name implies, the basic problem in this illness is that for some reason, the cat's liver fills up with fat. The liver isn't meant to store fat—its job is to help clean the body of toxic waste products. When fat builds up, the liver becomes less efficient. It may even fail to work at all, creating a life-threatening crisis.

A cat with hepatic lipidosis may lose his appetite, lose weight, become depressed, hide from you, and turn a distinct yellow color. This yellow color is called jaundice and usually indicates severe disease. Jaundice shows up first on the roof of the mouth and the inside of the ears. You can also easily notice it by looking at the whites of the eyes. If you see the palest hint of yellow or if your cat shows any of these signs, see your vet right away.

There's a strong link between a sudden lack of calories and severe hepatic lipidosis, which triggers life-threatening liver failure. You should never starve or fast a cat or make a major calorie cut to reduce his weight. In fact, many vets consider it an emergency when a cat misses more than one day's worth of meals.

A cat with hepatic lipidosis stands a good chance of recovery even if he's yellow. But it may take a lot of work to save him. Many of these cats will require intensive therapy at a hospital for several weeks and nursing at home for several weeks more. Treatment includes force feeding, fluid therapy, and treatment with a variety of drugs, depending on each cat's individual needs.

Obesity

Speaking of food, can you guess the number-one nutritional disease of cats? If you guessed obesity, you're right. Overweight cats are at high risk for hepatic lipidosis, diabetes, heart disease, lung disease, and arthritis. And obese toms tend to block more easily when they suffer from feline lower urinary tract disease— the internal fat makes the urethra very small and easily plugged.

The best way to treat obesity is to prevent it in the first place by feeding a proper diet and encouraging exercise. Once your cat is fat, it can be hard to take off the weight. To treat obesity, follow the advice in Chapter 4, Let Them Eat Cake: Not!

Vomiting

Cats seem to have rather tender tummies. Let them swallow a little hair or a few blades of grass, and chances are it will land on your carpet in just a few hours. While an occasional vomit rarely presents a problem, vomiting *can* be a sign of many serious problems. Kidney disease, liver disease, intestinal obstructions, and even poisons can cause a cat to upchuck.

So how do you know when vomiting is a serious problem? Mostly by getting to know your cat. Some cats religiously toss one hair ball each week, but others do it rarely. Get used to your cat's pattern, and if there's any change, report it to your vet.

In general, a single vomit or even two in a 24-hour period isn't particularly alarming as long as the cat feels fine. If you notice blood or suspicious foreign objects, such as a piece of string or pellets that look like rat poison, then seek immediate help. Do the same if your cat seems to feel sick, is running a fever, or is staggering or weak.

Even if your cat feels well, vomiting that continues over 24 hours indicates a problem. Your veterinarian will give your cat a full examination and may take x-rays to look for foreign objects and do blood tests to rule out infection, kidney disease, and liver disease. She'll also examine your cat's stool under a microscope to look for parasites. And she'll offer treatment designed to not only stop the vomiting but to cure the problem that made your cat nauseous in the first place.

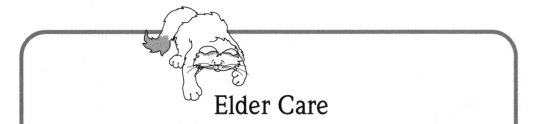

Elder Care

When cats age, they tend to slow down a bit, and they may be more prone to serious diseases, such as hyperthyroidism, kidney disease, and cancer. Unfortunately, the older a cat gets, the less likely he is to receive treatment, even for perfectly treatable conditions.

An owner of a two-year-old cat may rush to the vet when she finds a lump on her cat. A couple of days later, the lump is off and the verdict is in: benign. But when the cat is 15, that same lump might look like a death knell. "He's too old for surgery anyway," goes the thought.

But that's not necessarily true. Just as people are living longer and staying healthier, so are our pets. Old age isn't a disease; elder cats can respond to treatments as well as younger felines. And just as you wouldn't deny Grandma treatment, Grandpuss shouldn't be denied a chance for a cure, either.

Old-Age Diseases

When your cat's years roll into the double digits and she begins slowing down, you may be inclined to write it off as simply old age. In fact, it may be one of several diseases that tend to show up in elderly cats. The good news is that most of these diseases are quite treatable.

Kidney Disease

Kidney disease is almost epidemic in teenage cats, and no one really knows why. Some people blame a poor diet, others a poor environment, while still others say that cats today are simply outliving the life span of their kidneys. Whatever the reason, it's a fact that many elderly cats suffer from kidney failure.

Kidney disease may start years before it shows up in a cat. Only when three-fourths of the kidney is damaged does it begin to fail at its job of cleaning wastes from the blood. When waste products build up in the bloodstream, your cat begins to feel sick. At first she'll drink more water and urinate more frequently. Then she'll begin to lose a bit of weight. As the toxins build up she may feel weak, become anemic, and lose her appetite. She may also develop diarrhea and begin to vomit. Left untreated, she will eventually die.

The earlier you catch kidney disease, the easier it is to control. Treatment begins with fluid therapy, usually given into the vein over several days at the hospital. If the condition is very mild, fluid is sometimes given under the skin instead. This fluid support helps wash out wastes and gives the kidney a little rest and time to heal. Other medicines, such as antibiotics, B vitamins, potassium, and anti-nausea drugs, may be given if necessary.

If your cat does well after the initial therapy, he may go home with no more than a diet change. This seemingly minor treatment can extend the life of the cat remarkably—three or four years isn't uncommon. Although kidney disease usually can't be completely cured, the prognosis for control is good, especially when caught early.

Hyperthyroidism

It's very common for older cats to develop an overactive thyroid gland, which secretes much more thyroid hormone than the body

needs. Thyroid hormone speeds up a cat's metabolism: his heart beats faster, he burns more calories, and he wants more food. At first he feels pretty perky, but soon his body just can't keep up. He becomes ravenously hungry but still loses weight. He may begin to pace and howl. Eventually his heart will fail from the excess work.

The good thing about this disease is that it's quite treatable. Levels of thyroid hormone can be brought down to normal in three ways: with medicine, surgery, or radioactive iodine treatment. Decreasing the level of thyroid hormone brings the cat back to normal, too, and often can even reverse much of the heart disease caused by hyperthyroidism.

The three treatment options for hyperthyroidism all have benefits and risks. The correct treatment for your cat depends on many things, including your budget and your ability to treat your cat at home. Medicine is inexpensive but only controls the disease while it's given, so it's a commitment of time. Surgery is usually a cure, but there is the risk of serious side effects, such as damage to the parathyroid glands, which regulate calcium

> It's very common for older cats to develop an overactive thyroid gland, which secretes much more thyroid hormone than the body needs.

levels. Care afterwards is usually intense for the first week or more, and the price is much higher than medical treatment. Radioactive iodine therapy, on the other hand, is a definitive cure. After injections by a veterinarian and a hospital stay, you usually have no other treatments to give. But radioiodine can be quite costly. Let your veterinarian help you decide which option is best for your cat and you.

Cancer

The longer a cat lives, the more likely it is to develop cancer. *Cancer* is a terrifying word, and many cancers are deadly. But some types are quite treatable. For example, lymphosarcomas—tumors made up of a type of cell called a lymphocyte (a white blood cell that plays a role in fighting disease under ordinary circumstances)—that are caught as single tumors and don't seem to have spread have an average first remission time of 114 weeks, or over two years. Some of these cats are actually cured—the cancer doesn't re-occur. If it does, most cats can be given a second remission, with the expectation of achieving another year (or more) cancer-free.

Such excellent results are still the exception rather than the rule for most cat cancers. But veterinarians are becoming better at diagnosing and treating all forms of cancer, and board-certified veterinary oncologists can sometimes work miracles. If your cat is diagnosed with cancer, don't hesitate to ask your vet for a referral to a local oncologist or to the cancer center of a veterinary college near you.

Home Nursing Care

When you walk out of your cat's hospital, arms filled with medication, you might suddenly feel very much alone. It's just you, Kitty, and Kitty's medicine. And your cat's steely glare seems to warn you that medicine and cats don't mix.

It's true that some cats are almost impossible to treat. If that's your kitty, then you can always bring him by the hospital at medication time and pay the technician a dollar or two to pop the pills or put drops in your cat's ears for a week or so until he's declared cured. But with a little instruction, most owners find that treating their own cat at home really isn't so hard.

When you walk out of your cat's hospital, arms filled with medication, you might suddenly feel very much alone. It's just you, Kitty, and Kitty's medicine. And your cat's steely glare seems to warn you that medicine and cats don't mix.

Pills

Giving pills to a cat is basically a two-step procedure: opening the mouth and placing the pill. Opening a cat's mouth usually isn't hard, although it can feel awkward at first. I like to use my left hand to hold the cat's head and my right to actually pop the pill. If you're a lefty, use your right hand to hold and reserve your faster hand for maneuvering the pill.

First, grasp the cat's head with your left (nondominant) hand. Place your thumb and index finger on each of your cat's cheekbones, found below and behind her eyes. Take your little finger and lay it at the back of your cat's skull. Now, use your thumb and first finger to raise the head, and your little finger will act as a pivot point, helping to hold the head steady. Raise the head to a 40- to 50-degree angle, and you'll see your cat's bottom jaw drop open a bit. The job is half over.

When you see the jaw drop, it's pill time. While keeping a firm hold on your cat's head, grasp the pill between the thumb and first finger of your right (or dominant) hand. Take the little finger of that hand, press it on the small front teeth of the cat's lower front jaw, and gently push downward. Your cat's mouth will open wide. Look inside. Way at the back of the throat, you should see a nice V-shaped area that's created by the muscles of her tongue. I call this the pill slot. You can toss the pill in this slot with a flicking motion, or you can push it down with a finger. If you hit the slot, the pill is almost certain to be swallowed.

Did You Know?

A cat uses its whiskers to determine if a space is too small to squeeze through.

Once the pill hits the slot, close your cat's mouth. You can blow gently in her face or gently pet her neck until you see and feel her swallow. Once she swallows, let her go. But observe her for a minute more to make sure that she doesn't dump the supposedly swallowed pill on the floor. If she does, simply try again.

If your cat tries to claw away your hand, you can wrap her in a towel, or you can make a nice cat restraint by cutting the corner out of a pillowcase and placing her head through the hole. If the hole is the right size, her feet will stay safely tucked inside. Or enlist the help of a friend to hold down those wayward paws. Cats that bite the hand that pills them, especially if you're convinced it's deliberate, are dangerous. Let your vet help, or get him to give you liquid medication.

Dosing Liquids

Before attempting to give a cat liquid medicine, make sure that you read and understand the dosing instructions on the label. You'll also have to shake the liquid well to ensure that the drug is evenly distributed. Otherwise, your dose may be too weak or too strong. Then draw the liquid up to the appropriate fill line on the dropper.

Once you have medicine in hand, grasp your cat's head gently in the three-point hold described in preceding section on pills. With an index finger and a thumb on your cat's cheekbones, lift his head to a 40 to 50 degree angle—just until the bottom jaw drops open a bit.

Place the tip of the dropper into the side of your cat's mouth, between the upper and lower cheek teeth. Squeeze the dropper gently to put the liquid on your cat's tongue. If there's a lot of liquid—more than half a milliliter (0.5 ml) for a kitten or more than a milliliter (1 ml) for a cat—give it in small doses and let your cat swallow between each squirt.

Avoid the temptation to cram the dropper down your cat's throat as you give a vigorous squirt. A sudden burst of liquid far down the throat can go down the cat's windpipe, causing her to choke or develop pneumonia. The liquid belongs on the tongue.

Injections

In general, injections aren't do-it-at-home treatments. Some people are tempted to buy medicine or vaccines by mail order and shoot them into Puss themselves. But because veterinarians have noticed a link between a certain type of cancer and the injection of irritating substances, the wise owner will avoid injecting her own pets, even with vaccines.

If your cat becomes ill, you might sometimes have to give injections. For example, a diabetic cat must have insulin shots daily. If you're required to give injections, make sure your veterinarian demonstrates the right technique before you leave his office. Ideally you should give the first injection or two in front of your vet or his technician just to make sure you're doing it right.

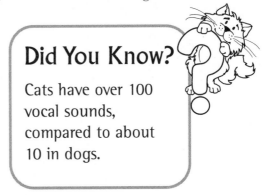

Did You Know?

Cats have over 100 vocal sounds, compared to about 10 in dogs.

Ear Medicine

If your cat develops an ear infection or is pestered by ear mites, chances are you'll be given drops to cure his problem. And cure him they will—*if* you can get them into the ear. Since giving ear medicine is very similar to ear cleaning, you'll find a detailed discussion of both in Chapter 9, Grooming.

8

Behavior Basics: Rules for a Happy Home

In This Chapter

- How Cats Get Along
- Learning to Live Together
- When Good Cats Do Bad Things

When we share a house with a person or pet, we expect them to obey a few basic rules. It's a reasonable request. Rules bring harmony and happiness to a home.

A cat may never win an obedience title, but all cats are born ready to adapt to the facts of life. Even the wildest feline lives within a strict set of natural laws. He quickly learns that he can't leap out of tall trees, for example, and that it's dumb to wrestle with skunks. Since cats adapt so easily to natural laws, they can learn to get along at home, too.

How Cats Get Along

It was long thought that cats didn't put much effort into getting along with other animals and people. They were believed to be solitary creatures who preferred, as the poet Kipling noted, to "walk alone." Today's behaviorists, however, realize that cats are actually quite social creatures. Cats may have complex rules of social interaction, but they do enjoy company.

Cats probably earned their solitary reputation from their hunting habits. They hunt alone for very practical reasons. A cat's main meals are hardly more than snacks—a mouse here, a grasshopper there. They don't catch enough to share, so solitary hunting works well.

> Left to their own devices, cats choose to live in loving, loose-knit social groups. The main wild colony is usually a set of mothers and their kittens, who range from newborn to adult.

Left to their own devices, cats choose to live in loving, loose-knit social groups. The main wild colony is usually a set of mothers and their kittens, who range from newborn to adult. One or more males will set up their ranges surrounding this group and take a personal interest in the family. The males range more widely than the females, but they stay nearby to protect the queens and kittens from danger.

Inside these social groups strong bonds form. Queens who give birth at the same time may actually form *matriarchal nests,* which is a scientific name for the cooperative nursing and rearing of young between several mothers. The feline social group is much like a sixties-style commune—existing for the mutual good but allowing each member a lot of personal freedom, too.

The Social Ladder

For the last several decades scientists have studied how cats interact. One of the most quoted early studies showed a very dog-like hierarchy system based on dominance. The top cat was the strongest, biggest, and meanest tom, who mounted every female cat to prove his "bossness." Each cat under his command aligned itself in a pecking order, from most to least dominant. When the top cat was removed from the study group, the next in line took over, mounted everybody, and began ruling the pack.

This study found a neat, linear feline hierarchy in cats' interactions, but that theory may actually be a myth. For one thing, the study looked only at cats in a laboratory setting, not in a natural one, so the pecking order may have been altered by stress and may not exist in nature. More important, no other laboratory or field study of feline society has found this neat hierarchy. The more scientists study cats, the more ways they find to describe feline social structure. In the end, the only crystal clear facts about cats' social structure are that cats interact in complex ways and that the social rankings may change over time and in different situations. Near the food bowl, cats often break down into a linear rank and file, with the meanest cat eating first and the most timid last. This also happens when cats become anxious or fearful for any reason.

Deferential Treatment

Most behaviorists categorize the normal cat social group as *deferential*. In other words, cats who know each other well generally defer to each other's wishes. If a compatriot nudges a cat out of one food bowl, she'll simply step aside—and may go nudge another cat out of another bowl. On the other hand, if a

detested cat walks by, chances are that the others will simply turn their heads and let him go about his business without a challenge. This understanding of and compliance with the wishes of others is a clear illustration of just how sociable cats can be.

Rules Cats Live By

Although cats learn most of the rules of their society from play and the silent guidance of others, some rules are actually written. Not in pen and ink, but in odor. For example, tomcats mark the outer edge of their range with urine, writing a rule that warns strangers away. Females mark, too, but they use urine only to claim hunting territory, keeping their nesting and living range clean. Cats also write rules and social notes by rubbing with their cheeks and chin or by depositing scent from the pads on their paws by clawing. These scents all post notice that the area is claimed by a cat—and that strangers should either turn away or act respectably while visiting.

> Cats also seem to take comfort from smells. When cats walk, the scent from their paw pads leaves behind an odor, marking commonly used paths.

Cats also seem to take comfort from smells. When cats walk, the scent from their paw pads leaves behind an odor, marking commonly used paths. Some observers have noted that an entire colony will have several paths, which all members tread. These paths aren't visible—they're scent trails that each colony member recognizes as a safe path through otherwise wild territory.

Learning to Live Together

Our house cats have the same basic instincts as cats in feral colonies. And they'd like to have the same social structure, too.

But when cats move in with people, the home range is limited, and cats give up the right to pick their colony members. In some cases, the stress of living with unloved compatriots can set up a linear hierarchy, where one cat is a tough boss cat, or—more commonly—where one is picked on, chased, and abused. More often, stress in a modern cat results in urine marking in the house. It's not bad behavior; it's usually just a cat trying to reestablish some rules when the living situation breaks natural feline codes of conduct.

Cat Obedience

Cats are barely domesticated, which means that they aren't yet born to do our bidding or live by our rules. Dogs have had over 10,000 years of living closely with humans and after all those years have become extremely compliant. Although cats have hidden in the shadows of our campfires for nearly that long, they never entered our lives as closely as dogs. Instead they hunted the vermin human camps attracted—and ignored human commands.

Only in the last 100 years have people brought cats out of the fields and firmly into their homes. That's hardly a burp in time—nowhere near long enough to breed the mindless compliance of the canine. Instead of blind obedience, what you'll get from a well-trained cat is a strong respect for your wishes and willingness to do his part to create a loving, peaceful

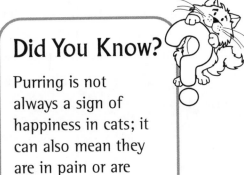

Did You Know?

Purring is not always a sign of happiness in cats; it can also mean they are in pain or are upset.

home. As long as the house rules don't conflict with his basic nature, your cat will happily heed them.

Of course, that leaves the burden on you—the higher intelligence in the house—to understand your cat's nature, to write reasonable rules, and to learn to communicate your wishes clearly. Given half a chance, your cat will be a quick student.

We've already learned that a cat's basic social nature is one of gentle comradeship and deference to others. Before we get into specific rules for your cat's behavior, let's take a little more in-depth look at how your cat speaks to you—and how you can communicate more effectively with your cat.

How Cats Communicate

In wild cat colonies, one basic means of communication is through odors. Wild cats leave notes for other cats in their urine, feces, and secretions from the anal glands and special glands on the cheeks, chin, and paw pads. Humans write in fairly emotionless ink, but the feline note card is chemically rich and may tell many, many things about the sender, including his feelings of fear, anger, virility, or weakness.

Indoor cats are expected to give up this very natural method of communication. We demand that they urinate and deposit stool in a place we pick for them. They are happy to do that—until they have a strong, emotional message to send to you. In most cases, a cat who quits using a litter box is trying to give you an urgent message—he may be sick or in emotional distress. Scent is one of a cat's most powerful tools of communication and should never be ignored.

> Although they have no "language" per se—no syntax and sentence structure—they have a varied and rich vocabulary.

Besides smell, cats have plenty of other ways to communicate. Although they have no "language" per se—no syntax and sentence structure—they have a varied and rich vocabulary. Some experts have tried to put words in a cat's mouth—a *mewl* means "pet me," while *rowwwl* means "I'm mad," for example—but feline communication isn't so cut and dried. The facial expression, the inflection, and the body posture speak in unison with the actual phonetic sound. If your ears, eyes, and mind are open when a cat speaks, you'll find yourself understanding almost effortlessly.

Cats use motion and body position to convey meaning. A cat with an arched back is most likely angry, but if she combines the same position with a few sideways hops, she's clearly saying, "Come and play." Feline body language is subtle and exquisite. Your cat will write paragraphs with the mere twist of a tail.

Cats do have several common gestures and sounds, and knowing a few will help you get started understanding your kitty. But if you truly want to communicate well with your cat, you have to get to know her. Only by paying attention to the whole cat can you come to understand all the nuances in her speech to you.

Body Language 101

A few postures and sounds mean pretty much the same thing from cat to cat. Learning what these mean is a first step in understanding cat speak.

Play with Me
- Belly up
- Standing up on hind feet, front paws in air
- Pounce
- Pawing
- Sideways skittle
- Squeaks and trills

You're Mine
- ○ Face rubbing
- ○ Head butting
- ○ Pawing or kneading

I'm Dangerous
- ○ Ears flat back
- ○ Eyes dilated
- ○ Back arched, tail erect and fluffed
- ○ Teeth bared
- ○ Shrieking yowl
- ○ Growls

I Want Something (Most Often Food)
- ○ Pacing
- ○ Weaving between your legs
- ○ Tail erect
- ○ Mewling, vigorous cries
- ○ Ears erect, whiskers forward
- ○ Direct stare

Talking Back to Your Cat

Good communication with your cat is based on a happy relation-

ship. A cat will defer to the wishes of those she respects. She'll take the time to listen and try to please you. Fear, anxiety, or discomfort blocks a cat's ability to communicate. Her mind will be only on fight or flight—not on learning or listening to what you say.

To build good behavior, reward Kitty when she's doing right. When she's calmly sitting on the floor, offer her a few unexpected treats. Or when she's sitting on your lap sweetly, offer her some gentle pats. By going out of your way to be pleasant to your cat when she's behaving well, you're creating a win-win situation—not only are you teaching your cat the behavior you prefer, but you're forging a loving bond.

Because no cat is perfect, sometimes you'll have to teach Kitty that what she's doing is wrong. This is where cat training gets tricky. Because you're big and strong and your cat is small, she can easily be injured and even more easily frightened during training. From observing a mother cat with an unruly kitten, you might think that violence is a natural training tool. It's true that the mother may bite and shake her kit-

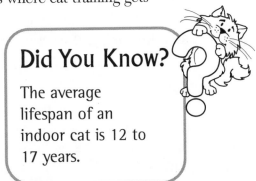

Did You Know?

The average lifespan of an indoor cat is 12 to 17 years.

tens. But what you don't see is the key—the canine teeth of cats have extremely sensitive nerves that give a cat instantaneous, precise control over her bite. The queen may look vicious, but she's only gripping, not harming, the kitten.

When people try to imitate a queen's physical punishment, tragedy can occur. A simple smack can crack ribs or even kill. A toss from the bed can break a leg. Even if rough discipline doesn't hurt the cat physically, you'll only teach her fear. A frightened cat *never* learns—she focuses on her own survival.

This isn't to say you can't correct your cat. Quite the opposite—correction is as essential to developing a cat's social skills as it is to a child's. But effective correction is done without anger, without pain or injury, and is aimed at humanely teaching your cat to stop a problem behavior. Effective correction is true communication—sending an understandable message from you to your cat and listening to the response you receive.

The best method to correct unwanted feline behavior is to startle her while she's involved with (or contemplating) a bad move. You can do this by using a loud, angry shout. A corrective shout startles but doesn't frighten a cat. It coincides with bad behavior and stops immediately when the behavior stops.

Other startle sounds include dropping a stack of books on the floor, blowing an air horn (at a distance), using an ultrasonic noisemaker, shaking an aluminum drink can filled with pennies, and shrieking as if you're mortally injured. The latter is especially helpful for a cat who attacks your feet or hands.

> To abolish bad behavior while keeping a good relationship, it's important that your cat link the punishment with the behavior, not with you.

Besides startling noises, some cats need physical cues, too. Far and away the best physical deterrent is a spritz with plain cold water. This is completely harmless to the cat but unpleasant enough that she will stop whatever she's doing. You can use a water pistol or spray bottle, but to be effective, the water must be used *only* when the cat is caught in the act.

To abolish bad behavior while keeping a good relationship, it's important that your cat link the punishment with the behavior, not with you. If you can, set her up with water sprinklers, invisible fences, Scat Mats (plastic pads designed to give a mild electric shock when stepped on), and upside-down mousetraps—all tools designed to give a cue *only* when the cat misbehaves.

Timing Is Everything

As you watch your cat's body language, it's likely that you'll eventually be able to learn the body language that comes just before misbehavior. If you can correct her at this point—just as she's poised to leap on that counter, for example—you have perfect timing. Your cat will be amazed at your mind-reading ability, and she'll be less likely to even think of bending the rules again.

The second-best time to correct a cat is while she's in the middle of the bad act. In the case of the counter cat, that would be either midleap or while she's cruising the counter.

After the bad behavior is over, there's no point in correcting it. Your cat won't understand the lesson; she'll just think you're having a frightening fit or attacking her for no reason. Don't ever correct after the fact—simply plan a way to catch her in the act next time.

When Good Cats Do Bad Things

For the average cat house rules are few, but they're important. The following section covers problem behaviors and how to correct them.

Litter, Litter Everywhere

If you're like 99.9 percent of cat owners, the one thing you demand of your cat is that he be tidy with his bodily waste. But this simple rule too often becomes a point of conflict. Veterinary behaviorists report that between 40 and 70 percent of their patients have litter box problems. It's also the number-one reason that veterinarians are asked to euthanize healthy cats.

Elimination doesn't have to be such a problem. Cats have a strong drive to mind their litter habits. Even in the wild, cats are fastidious with their waste. Given half a chance, a cat will use his box as zealously as a deeply religious person prays—never missing a single opportunity. So why, then, are litter box problems so widespread?

Why Cats Miss the Box

The biggest problem in litter box training is that owners often don't give their cats that half chance they need to behave. To most people, the litter box is just a nasty afterthought—something we put down and clean up only because we have to. We toss in any old litter, plop the box in a random spot, and then clean it every few days. Or weeks. Or even months. Then we can't understand why our cat refuses to use it.

The cat sees things differently. To him, the feel of the litter on his toes, the smell, the cleanliness, the safety, and the quietness of the box are supremely important issues.

To begin with, the box is where he puts his pheromone-filled urine and feces. They may be wastes, but they're filled with chemical messengers that tell much about who a cat is and even about his state of mind. Just as you wouldn't leave a personal diary out for every neighbor and houseguest to read, your cat prefers to keep his waste private from others, too. If too many other animals use the box or there's too much traffic around it, it's perfectly normal for a cat to tuck away his urine and stool in a more private place.

> Even if you've given your cat a clean, private litter box with a pleasant feeling and odorless gravel, a cat may miss the box when he feels ill.

Cleanliness is another issue. Even humans hate using a filthy Porta Potti, especially in midsummer, when the stench could choke a cow. And we don't have to get our feet in the filth, either. Imagine having a nose 1,000 times more sensitive than you do now and being forced to crawl into dirty litter. You don't have the luxury of washing your paws in running water, either. When you're done, you have to lick yourself clean. Nauseous yet? Well, this is exactly what we ask cats to do when we ask them to climb into a soiled box.

Even if you've given your cat a clean, private litter box with a pleasant feeling and odorless gravel, a cat may miss the box when he feels ill. If a cat feels pain when he urinates, he'll associate the pain with the box. If his condition isn't corrected quickly, it can be difficult to get him to go back into a litter box routine. Illness may also make a cat anxious, fearful, or distressed—all reasons for a cat to begin pasting chemical note cards around the house.

Cats will also avoid an unsafe box. Perching in a box puts a cat in a vulnerable position—he can't fight or flee very effectively while he's eliminating. In multicat households cats who quit using the box may be the ones who get pounced on or attacked when they need privacy. Or the box may be in a noisy throughway, and the sound of children's running feet makes a cat feel vulnerable. If a cat can't have peace in his toilet area, don't expect him to use the box.

Toilet Training

A kitten learns toilet habits between 4 and 14 weeks of age. He'll learn to scratch in the clay, develop litter preferences, and discover if the box is a safe refuge. Whatever elimination habits a kitten learns in this period usually stick with him for life.

To give your kitten the best start, make sure that you have a litter box ready before you even bring him home (see Chapter 3, Welcome Home!, to learn more about choosing a box and litter). When he first sets foot on your floor, show him his box and let him play in it and near it. In a little while put him into the box and help him scratch the litter around. This motion may start reflexive digging, and elimination usually follows quickly.

To encourage forming strong bathroom habits, it's best to keep the kitten in the same room as the litter box at first. Young kittens need to go quickly after they feel the urge, so it also helps to avoid accidents if you provide many boxes throughout the house when he's running free.

Older cats may come to you with litter box quirks already set in place. It's best to offer the adult adoptee several different kinds of boxes filled with several different litters. You should also confine him and his box in a room until he's proved himself reliable in the litter department.

Correcting the First Mistake

When a cat loses litter box training, acting quickly to uncover and correct the reason can usually turn the errant eliminator back into a happy litter user. The longer the behavior continues, the harder it is to cure.

The first step in finding a cure is a full physical examination. A cat who is sick for any reason may show his illness only in very subtle ways, and going out of the box is one of the first signs. Urinary-tract-specific diseases, such as bladder infection or feline lower urinary tract disease (FLUTD) (see Chapter 7, Emergencies and Illness), are a common cause of litter box misbehavior and if caught early can be corrected quickly.

Once your veterinarian has given Kitty a clean bill of health, you'll need to work on her emotions. The source of the problem can be difficult to figure out, but when the answer is found, cures can and do happen. For example, one of my own cats, Electra, had a problem with using her litter box. She wanted her paws pristine, and I was too busy as a student to clean the box daily. I also thought that one box was plenty for four cats—a basic mistake that many cat owners make.

Between the crowding at the box and the accumulation of filth, Electra gave up using it. After several unpleasant confrontations with my cat and after counseling from my instructors, I was able to strike a deal with Electra. I increased the number of boxes and worked harder at cleanliness. On her part, she agreed to give me fair warning of a dirty box. Many mornings I woke to the stomping feet of an angry cat across my hardwood floor. She'd make exactly three slow trips across the floor, and then—if I was foolish enough to lie in bed in spite of the warning—she'd find a cleaner place to pee. As long as I did my part, Electra did hers, and we lived happily ever after.

Tailoring Treatment

Each cat is unique, and so the reasons for litter box problems can be elusive and treatment must be tailored precisely to each cat. Although owners are essential to their cat's cure, it's often necessary to call in a veterinarian for help. For difficult cases, adding a board-certified veterinary behaviorist to the team can be invaluable. With different perspectives, each team member can help shed light on the particular cat's problems, and a cure is very likely.

Veterinarians can offer more than counseling. Besides curing a cat of any physical problem that may affect litter box habits, your vet can offer drug therapy for emotional problems. Diazepam (Valium) and buspirone (BuSpar) are two drugs that often calm anxious cats and improve litter box behavior. Amitriptyline (Elavil) in tiny doses can relieve interstitial cystitis—a painful, noninfectious bladder disease that frequently makes cats urinate all over the house from pain and anxiety. Behavior specialists may be more comfortable with drugs such as Prozac (fluoxetine), which can give relief to cats with obsessive-compulsive disorders (OCD).

> Veterinarians can offer more than counseling. Besides curing a cat of any physical problem that may affect litter box habits, your vet can offer drug therapy for emotional problems.

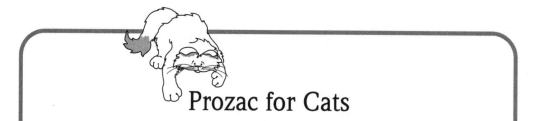

Prozac for Cats

If you think the image of millions of Americans swallowing pills to get a quick fix for the stresses of unhappy lives is disconcerting, how do you feel about medicating pets?

Many owners feel that treating a pet with anti-anxiety or antidepressant medication is little more than drugging a cat into unwilling submission, much like keeping mental patients "down" with Thorazine, a sedative. Medication may calm the cat, they say, but who wants to live with a fogged-out, drug-addicted feline?

Early behavioral medications, such as the barbiturates, were little more than kitty downers. But modern pharmaceuticals aren't chemical cover-ups—at least not when used properly. Like human behavior, cat behavior can go awry when brain chemistry changes. A drop in serotonin, for example, can cause compulsive self-mutilation. With proper medication, brain chemistry can be restored. Not only will the cat feel better, but the restoration of natural chemicals will actually bring her real personality to the forefront, not hide it under a blanket of drugs.

Because both feline pharmacology and behavior are such new, complex fields, don't expect your veterinarian to understand all the intricacies of the newer drugs. If your cat needs medication, ask for a referral to a veterinarian who has been board certified as a specialist in behavioral medicine. These veterinary behaviorists are the true experts on why and how cats have fun. And they usually have a cure for cats with behavioral problems.

Owners who go it alone, however, are often puzzled, angry, and ineffective at dealing with kitty litter box crises. As a result, thousands of cats are abandoned and euthanized each year. While investing in veterinary help does cost money, treatment is usually effective. And abandoning a problem cat and starting over with a new one in no way guarantees the same problems won't arise next time.

Why Cats Become Homeless

In her book *Clinical and Behavioral Medicine for Small Animals,* Karen Overall, a prominent veterinary behaviorist, states that only *one-third* of all pet cats remain in the same household for their entire life. In any given year 25 percent of all adult cats lose their homes—usually due to a behavioral problem. Given the fact that 50 to 75 percent of these cats will end up euthanized, behavioral problems are the number-one killer of adult cats.

The most common reasons that cats lose their homes are:

1. Spraying

2. Other indoor urine or fecal marking

3. Nervousness (fraidy cat)

4. Aggression to other cats

5. Aggression to people

6. Self-mutilation

Biting, Fighting, and Scratching—Oh My!

Owners don't like cats who scratch and bite—and for good reason. Not only is the behavior unpleasant to live with; the mouth of a cat is rich in bacteria. When a cat bites another cat or a person, infection often sets in, requiring vigorous antibiotic therapy.

Statistics say that 60 percent of cats will scratch, hiss at, or bite their owners at some point in their life. And although cats prefer to lead quiet, peaceful lives, they do sometimes fight among themselves. In her book *Clinical Behavioral Medicine for Small Animals,* Karen Overall, M.A., V.M.D, Ph.D., a respected veterinary behaviorist, says that

Physical Causes of Bad Temper

When your docile calico suddenly becomes a biting snake, it may not be just a passing mood. She may be suffering from one of several medical problems. The following is a short list of the most common diseases that may cause your cat to turn sour.

- Epilepsy
- Hyperthyroidism
- Lead poisoning
- Liver disease

- Meningioma (tumor of the lining of the brain)
- Pain from any reason
- Rabies (rare)
- Toxoplasmosis

during an average cat's life span, 80 percent of cats will hiss at another cat, 85 percent will swat, and 70 percent will occasionally fight. Indoor cats tend to fight less than outdoor, sexually intact cats. Taken all together, feline aggression can be a serious problem.

Taming the Attacking Beast

If you have an aggressive cat, it's extremely important to learn the first signs of his rising temper. A cat in full fight mode can be impossible to deal with safely, but fortunately, cats rarely attack completely out of the blue. The natural progression of aggression is a long process, full of subtle posturing and signals. By simply learning your cat's early signals, it becomes easy to avoid the attack.

Cats who attack people or other cats can inflict serious damage. The attack signals are clear to those who know cats but are often invisible to the owner. Rather than go round after painful

Training for Good Temper

Aggressive cats are made, not born. To ensure that you'll have a cat who respects you, start your kitten out following these rules:

1. *Never play rough.* Hand wrestling and biting in a one-pound kitten are cute, but they teach disrespect. By the time the kitten grows to an adult, you can bet he'll be drawing blood on a routine basis.

2. *Give the cat a good start in life.* In order to develop social skills, kittens need to grow up with their mother and siblings. If you raise an orphan, get him around other cats as often as possible. This will help teach him to have a gentle mouth and give him a sense of social rules.

3. *Human bodies aren't toys.* Even if you're not playing rough, allowing a kitten to nibble on your fingers or slap at your feet sends the message that you're up for abuse. If your kitten can keep her claws sheathed, it's fine to play gently. Otherwise she may play only with toys.

4. *Don't take the bottom-cat role.* If your kitten bites or bullies you, put him in a crate or separate room for a time-out or spritz him with water to make him stop. Many aggressive cats learned to boss their owners when young. As they get older and their tempers get shorter, they begin to answer any perceived challenge with an iron, unsheathed claw. Avoid this by being a kind, gentle owner but the unwavering boss of the house.

round with your Tyson of felines, enlist the help of your veterinarian or a veterinary behaviorist. With professionals on your side, chances are good that you can improve an aggressive cat's behavior and help to make him a gentleman again.

Understanding Your Aggressive Cat

Cats fight and bite for many reasons. To cure a cat's foul temper, it's important to understand the cause.

Lack of Socialization   Kittens who aren't exposed to people or other cats before 12 weeks of age or who have suffered from serious malnutrition are very unlikely to ever become cuddly, socially adept cats. This fact is pretty important if you have visions of taming a feral cat. Poorly socialized animals just don't understand normal cat or human body languages. They may strike out in fear or anger or simply not understand their own strength when they think they're playing.

Over time, a poorly socialized cat may adjust to one person or a very small group. Patience and low expectations are key.

Play   Kittens learn to sheath their claws in play as early as four weeks of age. Shortly after, they learn to temper their bites when wrestling with siblings. A kitten learns play skills up to 12 weeks of age, then begins to learn how to fight. When owners play rough with a young kitten, the kitten won't learn how to restrain herself—which is essential for a social, gentle cat. Do *not* wrestle or roughhouse with your kitten unless you enjoy the pain of bite wounds and can pay the cost of prescription antibiotics for post-bite infections.

It's normal for young kittens to want to play too rough—and it's up to you to teach them better. When a kitten latches onto

you, stop moving immediately. This tells the kitten you are no longer playing and usually causes the kitten to back off. If she doesn't, then startle her with a spray of water or a high-pitched, bloodcurdling shriek. The kitten will detach and leave at top speed. She'll also be cautious about putting the bite on you again.

Although rough play is expected and must be trained out of young kittens, when older kittens and adult cats persist in violent play, you need to learn to sidestep the attack. Most play-aggressive cats begin by stalking, then will crouch with a twitching tail before making the grab for your ankles. A spritz of water or startling sound will waylay the immediate attack. Repeated consistently, early correction will often do away with aggressive play entirely.

Fear   Fearful cats will run away if possible, but when cornered, they may become extremely dangerous. Confronting these cats head-on will get you nowhere. When living with a fearful cat, it's important that you know the signs that a cat is about to snap: raised hair, dilated eyes, arched back, hissing, and spitting. Teach these signs to your children, and give the order to simply leave the cat alone when they see any of them—it means she feels cornered and she's had enough.

Positive interaction with the cat when she's calm, including food treats, can often eliminate the worst part of fear aggression. Veterinarians can also offer medication that will quell some of the fear and allow positive training methods to reach your cat.

Pain   When a cat is hurt, it's normal for him to strike out to try to stop the pain. If your cat has a thorn in his paw and you grab his foot, he's quite likely to shriek and bite. Cats who have arthritis may be touchy over the hips or spine, and cats who have had their tails caught in doors often end up with "phantom pain" in the tail or spine. Even though veterinarians can find nothing wrong, these cats react with aggression when touched.

Did You Know?

In ancient Egypt, entire families would shave their eyebrows as a sign of mourning when the family cat died.

The treatment is straightforward: Alleviate the pain. Because many over-the-counter pain relievers can be deadly to cats, never treat a cat's pain by yourself. You'll need your veterinarian's help to discover and safely relieve the cause of your cat's aches and pains.

Inter-Cat Aggression   Cat-to-cat aggression is very worrisome to owners—and with good reason. A true catfight is loud, frightening, and destructive. The primary reasons for cat-to-cat aggression are squabbles over sexual privileges or territory, and these fights are most common between intact toms. Studies have shown that neutering cats before 12 months of age can decrease or prevent fighting by 88 percent and decrease spraying (often a form of aggression) by 87 percent.

> The primary reasons for cat-to-cat aggression are squabbles over sexual privileges or territory, and these fights are most common between intact toms.

In indoor households with spayed and neutered cats, inter-cat aggression can still occur. Many aggressive episodes are simply a swat after a veterinary visit or a hiss over a particularly tasty treat. These need no treatment. But when cats actually tussle or bite, then intervention is needed to prevent injury to the cats.

The saddest type of inter-cat aggression is the creation of a pariah cat. This unfortunate feline becomes the whipping cat of the household and can be mercilessly beaten day after day by one or more feline housemates. The pariah may be a socially unskilled cat, whose gaffs enrage the others, or she may have a medical problem that makes her smell or act oddly. Often no fault at all can be found with the pariah—she's just a convenient victim for aggressive cats.

Inter-cat aggression can be very difficult to cure. A veterinary behaviorist can often make the difference between success and failure. When dealing with aggressive cats, it's essential that the aggressor(s) and victim(s) be separated when their owner can't supervise them. Some experts advise keeping the more aggressive cat in a small room while allowing the victim full access to the rest of the house, enlarging the territorial rights of the undercat.

When living with aggressive cats, put a bell on each of them to help you keep track of their actions. Make sure each bell has a different sound so you'll be able to tell when the two cats meet—and if the bells ring in the sound of a chase, you'll be able to quickly intervene with a squirt of water to the aggressor or perhaps even a bowl of water dumped on his head.

Whenever the two cats share space peacefully, make sure to give positive reinforcement. Food treats are the reward method of choice for inter-cat problems. They can be evenly distributed at the same moment, and, unlike petting, rarely set off jealous attacks.

Maternal Aggression   Some queens are quite protective of kittens and can be downright dangerous to approach when nursing. The best treatment is usually just to leave the queen and her kittens unmolested. Given space and time, the queen will almost always be less protective by the time the kittens scramble out of the litter box at around three to four weeks of age. A queen who is consistently vicious at kittening time, however, should be considered temperamentally unstable and spayed to prevent passing any genetic temperament problems to another generation.

Did You Know?

Cats purr at about 26 cycles per second, the same frequency as an idling diesel engine.

Predatory Aggression Cats are natural-born hunters, and they *will* be aggressive to prey animals. There's not much you can do about this, other than keeping cats behind closed doors. If you insist on letting your hunter prowl, here are some ways to keep at least the birds safe. You can minimize bird hunting by hoisting wind chimes, flags, or loud bells around feeders as a signal to birds that the cat has been let out. Or you can try ringing the bird feeding area with an Invisible Fence—an underground electric fence that will keep out a suitably collared cat.

The most traditional "cure" for the hunting cat—putting a bell around her neck—is actually a bad idea. Most cats' hunting is done by stalking too slowly to ring a bell. By the time the cat is in position for a murderous pounce, the prey doesn't have time to react to the sound of the bell. When the cat trots or runs, however, the bell will ring and can interfere with a cat's hearing, making it hard for her to avoid dogs, cars, or other dangers.

Territorial Aggression Most territorial aggression is accompanied by urine marking behavior. Cats claim territory against not only other cats but also dogs, people, or any other animal that offends a cat's good taste. They may defend territory against one cat in the house but not another. The ramifications of territory are very complex and best dealt with as a team with your veterinarian. Drug therapy to lessen both anxiety and the need to control territory can help cure this type of aggression.

Redirected Aggression Redirected aggression is uncommon but can be especially unsettling since it's characterized by a vicious attack completely out of the blue. It occurs when a cat is highly aroused and upset but is prevented from attacking the object of his rage. He'll turn on whatever or whoever is handiest. And he may have no idea of the damage he's inflicting—he's simply out of control.

I was once the victim of such an attack. One morning I heard a catfight begin outdoors, a sound I knew would send Shorty, my recently neutered top cat, into a frenzy. I grabbed him and closed him into a windowless bathroom, trying to minimize the stimulation. As the fight escalated, I heard horrendous sounds inside the bathroom. Shorty was yowling and flinging himself against the walls in a rage. He wanted to get at those cats.

Frightened for Shorty's safety, I opened the door to peek inside. Out flew one hyped-up, angry cat. He latched himself around my leg, leaving deep gashes and bites that had to be treated at a hospital. I could see his shock when he realized he'd bitten his best friend. He dropped off and ran outside. We were both shaken—he didn't return for a full two days.

> Behaviorists often call this the "leave-me-alone" bite. It most often occurs during petting, when the cat simply tires of attention and wants you to stop.

Redirected aggression can rarely be either controlled or predicted. The best way to avoid such an attack is to stay away from any highly agitated cat. Although such an attack can be vicious, a reoccurrence is uncommon. Don't fear or destroy a cat, such as Shorty, who mistakes your leg for an enemy.

Status-Related Aggression Behaviorists often call this the "leave-me-alone" bite. It most often occurs during petting, when the cat simply tires of attention and wants you to stop. It's a strong method of controlling an owner. When control isn't an issue, such as during most of the normal daily routine, the cat may be quite friendly and loving.

The best treatment is to learn the signals that suggest the cat is about to bite or scratch: the angry flick of his tail, pinning his ears back, unsheathing his claws, and tensing his muscles. If you know when your cat is getting angry, you can defuse the situation before the cat is committed to violence. If you're petting your cat and his eyes glaze and his tail starts twitching, simply stand up and spill him from your lap. This avoids attack as well as puts the control in your hands. Don't ever swat the cat, flick him on the head, or otherwise physically challenge him—that's just playing his game and asking him to retaliate.

Fraidy Cat

No one likes to live with a cat who's constantly fearful. A cat who runs away from you isn't just sad—she's frustrating to live with. You'd like to pet her and play, but she insists on hiding under the bed, eyes wide, afraid of the world. It's no wonder that many owners finally give up on these pathetic cats and ship them away to a new home or turn them over to certain death in a shelter.

Most fearful cats got that way from improper socialization. They probably weren't given affectionate handling in the nest and weren't exposed to strangers or other stimulation before 12 weeks of age. If a cat's fears reach back to kittenhood, she may be impossible to cure. With a great deal of patience she may become a bit more mellow, but she'll never become truly affectionate and brave.

When adult cats are neglected, terrorized, or even held in loving but solitary homes for long periods, they may learn to become fearful. Given time and gentle encouragement, many of these later-in-life fears can be overcome.

Basic care for a fearful cat is to gently encourage her trust in you. For this to happen, you must be consistently calm. One noisy outburst or a sudden grab in her direction may undo months of work. It also helps to give liberal food rewards for good behavior. If she stays in sight when the neighbor rings the doorbell, toss her a tasty treat. For many cats petting is also a good reward.

With time and patience a fraidy cat may come slowly out of her frightened shell. She'll never become a social butterfly, but the gentle affection of a shy cat brings great though subtle rewards.

Attention Seekers

Does your cat greet you at the door with happy meows, then follow your every move the rest of the evening? Do you long for just one moment of peace, a moment when your lap is free of your feline friend? If this sounds like you, chances are you've purchased a highly demanding, energetic breed such as an Abyssinian or Siamese. Or you may simply own a young, highly energetic cat of any breed.

If you're surprised at your cat's need for attention, it might be because you had bought into the myth that cats are solitary creatures. Cats are truly social animals. Most can't cope with being left alone 12 to 16 hours a day in a house with no friends. It's a social wasteland and a total bore. A cat trapped in such a life may well try to save her sanity by making the most of every moment that you're home.

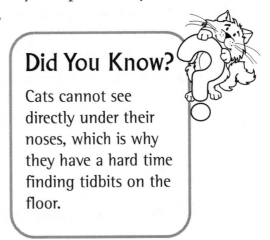

Did You Know?

Cats cannot see directly under their noses, which is why they have a hard time finding tidbits on the floor.

Occasionally older cats become hyperactive due to physical problems, such as hyperthyroidism. Or failing eyesight or hearing may make a cat feel insecure, prodding her to keep in close contact with her master. In adult animals sudden clinginess should always signal a visit to the veterinarian. If her neediness is a side effect of a physical problem, she'll return to her old self as she begins to feel well.

The best treatment for the overly demanding young cat is to increase her physical exercise. A tired cat is a mellow cat. When you come home, give her a nice greeting, then break out the toys. Toss her a ball while you watch TV and drag a string around during your aerobics tape.

> The best treatment for the overly demanding young cat is to increase her physical exercise. A tired cat is a mellow cat.

You might also consider enriching her daily grind. Buy her a window seat so she can watch the birds and beasts outside. Set up some climbing toys and a kitty condo so she can entertain herself. Put a Ping-Pong ball in an empty bathtub, or dangle some safe toys from doorknobs. You can even buy "video catnip"—movies designed to entertain cats.

If all this exercise and creativity wears you out, there's one simple solution. An energetic young playmate often cures the clingy cat.

Wool Sucking and Other Oral Aberrations

Some cats just love to suck, mouth, or eat weird things, such as sweaters, plastic, and clothing. While mouthing odd objects is part of normal exploratory behavior in kittens, adult cats generally don't like strange stuff in their mouths.

Wool sucking is most often seen in Siamese cats. It can become a real health threat if the cat actually eats the material it craves. Early weaning can sometimes be a cause of this problem, but not always. There's rarely a physical reason cats suck wool, although illness, such as intestinal obstructions or dental disease, may result.

If a cat is just beginning this behavior, putting foul-tasting substances on wool objects, such as jalapeño juice or Bitter Apple spray, might stop a habit from forming. Or if the object of desire is something like a sock, you could booby-trap it with a balloon inside (but make sure the cat can't reach the balloon fragments). Most of the time, however, wool sucking is a difficult habit to break.

Some behaviorists feel that more severe forms of wool sucking, ear sucking, licking, and pica (eating things they shouldn't) are a form of obsessive-compulsive disorder. Like human OCD, the behavior can be almost impossible to simply "train away" but may respond well to drug therapy.

More Greens, Please: The Plant-Eating Cat

Even though cats are carnivores, they do enjoy nibbling on greenery. Scientists don't think cats get any nourishment from plants—cats apparently chew simply for the joy of it. Most houseplants, even the dozen or so that are considered poisonous, aren't terribly dangerous to a cat. But a few can be deadly. If you have both plants and cats, you also need a handy reference to toxic plants. A good one is available through the ASPCA National Animal Poison Control Center (see Resources).

The best way to quash plant eating is simply to move the plants to a spot where the cat can't reach them, such as a porch or catless sunroom. If you want a little greenery in cat areas of your house, learn which plants are toxic and which aren't, then make sure that feline-accessible greenery is safe. Also, avoid using pesticides and fertilizers on plants that may attract a feline forager.

To solve a cat's urge to nibble, many owners grow a little indoor plot of wheat or rye grass or even catnip. If you start these tender plants from seed, it's essential to get untreated seed. Many grass seeds are treated with potent herbicides that can be deadly to a cat. Buy your seeds from an organic source or check out cat catalogs for safe, pre-planted containers.

> The best way to quash plant eating is simply to move the plants to a spot where the cat can't reach them.

Surfing the Counters

While almost no one seeks veterinary help to keep a cat off the counters, this habit does offend a lot of owners. Not only is it unsanitary to have a cat treading on food preparation areas, but the cat may snatch your dinner for a snack while she's prowling around.

To avoid counter surfing, start young. Even though a kitten on the counter is cute, try not to laugh or pet your precocious kitten if she finds a way to crawl up. Instead give her a firm "no" and put her down on the ground where she belongs. With repetition even the dullest kitten will soon realize her feet need to be on the floor for her to get praise, petting, and food.

For the older cat, one of the simplest ways to discourage counter surfing is to use double-sided tape (carpet tape works well). Cover the leading edge and several inches inside the counter with the tape. When Kitty's toes touch the sticky stuff, she'll leap down again immediately. Leave the tape up for several weeks or until the cat no longer tests the countertops. You may

need to repeat this lesson several times, because a few overly optimistic cats will test the counters once every few months, hoping
the sticky feel has disappeared. Most cats, however, will stay on
the floor forever.

9

Grooming

In This Chapter

- Grooming for Health
- Bath Time!
- Going to the Pros

Cats are naturally clean creatures. Even the least finicky feline devotes hours each day to preening and shining his coat. The average cat tends to bathe in short, efficient spurts—a five-minute lick after a meal or a 10-minute scrub in the sunshine. This quick-clean habit has crept into the English language. We say we're taking a "cat bath" when we spend just a few minutes to go from grubby to sparkling clean.

Although your cat will make tending his coat a major life goal, most cats will greatly appreciate your help. Indeed, some,

> The average cat tends to bathe in short, efficient spurts—a five-minute lick after a meal or a 10-minute scrub in the sunshine.

such as the longhaired Persian, simply can't go it alone. After all, brushes and combs are much more efficient grooming tools than tongue and paw.

Grooming for Health

Good grooming promotes good health. A daily groom will let you spot parasites, such as fleas or ticks, on your cat before they become a real problem. You'll also notice any changes in your cat's skin—scabs, lumps, and bumps—that should be brought to your veterinarian's attention. More than one case of breast cancer, which spreads quickly in cats, has been caught in time, thanks to a good grooming.

The bane of cats and carpets—the hair ball—can often be prevented simply by combing a cat every day. health.

The comb removes loose fur before your cat swallows it, so she's much less likely to vomit the hair back up or to develop a hair blockage in her intestines.

Grooming can be healthy for people, too. If someone in your life is allergic to cats, you can make him much more comfortable by bathing your cat—or even rubbing her down with a wet towel—once a week. A person's allergy to cats is caused by the proteins found in a cat's saliva and dander, which get trapped in the coat, not the hair itself. These proteins dissolve in water, so a bath will wash them away.

Besides all the health benefits, once you and your cat get into the habit, you'll find grooming is just plain fun. By using a comb just 10 minutes a day, you'll deepen your loving bond.

How to Groom

For the average cat, grooming is very easy, so plan on enjoying the session. Besides, cats are clever at reading emotions and are likely to give you exactly what you expect. If you expect a good time, you're likely to enjoy yourself, but if you plan on misery, your cat will pick up on your opinion—and make sure you're right.

To ensure a good time, start a grooming session by petting your cat, smoothing out her fur and adjusting her attitude. Once your cat is happy and relaxed, reach for the combs and brushes.

All the Right Tools: Basic Grooming Kit

○ Flea comb
○ Metal comb: fine for short coats, medium or coarse for long
○ Brush: pin brush for long coats, soft bristle brush for short coats
○ Nail clippers
○ Toothbrush
○ Cotton balls
○ Olive oil
○ Mild shampoo
○ Pair of scissors with blunt tip
○ Additional Things That Might Help
   ○ Chamois cloth
   ○ Rubber comb
   ○ Cat bathing bag
   ○ Window screen that fits inside your tub

Different Strokes for Different Coats

Your cat may have layers of lovely locks, an inch of thick fur, wiry hair, or be essentially hairless. Each coat type requires a slightly different care routine.

Shorthaired Cats

Short, dense coats normally require grooming once or twice a week to look their best. If hair balls are a problem, a daily groom may make them vanish.

The ideal grooming session starts with a flea comb. This is a metal or plastic comb with teeth placed tightly together. Tiny fleas can't wiggle through the teeth, so they become trapped as you comb. To use the comb, slowly run it through your cat's entire coat. Pay special attention to the favorite flea hiding spots: under the chin and behind the ears. Pick out the trapped fleas with your fingers, then deposit them in a jar containing either soap and water or alcohol.

> Short, dense coats normally require grooming once or twice a week to look their best. If hair balls are a problem, a daily groom may make them vanish.

Once you're convinced your cat is flea-free, it's time to remove the loose hairs from his coat. A fine- or medium-toothed comb works well on short hair. The right comb should pass smoothly through nonmatted fur yet provide very gentle friction. It's best to comb in the same direction as the coat lies—from head to tail. Ruffling the coat can remove a bit more loose hair, but many cats find it annoying.

An alternative to the comb is a rubber brush. This little hand-held brush looks a bit like a fingernail brush, except it's made out of rubber and has small nubs instead of bristles. Although the nubs don't reach the skin, they are excellent at removing loose hairs. Some cats who hate combs love these brushes.

Finish grooming by polishing the top coat. To remove the dust, dander, and bits of loose hair on the outer coat, stroke your cat from head to tail with a chamois cloth. Or you can use your hands in long, smooth motions along your cat's body. This hand-rubbing technique is used by fine grooms to make racehorses shine—and it works for cats, too.

Longhaired Cats

Longhaired cats require more care than shorthairs and a few different tools. But the technique isn't much different: deflea, comb or brush out, then finish by polishing the top coat.

A flea comb can be hard to use in longer coats. If the coat is thick or matted, the comb won't pull through easily, so don't try. But the flea comb should still be used around the ears, under the chin, and in the shorter fur around the neck to trap fleas lurking in these favorite hideouts.

The best grooming tool for the longhaired cat is a wide-toothed steel comb. The teeth should be at least an inch long to reach all the way through the fur. For really thick, luxurious coats you may need a comb with even longer teeth. Comb a longhaired cat the same way as a shorthaired cat: move from head to tail in slow, gentle strokes.

After straightening out the fur with a comb, many groomers like to use a pin brush—one with stiff nylon or metal bristles set wide apart—to remove loose hairs and lay the fur down in a soft look. Pin brushes are great at removing loose fur but will either skim over or get stuck in snarls. Brushing is no substitute for combing, so it's best to do both.

You may hear show groomers talk about "back brushing" their Persians. This technique involves taking small sections of fur and brushing it in the opposite direction to the way it grows (back toward the cat's head). This technique fluffs an already perfect coat and can give show cats a truly elegant look. But back brushing can create snarls and mats, and it feels uncomfortable to the average

cat. Unless you're interested in learning advanced show-grooming techniques, keep it simple. Combing and brushing in the direction that the hair lies will keep your cat's coat in tip-top shape.

For a final polish do a head-to-tail stroking with your hands or a quick brushing with a soft-bristled brush. Avoid using rubber brushes—they tend to break long fur. Chamois cloths won't hurt long coats but don't work as well on long coats as they do on short ones.

Medium-Coated Cats

The cat with a medium-length hair coat lies halfway between the sleek shorthair and the elegant longhair both in looks and in ease of care. How often you need to brush depends entirely on the thickness of the undercoat and the fineness of the long hairs. Cats who have very short, thick hairs combined with long, flyaway fine hairs (called a thick undercoat and a fine top coat) tend to snarl the fastest and so need more frequent grooming.

Groomers usually recommend treating a medium-length coat exactly like a longhaired one. Flea comb where you can, then comb the body with a medium-to-coarse tooth comb. Follow with a pin brush to remove loose hairs and to lay the top coat flat. To make your cat's coat shine, polish with your hands or a soft-bristled brush.

You should plan on grooming your medium-coated cat daily. If your cat's coat doesn't seem to snarl easily, you can cut back the brushings until you get to a less frequent regime that still keeps your cat looking great.

Curly Coated

Cornish and Devon Rex cats have an extremely short, silky, curly coat. They are generally very easy to keep clean. Just a weekly good hand rubbing or a polish with a chamois cloth is the best way to keep these cats' coats fit.

Hairless

Some cats, such as the Sphynx, are born virtually hairless. They may have a few fine hairs on the face, ears, paws, and tail, but basically the cat is bare from nose to tail. These cats can't be combed or brushed, but that doesn't mean they're groom-free. They may need even more care than your average short-coated cat.

Hairless cats tend to produce a lot of skin oils, which make them feel sticky and can cause them to smell bad. All cats produce a little oil, which spreads out over the hair coat to make it shiny. Hairless cats tend to overdo oil production, and they don't have any fur to spread it around. To remove this oil, you'll have to bathe your hairless frequently—once every week or two—depending on how fast he gets greasy. Use a mild shampoo, preferably one recommended by your veterinarian.

Show Cat/Purebred

Although grooming a mixed-breed cat is very simple, a few breeds have special coat care quirks. The Abyssinian, for example, has a short coat with a unique texture. These hairs may be broken and dulled by chamois or rubber brushes, not improved by them. If you have a purebred cat, ask your breeder or local breed club about special grooming needs.

> ## Did You Know?
>
> The catgut formerly used as strings in tennis rackets and musical instruments did not come from cats, but rather from sheep, hogs, and horses.

If you're planning to tour the show circuit, coat care becomes vitally important. For a cat to win ribbons, his coat must not only be flea-free and healthy but the grooming job must satisfy the discriminating eyes of the judge. Show-grooming rituals can be quite complex and vary from breed to breed. If you buy a show cat, find a grooming mentor—a breeder or groomer—to get the inside track on ringside grooming.

> Some medium-coated breeds require only a weekly brush, whereas some have thick fur that snarls as quickly as a Persian's.

Out, Out, Darn Mats!

If your comb catches in a mass of snarled fur, you've discovered a mat. These patches of tangled fur are not only unsightly but can be unhealthy, too. Large mats block air circulation to the skin and can cause it to become itchy, irritated, and sometimes infected. In outdoor cats a heavily matted coat can set up a home for maggots—the horrid little larvae of the common housefly. These feed on sick and dying skin and can kill a cat.

Small mats can often be removed by careful combing. Simply use patience to slowly separate the outer tangled hairs from the center of the mat. You can also trim small mats out of the coat with a pair of blunt-tipped scissors.

Larger mats come out most easily if they're split. To split a mat, use blunt-tipped scissors. Turn the tips parallel to the lie of the unmatted fur, and cut down the center of the mat. Split each mat once or twice to begin to shorten the tangled hairs, then use a comb. You'll find that the shortened hairs pull out more easily and that you can eventually remove the mat without losing a huge chunk of fur.

A mat of hair begins small and grows over days or weeks. Really bad mats can work their way right down to the skin. When this happens, the only safe way to remove the mat is by clipping.

Clipping matted fur is difficult and is best done by your groomer or veterinarian.

If the mats become wet or your cat begins to smell bad, you'll need a trip to your veterinarian for an emergency dematting. And of course, maggots are an extreme emergency—get your cat to your vet immediately for treatment. A maggot-ridden cat will not only be shaved but bathed and put on antibiotics. If the infestation is mild and the cat is strong, quick treatment will cure him.

Clipping the Coat

Okay, you've fallen behind in your grooming and your cat's coat is now lumpy with mats instead of luxurious and flowing. Or you're doing a great job but just plain tired of the daily routine that a long coat demands. You may begin to fantasize about trimming those flowing locks into submission and creating a shorthaired version of your beloved cat. But should you? What happens when you clip a cat?

Let's look at one family's choice.

Turkey and Crabber are two Himalayan cats living in Maryland. Their coats aren't particularly messy, but Tina and Jeff live in a small town house. The cat fur and weekly gifts of hair balls barfed up underfoot annoy Jeff, who likes a clean house. What's more, Turkey suffers from feline acne and allergies. Medicating his allergies with pills and facial scrubs has turned into a wrestling match that Turkey usually wins. When we spoke, Tina and Jeff were about to give up on their cats.

"They're sweet, but man, what a lot of trouble," said Tina.

"I'm just about over it," agreed Jeff.

When I mentioned shaving the two cats, the couple were skeptical. "So you want us to pay good money to make these cats look ugly," said Jeff. "I

don't know. Their looks are about all they have going for them right now."

The next week Turkey and Crabber showed up for a shave. The groomer gave them each a "lion cut"—a trim that leaves a ruff of fur around the neck, fluffy feet, and a full tail but shortens the body fur down to about half an inch long. When Jeff and Tina picked up the cats, they glared silently at the cats, then at each other. I wasn't sure what the baleful stares meant, so I didn't ask their opinion on the clip job.

A week later I called to see how the cats were faring. The reaction was effusive.

"This is great," said Tina. "They look wonderful now, and they feel like velvet. We're actually petting them all the time now."

"We haven't had a single hair ball, and we don't have to vacuum every day, either," added Jeff. "You know, Turkey's acne has cleared up—even without those darn pills."

A simple trim had allowed the couple to fall back in love with their cats.

Getting Clipped

A clip won't turn every messy Himalayan into a velveteen darling, but it can certainly help many cats and make life easier for their owners. A short coat with frequent baths can also help in controlling fleas, allergies, ringworm, and feline acne.

Although it's possible to clip at home, it takes time to learn how to use clippers, and the tools are pretty expensive. If your cat is matted, it's definitely a matter for a professional, not a beginner. It's best to take cats in need of clipping to a groomer or a veterinarian. If you want to learn to clip, ask to sit in while your cat is being groomed. The best way to learn the delicacies of handling a clipper is by watching.

Nail Care

The average cat has 18 toes—five on each front foot and four on each hind foot. A few cats, called polydactyls (which means literally "many toes") have a few extra, usually on the front paw. Each toe has a single nail, and each nail will need care.

New cat owners often fear trimming their cat's nails. In fact, it's usually a very easy job once you—and your cat—get used to the idea.

Trimming Tools

To make the job easy, start with the right tools. In any pet store you'll find a selection of nail trimmers. The most common type has a loop at the end and is called a guillotine-type cutter. To use it, you stick your cat's nail through the loop, then squeeze the handle to make the blade come down on the nail, lopping it off the same way Marie Antoinette lost her head. Another common type of nail trimmer is the scissors cutter. These trimmers look much like regular scissors, except the blades are hooked and thick, providing a strong, sharp surface for nail trims.

Although both of these types of nail cutters do cut nails, they both have drawbacks. The guillotine type tends to creak, squeak, and pinch the nails while cutting, which makes for a less than cooperative cat. The scissors type works well when sharp, but as the blades dull (which they do pretty quickly) they also tend to crush and squeeze the nail rather than cut it.

Did You Know?

Tests conducted at the Institute for the Study of Animal Problems in Washington, D.C., revealed that dogs and cats, like humans, are either right- or left-handed.

My favorite nail cutters are found in human beauty supply houses or pharmacies, not pet stores. For adult cats I like a sturdy, sharp, good-quality human toenail or hangnail clippers. The wedged blades are usually made of carbon steel and stay sharp for years. Unless they become dull, human-quality cutters clip cleanly and won't crush or pinch the nail. For kittens I prefer small human fingernail clippers, the two-inch-long squeeze type that are often attached to a key chain. The blades are quite sharp and are small enough to give a very precise trim—important when working on little toes.

Whatever your choice of trimmer, make sure that the blades stay sharp and the mechanism works smoothly. More expensive human trimmers can be sharpened, and the better guillotine types have replaceable blades. If your trimmer can't be sharpened, throw it away when it gets dull or begins to creak and squeak. If you don't, you'll only teach your cat that nail trimming is a painful and frightening experience.

Time to Trim

If you've never trimmed a cat's nails before, it's best to ask your veterinarian or her technician to give you a hands-on demonstration. Watching is worth a thousand words. If you're impatient or need a refresher course, read on.

To trim a cat's nails you first have to extend them from their sheath. To do this, put your cat's paw gently on the first finger of your hand. Lay your thumb on his first knuckle, then gently squeeze. The nail should slide forward quickly and smoothly. If your cat protests, you're probably squeezing too hard or in the wrong spot. Pet him, then try again.

Once you've mastered the claw extension, pick up your nail trimmer and get set to trim. Most cats will have a nail that is thick and flat near the paw, then ends in a downward, curving hook. You can trim this hook completely off. Position the nail between the blades of the clippers, then clip quickly and firmly. If you can't see a distinct hook, then take off only the sharp tip of the nail. You'll have to trim more frequently this way, but you'll avoid the quick that lies in the thick part of the nail.

If you do trim the quick, don't panic. Your cat may bleed, but he won't bleed to death. Dip the nail in a coagulant powder, such as Quik-Stop, to stop the bleeding, and let your cat rest in a quiet spot. If the bleeding is severe, call your veterinarian—he has more powerful cauterizing powders in his office. It's highly unlikely, however, that you'll cut the quick so badly you'll need medical help.

Novice nail trimmers (and novice cats) should start slowly. One paw at a time is usually all you and your cat can stand on the first session. If you start when your cat is a young kitten, work carefully, and make sure to give your cat plenty of petting (and maybe even a tasty treat) when you're done. That way, the nail trim should become just another simple grooming routine.

How Often to Trim

Most cat nails need trimming once every two to four weeks. But your cat is an individual, and his needs are unique. In general, kitten nails grow very quickly and are very sharp. They often need a tip trim weekly. The nails of elderly cats also grow fast and may need a weekly trim.

Ingrown Nails

If cats' nails aren't trimmed regularly, they can curve around and grow into the nail pad. This is extremely painful and can lead to infection. The good news is that overgrown nails are cured by clipping.

Clipping ingrown nails can be painful for the cat. The technique is a bit different from that for normal clipping, and ingrown nails need to be clipped very quickly to minimize pain. Let your veterinarian trim these nails rather than trying it at home. A few cats will have to be sedated to trim ingrown nails, but most of the time the job can be done quickly—and inexpensively—with the cat awake.

> If cats' nails aren't trimmed regularly, they can curve around and grow into the nail pad. This is extremely painful and can lead to infection.

Oh, Dear, Those Ears!

For the most part, a cat's ears are self-cleaning devices. It's not necessary to scrub them with each bath or on any routine schedule. In fact, the less you mess with them, the healthier the ears are likely to be. If your cat's ears are dirty, he should see his veterinarian before you clean. Dirty ears are usually the sign of an infection, ear mites, or allergies.

At times, however, you may need to clean your cat's ears. For example, it's a good idea to clean before you put any medication into the ears, so that the medicine can work more effectively. Or your cat may battle a low-grade yeast infection, and your vet may suggest routine cleaning to keep it in check.

Ear-Cleaning Equipment

The tools for ear cleaning are very simple: cotton balls and olive oil or a commercial ear cleaner.

Although cotton swabs (such as Q-Tips) might seem like the right tool, they aren't. By using cotton on a stick to probe into the ear canal, you're much more likely pushing bacteria and debris deep into the ear—right where it shouldn't live. You're not likely to rupture an eardrum, but you may very well cause an infection or make one worse.

Cleaning Them Out

Before you begin to clean, warm the olive oil or ear cleaner slightly to take off the chill. The safest way to warm is by setting a jar of cleaner in a cup of very warm water for ten minutes or so. The perfect temperature is baby-bottle warm—a drop on your wrist should feel neither warm nor cold. Don't use the microwave to warm ear cleaners. It warms unevenly, causing hot spots that could scald your cat.

To clean, put one drop of olive oil or one squirt of liquid ear cleanser deep into the ear. Ideally, you'll drop it into the round opening of the ear canal. Quickly do the same to the other ear. Then take your cat's head in your hands and give a gentle but firm massage on the base of her ears. Try to massage for a full minute to allow the cleaner to reach the deepest part of the ear.

After the massage, leave your cat alone for about five minutes. She'll shake her head vigorously, which helps move the debris out of the depths of the ear into the outer canal. After five minutes collect your kitty back into your lap, and use a cotton ball to remove all the moisture, dirt, and debris that you can see.

If your cat needs ear medication, it's given the same way as cleaning: warm, instill, and massage. For medication skip the cotton ball removal. Simply let the medication rest in the ear for at least six hours. After that, you can remove debris that collects in the outer ear.

Teeth, Glorious Teeth

Cats are blessed with extraordinary teeth. They are sharp, sensitive, and strong. Their razorlike shape even makes them partially self-cleaning. In other words, when a cat eats, the action of kibble, gristle, or meat scraping against the smooth tooth surface tends to act like floss—removing plaque and debris.

Although the shape of a cat's teeth minimizes dental care, her teeth aren't totally care-free. The cat was designed by nature to live only a few years, so long-lasting teeth weren't written into the feline genetic code. After the age of two or three cats begin to have noticeable plaque and tartar buildup. After the age of eight almost every cat has hard tartar that requires a professional dental cleaning.

Healthy Teeth for a Healthy Cat

Plaque and tartar are enemies of good health. Plaque is a soft buildup of food and mineral deposits that harbor bacteria, while tartar is a heavy buildup of minerals. Tartar rubs and irritates the gum line and may make it painful for a cat to eat. Bacteria live in tartar as well as plaque, and these bacteria can spread to other parts of the body, such as the heart or kidney, and cause serious illness.

> To keep your cat's mouth healthy, it helps to brush her teeth. It's ideal to brush daily, but few owners actually manage to do it that often.

Break Out the Brush!

To keep your cat's mouth healthy, it helps to brush her teeth. It's ideal to brush daily, but few owners actually manage to do it that often. Although more is better, even once a week will benefit your cat's health.

Before you begin to brush, teach your cat to enjoy a gum massage. It may sound odd, but most cats become completely mesmerized by a gentle gum rub. Start by gently petting her cheeks and chin, then begin to massage them with a firm but gentle motion. When your cat's purring and relaxed, slip your index fingers onto the gums near her canine teeth, rubbing gently.

Once your cat adores gum rubs (or at least tolerates them), begin brushing by wrapping a warm, moistened piece of terry cloth or gauze around your finger. Simply rub her gums as usual to remove much of the soft plaque and debris. Give extra attention to the large cheek teeth, especially the upper ones. This is where brushing can do the most to delay tartar buildup.

Advanced brushing techniques include using a toothbrush and feline toothpaste. The brush should be small and soft, and the toothpaste should be made for felines—human toothpaste can be dangerous for cats. Both can be purchased at your veterinarian's office, in pet stores, or from catalogs.

Tooth Trouble

If you notice that your cat's teeth are discolored, if her gums are red or bleeding, or if she seems in pain when you touch her mouth, she may have one of several dental diseases. A sick mouth will soon make your cat sick, so be sure to let your veterinarian take a look right away. Most dental diseases can be quickly treated for a complete recovery.

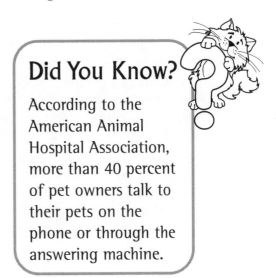

Did You Know?

According to the American Animal Hospital Association, more than 40 percent of pet owners talk to their pets on the phone or through the answering machine.

Ten Tricks for a Happy Bath

Cat bathing doesn't have to be a martial art. To make it pure pleasure—or at least reasonably stress-free—try these tricks.

1. Trim the nails. Neatly trimmed nails can protect your arms from angry feline protests, lowering the stress of bath time. It's best to trim the day before the bath. This not only gives your cat time to get over the indignity, but she'll also have groomed away any sharp edges the trimmers left behind.

2. Clean the ears. Ear cleaning isn't mandatory, but if you're going to do it, clean the ears a half hour before bathing your cat. Cleaning can be a messy job, and the bath will wash both cleaner and ear debris out of your cat's fur.

3. Premix the shampoo with water. Mixing shampoo in warm water before the bath avoids gobs of shampoo stuck in the coat and the shock of cold shampoo on sensitive feline skin. You'll cut your rinse time in half and have a happier cat.

4. Restrict escape routes. If wide-open spaces beckon your cat, chances are he'll try to take off to a more peaceful—and waterless—place. It's best to bathe a cat in a bathroom or another area that's small but not extremely restrictive. If his view is limited, he'll be more likely to sit quietly in the sink.

5. Test the temperature. When the bath is the perfect temperature, a cat barely knows he's getting wet. Cat bath temperature can be measured just like that of a baby's bottle—put a few drops on the inside of your wrist. If you can barely feel it—if it's neither hot nor cold—you've got it just right.

6. Quiet, please! The sounds of splashing, shouting children and barking dogs are unnerving even to a dry cat. Add water, and your cat will do his best to disappear. Silence or soft, gentle sounds—such as singing or chatting happily to your cat—help create a peaceful bath.

7. Stay calm. If your dentist seems nervous when he picks up the drill, are you going to open your mouth? No way! If you're nervous, your cat will pick up on your mood and do the smart thing—leave. Breathe deep, think of flowers, and have fun. Your cat will relax, too.

8. Easy on the face. No one likes blasts of water in their face, and your cat is no different. Water doesn't belong in ears, eyes, and nose—even a cat

knows that—so stray splashes are sure to make any cat protest. Use a sponge around the face, and rinse gently to avoid splashing.

9. Make it fun. Cats are sensual creatures, so a bath can be a wonderful experience. Warm water, a gentle massage, loving words, and maybe even a gourmet treat when it's over can all override your cat's natural dislike of water. Don't be a rough scrub machine—be a loving owner—and you'll create an easy-to-bathe cat.

10. Don't push. If your cat is truly frantic, start slowly. Let her look at the water and praise her at first. Once she can cope with that—whether it takes days or weeks—set her into a tub, pet her, and then let her out. Take your time and teach your cat to enjoy the bath. Cats and water really can mix.

Most cats will require periodic professional dental cleaning to remove tartar buildup. Since your cat won't open wide on command, she'll have to be put under general anesthesia to have the work done properly. This sounds scary, but modern anesthesia is very safe when given by trained hands. The benefits of healthy teeth are enormous and far exceed the small risk from the dentistry.

Bath Time!

Perhaps the most dreaded chore of cat ownership is the bath. It's true that cats don't take to water like ducks. But even a duck will quack and bite if he's plunged into a tub and swooshed around without regard to his feelings. If you bathe your cat with respect, patience, and gentleness, she'll accept the ritual with minor complaint. She might even like it.

To make bath time a happy experience, it helps to start young. Bathing your kitten every few weeks—even if it's just a short dip in plain water—and giving her a few delicious treats afterward will go a long way toward making her a happy bather for the rest of her life.

Why Should I Bathe My Cat?

Fortunately, the average cat doesn't need a bath very often. They don't get bathed on schedules; only when they need to have their fur cleaned. Since your cat is probably a fastidious feline, that may be as rarely as once a year or less.

Sometimes, however, your cat simply needs a bath. If you own a hairless breed, for example, you'll be bathing your cat every week or two to keep her oily skin clean. Show cats are bathed before every trip into the ring. Many medical conditions—such as allergies, fleas, and ringworm—can be treated by bathing. And if your cat walks in a poison such as oil or antifreeze, a fast bath may actually save her life.

Bathing Needs

The tools for an average cat bath are simple: a bathtub or sink, a handheld shower massage or spray nozzle, a shampoo that's labeled for use on cats and kittens, two unbreakable cups or jars, a sponge, and plenty of patience. Optional items include a figure-eight harness and leash to help restrain a jumping cat and a window screen to insert into the tub for your cat to grab onto so that

she feels more secure. You can insert the screen flat in the bottom of the tub; most often, however, the screen is placed at one end of the tub with one end on the tub's bottom and the other propped against the wall. If the screen slips, you may also need a plastic bath mat to give the bottom some traction. I personally find screens to be more trouble than help, but a few friends swear by them.

Cat muzzles aren't safe in the tub—a blindfolded cat may inhale water and choke. Grooming loops that wrap around a cat's neck and attach to a wall are also risky—a frantic cat may strangle himself. If your cat isn't cooperative, ask a friend to help, and avoid dangerous restraints.

On to the Bath

The key to a peaceful bath is water temperature. Cats have extremely sensitive skin, so water that's too hot or too cold is sure to send Kitty jumping claws out for the ceiling to escape. The right temperature is exactly the same as that of a baby's bottle. That means the water, placed on your wrist, should be almost impossible to feel—neither hot nor cold.

> The key to a peaceful bath is water temperature. Cats have extremely sensitive skin, so water that's too hot or too cold is sure to send Kitty jumping claws out for the ceiling to escape.

When you've adjusted the water temperature, put a couple of inches of water into your tub or sink. You're aiming to get enough water to reach your cat's belly, but not much more than that. Once the tub is filled, turn off the water and pick up your cat. Take a firm hold on the scruff of her neck (the perfect hold for a fractious cat—she can wiggle but can't scratch or bite you). Then lower her gently but swiftly into the water as you speak admiringly and lovingly to her.

Give your cat a few minutes of praising and petting, then begin to wet her skin. You can use a cup to dip the bathwater and pour it over your cat. Better yet, put the shower massage or nozzle right up against her skin and turn it on (make sure the temperature setting is correct first!). If you spray from a distance, the sound and the feel may make your cat protest, but held close to the skin, the nozzle provides a soothing massage-like action.

Once your cat is well soaked, pour on the shampoo. When used straight from the bottle, shampoos tend to be chilly and often go on in thick gobs that are hard to rinse out. To make life easy, mix a capful of cat shampoo in a pint of warm water. This premixed shampoo allows even distribution over the coat, rinses out quickly, and avoids the thrill of cold shampoo against warm cat skin.

The shampoo should be poured evenly over your cat's body. If you're washing her head—for nonmedical baths this is usually unnecessary—sponge just a little shampoo onto her face, avoiding her eyes, ears, and mouth. Once she's thoroughly shampooed, massage her gently for three to five minutes. Most cats love a whole body massage, so go slowly and rub her gently until you feel her relax. Many cats will even purr—even though they're soaking wet.

Rinse Her Well

The rinse is the single most important part of the bath. Poorly rinsed coats are dry and itchy. If your cat will tolerate the shower massage or spray nozzle, use it. Press it gently against her body to minimize scary noises and splashing.

For the most effective rinse, start at the highest point on your cat—the back of her head—and work to the lowest point, pulling the nozzle down the coat as if you were brushing her. Use a clean sponge and clear water to rinse her face. Avoid splashing water in her eyes, ears, mouth, or nose.

Some cats won't tolerate the noise of a shower massage or spray nozzle. If this is your cat, you'll have to use tub water and a cup to rinse. To do that, drain the tub and remove your cat to a quiet place (you can wrap him in a towel and put him in a crate) while you refill the tub with clean water. Put him back in and use a cup to pour water over him. You'll have to use your fingers to massage in the clean water and rinse out the soap.

Hanging Him Out to Dry

Once your cat is clean and rinsed, let the water run out of the tub or sink. Use the side of your hand like a squeegee over your cat's coat to remove the excess water from her fur. Pat her gently with a large dry towel to remove as much moisture as you can, then let your cat free inside the house. She'll seek out a quiet spot to finish drying.

If your cat tolerates the noise and the sensation, it's fine to use a hair dryer to hasten the process. Just make sure that you use medium or low heat, and keep it moving because cat skin can burn easily. Also, never point a dryer at a cat in a cage and then go off and leave him. Not only might you burn your cat, but the temperature inside the cage can rise quickly, causing your cat's body temperature to rise. If this happens, your cat can die.

Your cat shouldn't be put outside until his coat is dry, especially if the day is cold. His coat is his insulation, and a wet cat will chill quickly. Even on the fairest day a wet cat will be distracted by the urge to dry off and pull himself together. While he's busy with his fur, he's at risk for surprise attacks from outdoor dangers, such as a cat-mauling dog. It's safest to keep a wet cat inside.

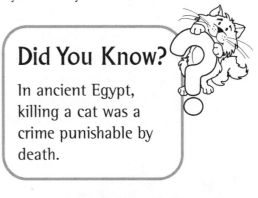

Did You Know?

In ancient Egypt, killing a cat was a crime punishable by death.

Going to the Pros

Okay, you've read all about grooming your cat, but you're still unconvinced. Do you have to groom your cat yourself? Can't you just take him to a groomer?

The answer is: Sure, you can. If you own a longhaired cat and intend to keep his tresses long, however, you'll have to learn to manage his daily combing. And you should try to tackle the tooth brushing at home, too. Other than that, your groomer or veterinarian will be happy to help you out.

Cantankerous Kitties

Don't feel that you're admitting defeat if you can't groom your cat at home. It's simply impossible with some cats. My own cat, C'hi (rhymes with *shy*), was a prime example. She was a dignified lady, and I could do anything at all with her—except trim her nails. Of course, being a veterinarian, I was determined to take care of this small task on my own.

The day I admitted defeat was the day I counted six people, plus myself, all trying to hold a different part of my enraged beast. She was still managing to best us all. To this day I can't imagine how 14 hands fit on a 10-pound cat all at once. After we had all recovered, I took C'hi to a friend of mine who happened to be a veterinary technician at the local veterinary college. She's

a tiny thing—just over five feet tall, and only has two hands—but she was happy to give a nail trim a try. She shooed me out of the room, and within five minutes C'hi was purring contentedly and all the nails were neatly trimmed. And there had been no bloodshed or caterwauling.

How Much Should a Groomer Do?

When you take your cat for a visit to the groomer, you probably expect her to make your cat clean and beautiful. This includes brushing, bathing, dematting, and clipping the coat as well as trimming your cat's nails.

Most groomers stop at coifing and caring for your cat's coat, but some offer skin care advice, treat ear infections, clean teeth, and sell nutraceuticals (food or nutrients that are touted to treat illness) or medicinal products. Some even administer drugs to sedate a cat while grooming.

Although it's nice to have a groomer who cares about your cat as a whole, when she offers services beyond plain coat care, she's practicing veterinary medicine without a license. Not only is this illegal in every state; it's risky for your cat. Bad advice may delay proper care or cause you to try products that could injure or kill your cat.

Sedation or anesthesia is particularly dangerous in the wrong hands. No groomer is trained to handle the risks of putting your cat into a sedated state. What's more, it's criminal for a groomer to handle controlled drugs. Federal and state laws restrict the use of most anesthetic drugs to licensed, trained medical professionals.

Dentistry is also particularly risky. Not only is it impossible to do a thorough dental cleaning with handheld instruments in an awake cat, but an improper cleaning may cut your cat's gums or damage her teeth. It may also cause bacteria to shed throughout her body, precipitating serious illness.

Avoid groomers who go beyond coat care. When your cat has health problems, he needs a veterinarian, not a hairdresser.

How did it happen? I don't know, but Karen was C'hi's pedicurist for years. There's no shame in calling for help when you need it!

Of course, no two cats are alike. Some cats loathe strange hands and will literally attack strangers but purr contentedly as their owner grooms. If you have one of these cats, learning to groom at home will save everyone a lot of grief.

How to Choose a Groomer

Just as in every profession, there are good groomers and bad groomers. Some will pamper your cat, praise him, and pet him; others will tie him up, fight with him, or reach for the tranquilizer before even saying hello. Obviously, the kinder the groomer, the happier your cat will be—and the safer he'll be in her hands, too.

So how do you find the right groomer?

Attitude Is Everything

Cats are sensitive creatures. If they are handled roughly or suffer personal indignity—even something as mild as unkind words—they'll protest. When treated with kindness, however, most cats will melt—or at least submit—to a grooming in good humor. A good cat groomer knows this and caters to her cats like a grandmother dotes on her grandkids.

Your first impression of the groomer will probably be by phone as you make the initial inquiry. Her voice shouldn't harden when you say the word *cat,* nor should she hasten to assure you that tranquilizers are absolutely in order. Instead, a groomer with the right attitude should sound pleased to hear about her newest customer in a cat suit and spend some time telling you about the way her shop handles felines. If she has cute cat stories to tell, make an appointment—you're likely to be pleased.

When you bring Felix in for his hairdo, watch your groomer and her staff (if she has helpers) for their reactions. It's important that they at least look at your cat, not just jerk the carrier out of your hand and take off. Better yet, they'll say a few kind words to your cat and ask you about his personality. Getting to know him will help make the grooming smooth.

If you find at any point that you just don't like the attitude of the shop, retrieve your cat and retreat. There are lots of groomers out there, and some of them do indeed love cats. Don't settle for anything less.

Check the Setup

When you make your grooming appointment, let your groomer know that you want to visit both the grooming and the caging area of her shop. If she's proud of her facility, she should be willing to let you look around. Don't expect her to let you poke around unchaperoned, however. Her insurance probably doesn't cover her if you're hurt in her shop or if you accidentally open a cage door and lose someone's pet.

During your tour check on simple items such as cleanliness. Expect hair on the floor, but a week's accumulation in corners or feces in cages are warning signs of unsanitary practices. If cage dryers are in use, check to make sure they're running only on low—not high—heat and that the animals are still wet. Hot dryers can kill caged animals.

While you're visiting, check to see if cats are caged in the same room as dogs and if the tub is in sight of potentially barking dogs. Little unnerves a cat as much as having a stranger clip and bathe her—unless it's being wet and helpless in front of a cacophony of hounds from hell. Ideally, your cat groomer will keep cats out of view of her canine clients—and away from their loud barking, too.

Take a look at her tub, and see if it's cat friendly. She should have a spray nozzle available, and the better shops will actually have a temperature regulator on the faucet. This helps your groomer know exactly how hot or cold the water is before she sprays your cat. Also, check out the restraint devices. If there are cat muzzles near the tub or the groomer says she attaches a cat to the wall with a neck loop, go elsewhere. These are risky to use on cats.

Hair or Fur?

These two small words often cause big confusion. Does your cat have hair or fur? And what's the difference?

According to Webster's Dictionary, *hair* means "a slender threadlike outgrowth of the epidermis of an animal," while *fur* comes from an old French term meaning "the hairy coat of a mammal." Either word can be properly applied to the soft, luxurious stuff that covers your cat's body.

While you're checking restraints, ask her about her attitude regarding anesthesia. Never, ever allow a nonveterinarian to sedate your cat for grooming. If a vet comes in to administer anesthesia, make sure that he stays on the premises until the cat is awake—and get this promise in writing. Anesthesia is unnecessary in most cats and is used only for the convenience of the groomer. If your cat is truly a bad actor and requires anesthesia, get him groomed at your veterinarian's office to minimize the very real risk from poorly managed sedative drugs.

Check Her Skills

Although attitude is everything, you'll expect your groomer to have some experience in handling, grooming, and clipping cats, too. Look on the walls for pictures of happy, beautiful cats—groomers often hang photos of their best customers. Also check the walls for certificates such as a membership in The National Dog Groomers Association of America, Inc., the largest groomers' association in the United States (there's no association strictly for cat groomers). You may also find a diploma from a school of grooming. If she has trophies from cat shows sitting around, you've found a feline beautician with plenty of cat experience.

Veterinarians as Groomers

Your veterinarian is an important member of your pet care team, and this includes coat care. You can expect your veterinarian to offer advice on every aspect of maintaining a healthy coat, from the vitamins and nutrients that nourish the fur to medical conditions that make a cat's skin sick. She can even point out the best, safest shampoo for your cat. And when your cat's coat is in desperate shape or he must have anesthesia in order to get cleaned, most veterinarians are willing to bathe and clip, too.

However, not all veterinary hospitals will offer routine well-cat grooming. Most hospitals prefer to focus their skills and expertise on the sick cat rather than a job that requires less extensive education. Some veterinarians do offer grooming services by hiring groomers to work in their hospitals, which can be an excellent arrangement. Others will refer your cat to a groomer who they respect. Make sure to ask your hospital's position on grooming and if they can give you a referral. It's an excellent way to find a reputable and kind coiffure for your cat.

10

Your Cat—Part of Your Family

In This Chapter

○ Children and Pets
○ Caring for a Cat Bite
○ Pets and Your Health
○ Cat Allergies
○ The Aging Cat

In early days of our country, a cat was a valued commodity. Every farmer and most home owners kept at least one feline. Cats were so important that they were hot items in the gold rush of 1849. Prospectors usually bought a cat in the East, then nurtured it carefully on the long journey to their California mine. But colonists and forty-niners didn't value cats as companions. They were working hunters who protected human food from the teeth of hungry rats and mice.

Even today some cats are kept as commodities. They live in a barn, hunting mice, or they create kittens to fatten their owner's pocketbook. But the primary job of today's feline is that of companion. More than anything else, cats have become our friends and part of our family. They share our homes, our hearths, and our hearts.

Such closeness is cause for celebration but it may bring complications. Can cats mix with babies, toddlers, teenagers, or a person suffering from AIDS or undergoing cancer chemotherapy? And if you're allergic, do you really have to get rid of your cat?

Children and Pets

Kids and cats can be a natural match. Both are energetic and playful and love to share adventures. Besides, there's no cuter image than a kid and his cat cuddled up together on the couch. Sharing a life with a cat can teach a child tenderness, respect for living things, and consideration for the feelings of others. Even more important, a cat can be the source of unconditional love. When no one else seems to care, a cat can be your child's own special and forever friend.

> Sharing a life with a cat can teach a child tenderness, respect for living things, and consideration for the feelings of others. Even more important, a cat can be the source of unconditional love.

But the combination of cats and kids isn't always idyllic. Kids can be pretty hard on a cat or kitten. Cats and kittens are, after all, small and relatively helpless—perfect victims for cruel kids. Cats sometimes suffer at the hands of even kind children, who may forget to put food in the bowl or may step on a tail in a rush to go play outside. On the flip side, cats have sharp claws and can often—quite innocently—scratch a child in the course of handling or play. And if a cat is hurt or frightened, he's likely to leave deep bites and deliberate claw marks.

With care and parental watchfulness, cats and kids can get along without harming each other. The golden rule: Cats and children should never be left alone without strict supervision. This is particularly important for babies, who aren't yet strong enough to push a loving cat away, and during the toddler years, because even a well-meaning two-year-old can easily squeeze a cat to death in a warm embrace. But you should also keep a close eye on your older child. Even teenagers can have appalling lapses in judgment, especially in front of their peers. No matter what a child's age, being with a cat is a *privilege*, not a right. Emphasize that your child must play nice with the cat or not play at all.

Cats and Babies

You may have heard a lot of myths about cats and infants. The most common are a cat will steal a baby's breath, he'll make the child sick, or he'll steal the baby's soul. These scary notions all date from the Middle Ages, when the Catholic Church linked cats to witchcraft and demons. Cats became viewed as little demons themselves, killing babies, stealing souls, and wreaking mayhem of various sorts. In retaliation for this and other mythic crimes, the church and many governments attacked cats, roasting them in giant bonfires at religious and political events.

Like these gruesome feline tortures, the legends of feline demonism should be forever put to rest. Your cat isn't interested in your baby's breath or her soul. And he has no desire to make her sick. As a matter of fact, most cats would like nothing more than to stay far, far away from the funny-looking little thing that makes such high-pitched noises. The few that aren't driven away tend to be motherly. Ace, my own cat, wanted only the best for my newborn baby. If I didn't immediately answer his middle-of-the-night cries, she'd jump on me, meow, and pace until I managed to stagger out of bed and tend to his needs.

That's not to say a cat should be given free rein with an infant. Cats have sharp claws and can inadvertently scratch your child. And there is, truly, a risk of a cat's smothering a baby—albeit completely unintentionally—if the cat is allowed into a baby's crib. A small infant can't roll away from a cat, push him off, or even turn her head away for a breath of air if the cat cuddles too closely. For these reasons, cats should never be alone with babies or allowed in the crib. A closed door, a child's gate across the nursery doorway, or a specially designed crib cover (a snug-fitting netting) can all be used to keep your kitty out of the crib.

The Child Who Torments

Young children who torment a cat are *usually* not trying to inflict real harm. They think it's funny to chase a cat and—if they consider the cat at all—may even think that he's enjoying the game, too. Youngsters also explore their world in mysterious ways, like experimenting to see if whiskers crackle when burned or checking out what happens if a cat spends a few minutes in a microwave.

It's hard to imagine that a child has no idea he's hurting a cat, but very young children often simply cannot grasp the concept of another's pain. Only careful monitoring of cat-kid interactions will prevent harmful explorations. If your child is particularly curious, keep your cat in a childproof cage or a locked room except when you're there to supervise. Sitters and siblings can't always be trusted to take your cat's welfare as seriously as you do, so don't count on them to watch Kitty's whiskers, either.

Unfortunately, a few children are just plain malicious. They actually delight in causing fear and pain to a cat and will watch for every opportunity to hurt one. These deeply troubled children may have been sexually or physically abused even if their parents seem nice or—if you're the parent—if you aren't aware of such abuse. Children who have a pattern of abusing pets can carry this cruelty into adulthood and may end up injuring others. The career of most serial killers began with repeated animal abuse.

What can you do if a neighborhood child—or your own—is a malicious child? Whatever you do, don't ignore it. If he's a neighbor's child, tell his parents your concern. You may also need to talk to the child's teachers, to local social services, or even to the police. If you're the parent, first of all, don't allow your child around pets. More important, make sure your child and family get counseling. Ignoring the problem will *not* make it go away, but facing the underlying problem can save not only other cats but your child as well. Professional counseling can usually cure these kids, often very quickly.

Did You Know?

The size of a cat's pupils is related as much to the cat's emotions as to the degree of light. A cat who is frightened, excited, or is about to pounce will have large, round pupils, while a contented or sleepy cat will have narrow pupils.

The Cat Who Attacks

Cats can sometimes torment children, too. Most of the time scratches on your child are the result of play or accident—such as when a sharp-clawed cat launches off a lap. Simply keeping the cat's toenails trimmed can minimize these accidental scratches.

Scratches are also accidentally given in rough play, which kittens in particular love to instigate. Fortunately, kittens can be trained out of rough play simply by refusing to play back. When attacked, your child should walk away or place the kitty in a crate until she calms down. Encouraging rough play, on the other hand, can create a man-eater, who has no respect for human flesh. Never allow your children to use their hands to wrestle with the cat. Instead stuff a sturdy sock with cotton and catnip and let Kitty vent her wrestling energies on that.

Bite wounds and frequent scratches are usually a sign that the child has been hurting or frightening the cat. It's natural, normal, and reasonable for a cat to strike out in her own defense, so don't automatically blame the cat if you see such wounds on your child. Teach your child that your cat means "leave me alone" when she's wiggling to get away, meowing when held, hissing, flattening her ears, or twitching her tail. If your child can respect your cat's language and appreciate her natural reaction to pain, he won't get scratched.

> Never allow your children to use their hands to wrestle with the cat. Instead stuff a sturdy sock with cotton and catnip and let Kitty vent her wrestling energies on that.

Although most scratches are accidental or justifiably defensive, you may—rarely—come across the feline version of a sociopath. This is a cat who will stalk, attack, and injure people. Such cats aren't playful kittens but adult cats who aim to hurt. They may attack all humans equally or focus their loathing on a particular person. Sociopathic cats sometimes improve with treatment by a veterinary behaviorist. But no human—especially a child—should suffer at the fangs of a cat. Confine the cat away from the object of his attacks or have him humanely euthanized.

Caring for a Cat Bite

If you own a cat long enough, you're likely to pick up a scratch or even the occasional bite. Although these are minor wounds, they aren't completely risk-free. A cat's mouth harbors a host of bacteria, many of which can cause infection. And rarely, a cat's claws might be home for *Bartonella,* the agent that causes cat scratch fever.

Cat scratches can be cared for at home. Clean the scratch well with an antiseptic scrub containing povidone iodine or chlorhexidine or with just plain soap and water. "It doesn't matter so much which cleanser you use, but it's important that you irrigate the wound very well and use plenty of water," says Harvey Steinfeld, M.D., a family physician in Shady Side, Maryland. But call your physician if the site becomes red and inflamed or if you feel generally ill and your lymph nodes begin to swell, since these symptoms are signs of cat scratch fever. A round of antibiotic therapy will get you well quickly.

Cat bites are more serious than scratches. "Almost all cat bite wounds become infected," says Dr. Steinfeld. "Cats' mouths harbor a particularly nasty bacteria called *Pasteurella.* It can cause a real problem, but normally it's easily treated with antibiotic therapy." He recommends that you clean the wound at home, then contact your physician within 12 hours to begin treatment.

Of course, the worst-possible result of a cat bite is rabies, which can be passed from a rabid cat to a person through saliva. Rabies is a fatal disease once signs develop, but fast action (a series of injections) can stop it from developing in a person who has been bitten by a rabid cat. If you or your child is bitten by a cat with an unknown rabies vaccination history— such as a stray or neighborhood wild cat—try to capture the cat if you can safely do so. If you can, take it

to your vet, who will quarantine the cat or, if it appears ill, may euthanize it and send the brain to the local health department laboratory to examine it for rabies. This test is usually free. Also, immediately visit your physician, who can help assess your risk of rabies and suggest proper treatment if necessary.

Pets and Your Health

Owning a pet can be beneficial to your health. Studies have shown that petting an animal can lower blood pressure, calm nerves, and improve the psychological well-being of patients suffering from a whole host of physical and emotional ailments. Any cat owner knows that life shared with a well-loved cat is more fun than a catless life, but some experts also suggest that bonding with a pet can help you live a longer, healthier life as well. Even the short visit of a therapy cat to a nursing home can bring a little ray of joy and emotional healing into otherwise catless lives.

Despite the benefits that living with a pet brings, you may have some health worries about it, too. Can I catch some awful disease from my cat? Will cleaning the litter box harm my unborn baby? If I'm allergic, should I get rid of the cat? If my immune system is impaired, can I live with a cat at all?

Things You Can Catch from Your Cat

"Get rid of the cat" is almost a mantra for a small set of physicians, who love to blame cats for a myriad of diseases, most of which are rare or even mythical. The veterinary response to this cat-killing refrain is generally something like this from a colleague of mine: "Listen, I'm sick of that. I'll get the oil to boil that M.D. in if you'll get the match."

Medical Myths

If it happens again, I'll scream. I spoke to a woman who said she's upset because her physician told her that her son got pinworms from the family cat. Should she get rid of the cat? While we veterinarians respect our human-treating counterparts, sometimes we just can't figure out where physicians learn this stuff. Here are the top three mythic diseases blamed on cats:

Parvo 19

In humans the parvovirus called parvo 19 causes "Fifth Disease." It's most common in children and is usually mild; symptoms are a rash, fever, and achiness that goes away without further treatment. Parvo 19 has also been implicated as a cause of some early miscarriages. Some physicians think that this virus is the same as canine or feline parvovirus. Cats do get sick with parvovirus—it causes panleukopenia—but it's *not* parvo 19. Not a shred of scientific evidence suggests that feline (or canine) parvo has ever infected people, and strong evidence exists *against* cats and people sharing this infection.

Pinworms

The pinworm is a tiny white worm that lives in the intestines and can cause your child's rectum to itch. You might find the worm in a diaper, in underwear, or on bed linen. If this happens, your pediatrician may blame your cat.

Don't go home and boot the cat—educate the physician. First of all, feline pinworm infestation is exceedingly rare. Second, the pinworm is extremely species-specific. In other words, the pinworm of horses likes to live in horses, and cat pinworms live in cats. They won't infest your child. Your child caught pinworm from another infected child, not a pet—so check out your child's friends and playmates.

Strep

Another favorite physician fallacy is linking pets with strep throat. It's true that cats and dogs normally have some forms of strep living in their throats and mouths. But the causative bug in people, Lancefield's Group A Strep, isn't found in dogs and cats. It's hard to get physicians to buy that this is a myth, however, because—very rarely—strep A has been cultured from the throat of dogs. Although the reports also suggest that the dog caught the bug from children, not vice versa, and didn't pass it back, that fact got lost somewhere in translation.

Given the fact that physicians are so adamant on this one, most vets will simply roll their eyes, culture your pet's throat, and treat the pet with antibiotics, which are unnecessary except to satisfy everyone's mind. While you're shelling out $100 or so to treat this phantom problem, make sure to buy fresh toothbrushes for the child (a step that's often overlooked when infections reoccur) and check to see if any friends are carrying the bug, too.

At the root of this mantra, however, are some legitimate concerns. It *is* possible to catch a few diseases from your cat. A normal immune system and washing your hands after handling the cat will protect you from almost all cat-transmitted diseases, but a few diseases may cause a problem, anyway. Cat owners should be aware of the risk of rabies (discussed above and in Chapter 6: What Bugs Your Pet?), cat scratch fever, ringworm, and toxoplasmosis. If you're immunosuppressed, you may also have to guard against the rarer cat-transmitted bugs, such as giardia and salmonella.

Cat Scratch Fever

Cat scratch fever is the common name for infection with *Bartonella* bacteria. People usually get the disease when they're

scratched by an infected cat, most often a kitten. If you catch cat scratch fever, you may feel achy and sick like you would with the flu, and your lymph nodes may swell.

Although cat scratches are common, cat scratch fever is rare. In fact, it's pretty hard to get the disease if you simply take the precaution of washing the wound well with plenty of soap and water. For the few people who *do* get sick, antibiotic treatment is quite likely to result in a rapid, complete cure. Studies have shown that a small percentage of people who contract cat scratch fever had *no* history of exposure to cats, so felines aren't always the culprit in this disease.

> Although cat scratches are common, cat scratch fever is rare.

Toxoplasmosis

If you're a woman of childbearing age, you've probably heard of the disease called toxoplasmosis. It's caused by *Toxoplasma gondii,* a tiny, one-celled parasite. This parasite can live quietly inside your cat's intestine, but when it infects other animals, it travels throughout their body and causes problems. If you catch toxo and your immune system is healthy, chances are you'll feel a little achy and tired—if you notice you're sick at all.

The real problem arises when a woman becomes infected *for the first time in her life* during the first trimester of pregnancy. In this thankfully rare scenario, toxo can attack the fetus and cause miscarriage or terrible birth defects. It's this fear that causes physicians to counsel pregnant women to simply "get rid of the cat." This advice is extreme and rarely necessary.

A cat catches toxo *only* from eating raw meat from an infected animal. If the cat lives indoors, she *can't* catch the disease unless you feed her raw meat or she's catching house mice. Even outdoor, hunting cats rarely catch toxo simply because it's not that common in mice. If your cat does become infected, it's still not that easy for her to pass the disease along to you. When a cat becomes infected, she will shed the organism in her stool only for one to three weeks *in her entire life.* Once the organism spends a little time inside a cat, the cat responds by controlling it and can no longer spread the disease to people. Even if a cat becomes reinfected later, she won't be able to give the disease to you.

What physicians often neglect to say, as they are condemning the cat, is that the most common way people catch toxoplasmosis is from their *food*. Humans, like cats, can easily become infected by eating undercooked or raw meat. It's also possible to catch toxo from soil brought in on garden or store-bought veggies. Cooking all meat to 160 degrees, washing veggies well before eating them, and washing your hands after handling raw food will prevent more than 90 percent of all human toxo cases.

> What physicians often neglect to say, as they are condemning the cat, is that the most common way people catch toxoplasmosis is from their *food*.

If you're planning to become pregnant, ask your physician to draw blood for a toxoplasmosis titer. If you have a positive titer *before* you conceive, your baby isn't at risk. If you're negative, however, you'll know to take precautions, such as letting someone else clean the litter box during pregnancy, keeping the cats indoors, and using caution while preparing and eating meat.

Worms

In general, the parasites that live inside your pet won't take up residence inside you or your child. However, hookworms or roundworms can cause a rare problem called larval migrans. The worms themselves live peacefully inside your cat's intestines, but they lay eggs, which pass into the environment through your cat's stool. When the stool—and eggs—lies on warm ground for several days, the eggs hatch, releasing hungry little larvae. These larvae want to move into a dog or cat, but if a child walks barefoot over them or plays with infected dirt, the larvae might look for a home in him, penetrate his skin, and cause itching sores. Worse, the larvae can sometimes travel through his muscles and internal organs, causing serious problems for the child.

Don't Get Rid of That Cat!

One day two very beautiful cats and a very distraught owner came into my office. She wanted me to euthanize both cats, on the order of her husband's physician. Her husband had an unusually bad case of toxoplasmosis and was very sick. "Get rid of the cats," the doctor directed the poor woman. "They infected your husband and are a health risk for you, too."

After a long heart-to-heart, the owner allowed me to pull blood to test for toxo in her cats rather than inject them with the killing solution. Both were *negative*—they'd never been infected in their life. Armed with that information, the physician hunted a little further. Turns out the husband loved to eat his lamb quite rare—almost lamb tartar. He plainly was infected from his food, not his cats. Fortunately the husband got well quickly, and his innocent cats were spared execution. And, I hope, the physician will look for evidence before he blithely condemns a cat again.

If you're confronted by a physician who suggests the cat must go, make sure to run the reasoning by your veterinarian, who might well understand the disease better than the M.D. You'll also find authoritative information from the Centers for Disease Control in Atlanta, Georgia. They have several fact sheets on diseases shared by cats and the people who live with them.

Larval migrans is *very* rare in the United States, although it's more common in developing nations where personal sanitation is poor. The reason that the disease is important to the average cat owner, despite its rarity, is that larval migrans is completely preventable. Public health officials recommend deworming kittens (and puppies) frequently, starting as young as two weeks of age, to kill the worms before they can reproduce. They also recommend that children wash well after digging in soil or running barefoot. You can minimize the risk of catching this disease by putting a cat-proof cover on your child's outdoor sandbox to keep stray, unwormed kitties from using it as a litter box.

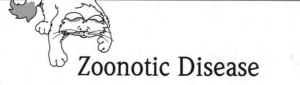

Zoonotic Disease

A zoonotic disease passes from animal to person and sometimes back again. The following is a list of diseases and agents of disease that may be passed from cat to human.

○ Rabies

○ Toxoplasmosis

○ Cat scratch fever

○ Ringworm

○ Hookworm and roundworm larvae

○ Salmonella (bacterial diarrhea)

○ Cryptosporidium (an intestinal parasite)

○ *Neospora caninum* (a parasite similar to that causing toxoplasmosis)

○ Giardia (an intestinal parasite)

Ringworm

Ringworm is caused by a fungus that grows in the hair and skin. It's highly contagious to all mammals, including cats, dogs, and people. You can not only catch ringworm from your pets; you can catch it from other people, too. And you can bring it home *to* your pets.

Fortunately, ringworm is usually easily diagnosed and easily treatable. For more information, see the discussion in Chapter 6, What Bugs Your Pet?.

Lyme Disease and Rocky Mountain Spotted Fever

Your cat may catch these diseases, and so may you. But you won't pass them directly back and forth. Lyme disease and Rocky Mountain spotted fever are passed by the bite of a tick, which then drops off and doesn't feed again for a long time. If your cat develops any tick-borne disease, she's warning you that there are infected ticks living near your home. This information can protect your family if you step up tick-control measures to rid your yard of danger. But don't shun the cat—she's perfectly safe to handle.

Pets and the Immunosuppressed

When you're grievously ill, a cat can be your only friend. The warm purring and constant love of a cat are often essential therapy—a connection with life and vitality that can literally help you hang on to the will to live.

In a 1989 survey of health care providers treating HIV-infected patients in community-based settings in San Francisco, 97 percent of respondents indicated that companion animals were a major source of support and comfort for patients. Seventy-six percent of the survey participants felt that the benefits of pet ownership probably outweighed zoonotic (pet-to-people-disease) risks, although only 21 percent of respondents felt comfortable with their level of knowledge of zoonotic disease.

If you have AIDS or are planning immunosuppressive cancer treatments, you may be concerned about the risks of owning a cat. Just when you need warmth, purrs, and love, your physician may demand you get rid of your cat. As you face your own mortality, you may be faced with the absolutely devastating pain of having to euthanize your best friend. The consequences of these emotions may be much riskier than continuing to live with your cat.

Before you accept your physician's demand for the demise of your cat, ask for other opinions. In particular, you may find a local Pets Are Wonderful (PAWS) group especially enlightening. These groups celebrate the real therapeutic benefits of sharing your sick days with a loving pet and are generally great sources of information as well as emotional support.

If you're ill but wish to continue living with your cat, follow these steps to help keep yourself healthy:

○ Keep your cat inside. If she's indoors, she's not going to catch giardia, salmonella, cryptosporidia—all organisms that can cause severe diarrhea in people with weakened immune systems. Also, she can't catch toxoplasmosis from hunting.

○ Routinely screen your cat's stool for parasites.

○ Be meticulous about flea and tick control. Fleas have been implicated in passing cat scratch fever to cats, who can then infect you. Ticks can pass several potentially fatal diseases to you during feeding.

○ Before adopting a cat, have her screened for toxoplasmosis and ringworm.

○ Wash your hands after handling your cat or her litter box.

○ Don't let your cat lick your wounds.

○ Keep your cat's nails trimmed short or declaw him to prevent scratches. You can also have nail caps, such as Soft Paws, applied to your cat's nails to keep him from scratching you.

○ If you're scratched or bitten, wash the wound immediately with a disinfecting solution, such as a povidone iodine (Betadine) scrub. Then phone your physician. Cat bites and scratches can become infected very quickly, especially if your immune system is weak.

○ Keep your cat up-to-date on all necessary vaccinations, especially rabies.

○ If your pet becomes sick, have him diagnosed and treated right away. If he develops diarrhea (a possible sign of toxoplasmosis, salmonella, or giardia, to name a few diseases), have someone else clean the box. Or use disposable latex gloves and a particle mask and wash well afterward if you must do it yourself.

○ Don't feed your cat raw eggs, unpasteurized milk, or raw meat. These can be a source of disease for both you and your cat.

Cat Allergies

With immunosuppressive diseases you worry about catching disease from cats because your immune system is weak. On the other hand, when your immune system is overactive, you develop allergies. Cat allergies are very common—right up there with ragweed and tree pollen—and can complicate life with your cat.

If you suffer from runny eyes, sniffing, or sneezing when you're around a cat but feel great in a cat-free zone, you probably have a cat allergy. Before you blame the cat, however, let your physician confirm your suspicions with a complete set of allergy tests. Most of the time you'll find you're not just allergic to cats but to several things. You'll want to seek treatment for all allergies, not just the cat, if this is the case.

Of course, even if, like me, your allergy tests are positive for over 20 allergens, the first words out of your allergist's mouth will be—you guessed it—"Get rid of the cat." In the eyes of allergists, cats are totally disposable. Most allergists really can't understand why you'd want to live with a cat if your body overreacts to his dander. Of course, if you were allergic to a spouse or child— the other loved beings who share your house—you wouldn't hear such a quick condemnation. Instead you'd work around the problem. In most cases it's possible to work around cat allergies, too.

Even if you get rid of the cat, it's a fantasy to think you'll live in a cat-allergen-free zone. Cat allergen (the little bits of protein that cause an allergic reaction) is literally everywhere. It's been found in

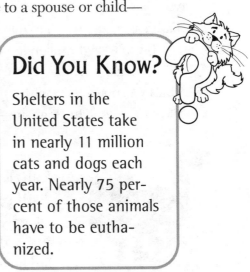

Did You Know?

Shelters in the United States take in nearly 11 million cats and dogs each year. Nearly 75 percent of those animals have to be euthanized.

school buildings that have been closed for years, presumably brought in on the sweaters of little girls and boys decades before. And it's been found even at the North Pole, far from the padding of any feline feet. So eliminating your own cat only diminishes the amount of allergens you live with daily—it doesn't eliminate them entirely.

Besides, unless your allergies are very severe or you suffer from dangerous bouts of asthma, you can usually manage to live in comfort with your cat despite allergies. To do this, first eliminate as much allergen as possible. Second, treat the cat allergy. Third, treat all other allergies you may have. Fourth, keep your general health good with exercise and excellent nutrition.

Eliminate Allergen

Your cat's body and even her hair aren't what cause your allergies—it's the allergens that your body objects to. These bits of protein are found in dander and saliva, and they dissolve completely and quickly in plain water. This means that by simply bathing the cat, you can literally wash your allergies right down the sink. A weekly bath has been proven to markedly reduce allergic reactions to cats.

If you're highly allergic, you may have to enlist some help so you don't actually handle the cat yourself. You can hire a groomer, charm a spouse, or enlist a neighbor to help out. The bath doesn't have to be long or dramatic—wet the cat, use a small dab of a mild

shampoo, rub it in, then give a good rinse with plenty of water. A routine allergy-reducing bath can be over in about five minutes.

If your cat is impossible to bathe or your allergies are mild, try simply toweling her off with a damp rag. I've seen veterinarians who are highly cat allergic send in a technician to wipe off patients before the exam. This 10-second wipe allows the vet to touch and handle the cat without problems. Because a damp wipe isn't as complete as a full bath, you'll have to repeat it often—every day or so—to get good relief at home.

Another way to reduce allergens is to use air filters to physically trap the saliva-covered hair and the larger bits of dander. You can purchase room sized-filters, or you can have a filter built into your central heat and air duct. Room-sized HEPA-type filters are the very best at removing allergens. Avoid ozone-generating air "purifiers." Although salespeople may tout them as being "good for" allergies, they *don't* remove allergens when used as directed. In fact, the Environmental Protection Agency regards ozone as air pollution and states that ozone generators shouldn't be used in the presence of people or animals.

Treat the Cat Allergy

Allergists, despite the fact that they often view cats as four-legged balls of allergens, can be wonderful allies. An allergist who is willing to work with you can offer medications to help quiet your immune system so that you react less severely to your cat. They can tell you how to control dander inside your house and offer a series of hyposensitizaton shots designed to make your body adapt to exposure to cats. If you make it clear that removing your cat is a last, not first, resort, you'll probably find that your allergist can make you much more comfortable. If he refuses to work around the cat, find another allergist who will work with you.

Treating Other Allergies

Imagine a party where everyone's sitting around, having a great time. Then the door opens and in comes a really annoying guy.

He's a pain, but everyone can tolerate one rude person. Pretty soon a couple more insensitive brutes stomp in. The atmosphere changes, and the party gets uncomfortable. When one more clod enters, there's no more room for tolerance—fights break out and chaos reigns until the rude guests are either ejected or an understanding is reached.

If you're allergic, your immune system resembles this party. It's buzzing along happily, and in comes one allergen. It's kind of annoying, but no big deal, so there's no reaction. A few more minor allergens show up, and your body may start to feel a bit run down. In walks the cat—another allergen—and it's just one too many annoyances. Your eyes run, you sneeze, and you feel awful.

This is the *threshold effect*. Your body can normally handle a few allergens, maybe a few house-dust mites and wool carpet, but at some point the immune system won't take any more. The cat may not be the only problem—just the last straw.

The point is, if you want to keep your cat, make sure you control your other allergies. You can control your house-dust mites, an allergen that's even stronger than cat, by meticulous housecleaning and frequently washing your bedding in hot water. Or you may discover that removing your down comforter quells your feather allergy. With other allergies controlled, many people suddenly find that cats no longer bother them, either.

Taking Care of Yourself

Picture the party again. Imagine the scene if everyone there were suffering from hangovers, insomnia, and ill health. They wouldn't have a lot of patience—it would probably take just one bad word to get a big reaction. In the same way a healthy immune system—one that lives in a well-nourished, well-rested, well-exercised body—can better take everyday insults without overreacting.

Psychic Cats?

Do cats communicate through extrasensory perception? Some say they do. The famous psychic Jeane Dixon, in her book *Do Cats Have ESP?*, admits that she's one of a host of cat owners who "talk" to their cats—and enjoy the close emotional bond that results.

If you own a cat, you've probably received a message or two—whether or not you realize it. For example, you gaze at your cat and feel deep love coming from her. Or you may find yourself thinking, out of the blue, that the cat must be terribly hungry right about now. You may even suddenly put down a book, dead certain that if you don't clean that litter box right away, your cat is going to pee on the floor.

If these scenes sound familiar, you might want to try to improve your psychic connection. If you wish to hear what your cat has to say, simply relax, pay attention, and throw preconceptions aside. The time will come when your cat finds you and gazes deep into your eyes. If you're very still and your mind and heart are open, you may hear what she has to say.

If you're plagued by allergies, take a careful look at your lifestyle. Improving your overall health can sometimes, almost magically, make the symptoms of allergy disappear. In my case, nurturing general good health quells my cat allergies quite nicely, allowing me to live and work with my beloved feline friends.

The Aging Cat

When Nature designed our lovable cats, she gave them one serious design flaw—a short life. Because our lives are so long and a cat's so short, chances are pretty good that you'll be around to witness, all too soon, the aging of your cat.

Aging is inevitable, but it doesn't have to be a sad time. It's a natural part of the circle of life. Older people often experience great inner joys as their bodies slow down, forcing them to rest and enjoy the simple pleasures that they ignored when they were young and vigorous. The older cat, too, gives up being the curtain-climbing athlete in favor of basking in sunshine and curling up on a loving lap. You may see a touch of gray in the fur or notice a slower walk and be sad because you know her life is shortening. But you can bet your cat isn't worrying—she's living for today. And it's a good day, too.

> Aging is inevitable, but it doesn't have to be a sad time. It's a natural part of the circle of life.

Age Stages

Veterinarians define a *senior* cat as between the age of seven and 12 years of age. During these years expect to see your cat's metabolism slow down. He'll exercise less, and his waistline may expand. Most senior cats benefit from a diet that's lower in calories, lower in protein, and lower in fat than that of their athletic counterparts. A few cats, especially late in the senior years, may need to actually increase calories to keep weight on. Of course, let your vet recommend any dietary changes to make certain they're right for your cat.

Good dental health helps to keeps your cat healthy, too, so make sure to pay attention to his teeth. It's very likely your senior cat will need a professional dental cleaning—perhaps more than once—to keep a healthy mouth.

Cats over 12 years of age earn the title of *geriatric*. Although many cats thrive into their late teens or even twenties, it's a common time for health problems to crop up. It's normal for geriatric cats to move more slowly and lose the sharp hearing of their youth, but these years aren't normally just a steady decline in health. In other words, if your geriatric cat begins to limp, lose weight, or weaken or changes bathroom habits or the amount of water she drinks, it's more likely the onset of a treatable disease, not normal aging. During these years it's essential to work closely with your vet. Call whenever you notice a change in your elder cat.

The Passing of the Cat

Nothing is harder than losing a beloved friend, whether he walked on two legs or four. Although it may be hard for non-cat-owning friends to understand, the grief felt when a cat passes away is in fact often as strong as the grief felt over the death of a human. It can even be greater, especially if your cat helped you live through troubled times, when no human heart opened in your support. If you're saddened by the passing of your cat, don't be ashamed or minimize your pain. You're entitled to grieve for a friend.

Euthanasia

The loss of a beloved pet is often complicated by a huge decision—should I euthanize my pet? And if so, when? Ending your cat's life with a painless, humane injection can be a great kindness and spare your cat a great deal of suffering. However, the decision can be a great burden on you. When the time draws near, share your questions with your veterinarian. She'll share her experiences with you and should help you come to grips with the decision.

When you're coping with the issues that surround a pet's death, you can also call one of several pet grief hot lines. They can help you sort through the difficult days both after—and before—your cat's passing. The days and months leading up to death, especially when a cat is battling a long-standing disease, are often filled with "pregrief." This is a very painful, very confusing emotion. You grieve for the impending loss of your friend, yet you either feel foolish or don't realize what you're going through because, after all, your cat is still alive. It's hard to cope with, but the people manning hot lines understand this tough emotion, too. You may find great relief in speaking to someone who will understand and care about your problems. Also, because the lines are anonymous, you may be able to express fears and questions that you would hide from friends and family.

Making the Decision   "You'll know when the time comes." Those words echoed in my head as I watched my beloved cat, C'hi, struggle with a multitude of diseases. She was the miracle cat. She was diagnosed with feline leukemia as a youngster and given a few months to live. But she carried the virus for life—for 16 years—without a second thought. In middle age she developed a vaccine-induced fibrosarcoma, a viciously spreading tumor. I was advised by the surgeon to put her to sleep, but I insisted he give my cat the best surgery possible and let her recover to live out her days. He did, and the tumor never returned.

Now C'hi was 17. We had struggled with kidney failure for years, then hyperthyroidism, then high blood pressure and heart disease. Drug therapy became complicated—we walked a delicate tightrope, trying to balance the hormone with the failing kidneys. If her thyroid levels got too low, her kidney function declined. Also, we needed to control her blood pressure to help her heart, but the kidneys actually appreciated the higher blood pressure. It helped them do work that they were really no longer able to do on their own.

Over the final months I kept looking to my cat for a signal, something to tell me that this cat had had enough—that she was in pain, she no longer wanted to live, or she hated life. I knew my cat very well, and I was certain that I would know when the right time came. But all I saw was a cat who had a total, utter, and peaceful faith in me. She had sick days, but she never seemed willing to quit.

One day my beautiful friend tried to walk to me and staggered and fell. I quickly examined her, and the truth was obvious—her vital signs were flagging. Death was imminent. She was confused and frightened, but she still tried to comfort my fear, pushing her way into my lap and purring. I called a veterinarian friend, who came and mercifully ended my friend's life with an injection as I held her on my lap. It was terrible to be unable to save my friend, but it was wonderful to ease her passage.

The point of the story is that despite your best intentions, you may *not* intuitively know the right time. Many cats do signal that they're miserable and want to quit. Others, like my C'hi, put their faith in you and are willing to endure anything, silently, rather than give up on the relationship you have.

In retrospect, I would have liked to have spared C'hi that last day of staggering and suffering. I berated myself not only for my failure to save her—which was a blatantly impossible task—but also for waiting just a little too long to release her spirit from her suffering body. I know that I couldn't have predicted the moment that

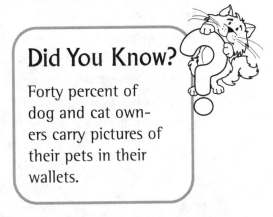

Did You Know?

Forty percent of dog and cat owners carry pictures of their pets in their wallets.

C'hi's body would suddenly shut down, either. In the end, I know that I did my wholesale best for my dear friend. That knowledge is what brings comfort when I think on my cat's last days.

When struggling with your cat's last illness, it's important to re-member that *you* are the one who lives on. When coming to the deci-sion to euthanize your cat, take it a day at a time. Pray, ask your vet for advice, talk to others. Call the grief hot lines, and pray some more. It's enormously important that regardless of the day you choose to relieve your cat's suffering, you believe with all your heart that you did the best you could. After all, that's all your cat would ever ask of you.

The Cat Came Back

Does anyone who's shared a life with a cat, and experienced cats' vitality and individuality, really believe that it's all over when the last breath is drawn?

Although some religious leaders rage at the thought of beasts having souls, most of the greatest figures in religion give hints that animals, too, are more than just sinew and bone. The prophet Mohammed cut off a sleeve of his robe rather than wake his cat, who slumbered peacefully on the sleeve. Buddha taught respect for all living creatures. And the Christian Bible speaks of God's awareness of each sparrow in the field—surely evidence that he deems animals of great importance.

Of course, there's no proof that the spirits of cats live on after their death, no more than we can prove that human souls pass to heaven or hell. It's a matter of faith and of personal experience. Al-

though I'm a scientifically minded skeptic by nature, it's obvious even to me that the essential cat—whether you call it spirit, soul, or energy—is greater than her body. When I've held dying cats, I've felt this energy leave the body. It's quite distinct from the stopping of a heart, a brain, or breathing.

People—all of quite sound mind, thank you—have also shared with me some wonderful experiences. One friend is convinced that her own beloved cat returned in the form of a kitten—a kitten who was born a few days after her cat passed away. Not only did the kitten have all the mannerisms of the elder cat, but she slept in the same spots, many of which were difficult to crawl into, and enjoyed the same favorite morsels. Another friend, who owned a most extraordinary and famous cat, one who spent her life performing on television and in movies and making personal appearances in front of sick and underprivileged children, is convinced that her cat lives on—although her body died years ago. In fact, my friend says the cat helps write a column on cat care and training, nudging her owner's mind and spirit to come up with helpful answers to tough questions.

After your beloved cat has passed away, you may feel footfalls on your pillow, only to look and see blank air. Or you may hear a rumbling purr in your ear and feel the weight of a cat on your chest—but when you reach to stroke the familiar fur, touch nothing. Or while deep in a dream, your cat may quietly appear, gazing lovingly at you and leaving you to awaken with a peaceful, happy heart. If this happens to you, don't overanalyze the situation. Most likely, you're neither crazy nor making it up. You may indeed have received a paw pat from the other side.

> After your beloved cat has passed away, you may feel footfalls on your pillow, only to look and see blank air.

Your life with your cat begins when you take her home, possibly as a fluffy kitten, maybe as an older matron. During the good days and the bad, the seasons pass and love builds. Eventually death demands a separation. It's simply the passage of life, but not necessarily the end. The bond of love between a cat and her best friend doesn't die in a year, or two—or even 15. The bond between friends lives forever.

Resources

Breed Information, Clubs, Registries

Cat Fanciers Association, Inc.
Box 1005
Manasquan, NJ 08737-0805
(732) 528-9797
www.cfainc.org

The International Cat Association, Inc.
Box 2684
Harlingen, TX 78551
(956) 428-8046

Tatoo-A-Pet
6571 S.W. 20th Court
Ft. Lauderdale, FL 33317
(800) 828-8667
www.tattoo-a-pet.com

Cat Publications

The Cat Who Cried for Help: Attitudes, Emotions and Psychology of Cats,
Nicholas Dodman, B.V.M.S., M.R.C.V.S
Bantam Books

Cats in the Sun, Leslie Anne Ivory
Illustrated stories of cats
Puffin Pied Piper Press
Direct Book Service
(800) 776-2665
www2.dogandcatbooks.com/directbook

First Aid for Cats, Bruce Fogle
Penguin, USA

Infectious Diseases of the Dog and Cat,
Craig E. Greene, Editor
W B Saunders Company

Pet First Aid: Cats and Dogs, Bobbi Mammato, D.V.M.
Mosby Year Book

Six-Dinner Sid, Inga Moore
Fat-cat humor
Aladdin Books

Fun, Grooming, Obedience, Training

American Grooming Shop Association
(719) 570-7788

Animal Behavior Society
Susan Foster
Department of Biology
Clark University
950 Main Street
Worcester, MA 01610-1477

Cats United
Health tips, grooming tips, and more
www.catsunited.com

Fat Cats, Inc.
73 Troy Avenue
Colchester, VT 05446
(802) 655-1300

Flea News
Biannual flea newsletter
Iowa State University, Department of Entomology
411 Science II
Ames, IA 50011-3222
(515) 294-7400
http://www.ent.iastate.edu/fleanews/aboutfleanews.html

Grooming Supplies Catalog
Pet Warehouse
P.O. Box 752138
Dayton, OH 45475-2138
(800) 443-1160
www.petwhse.com

Intergroom
Professional society of dog and cat
    groomers
www.intergroom.com/directory/
    prof_directory.htm

Snuggle Kitties
Soothe those separation jitters
ChilsonRoth, LLC
P.O. Box 6805
Snowmass Village CO 81615
(800) 463-4107
http://snuggleme.com/

Grief Resources

books...
Cat Heaven, Cynthia Rylant
The Blue Sky Press/Scholastic
Written for kids, but wonderful for
    any age

Cold Noses at the Pearly Gates,
    Gary Kurtz
Privately published
A book about animal afterlife

grief hotlines...
Chicago Veterinary Medical Association
(630) 603-3994

Cornell University
(607) 253-3932

Michigan State University
College of Veterinary Medicine
(517) 432-2696

Tufts University (Massachusetts)
School of Veterinary Medicine
(508) 839-7966

University of California, Davis
(530) 752-4200

University of Florida at Gainesville
College of Veterinary Medicine
(352) 392- 4700

Virginia-Maryland Regional College of
    Veterinary Medicine
(540) 231-8038

Washington State University
College of Veterinary Medicine
(509) 335-5704

Humane Organizations and Rescue Groups

American Humane Association
63 Inverness Drive E
Englewood CO 80112-5117
(800) 227-4645
www.americanhumane.org

American Society for the Prevention of
    Cruelty to Animals (ASPCA)
424 East 92nd Street
New York, NY 10128-6804
(212) 876-7700
www.aspca.org

Animal Protection Institute of America
P.O. Box 22505
Sacramento, CA 95822
(916) 731-5521

Humane Society of the United States
2100 L Street, NW
Washington, DC 20037
(301) 258-3072, (202) 452-1100
www.hsus.org/

Massachusetts Society for the Prevention of Cruelty to Animals
350 South Huntington Avenue
Boston, MA 02130
(617) 522-7400
http://www.mspca.org/

SPAY/USA
14 Vanderventer Avenue
Port Washington, NY 11050
(516) 944-5025,
  (203) 377-1116 in Connecticut
(800) 248-SPAY
www.spayusa.org/

Medical and Emergency Information

American Animal Hospital Association
P.O. Box 150899
Denver, CO 80215-0899
(800) 252-2242
www.healthypet.com

American Association of Feline Practitioners (AAFP)
2701 San Pedro NE Ste 7
Albuquerque, NM 87110
(505) 888-2424
www.avma.org/aafp/default.htm

American Holistic Veterinary Medicine Association
2214 Old Emmorton Road
Bel Air, MD 21015
(410) 569-2346
www.altvetmed.com

American Veterinary Medical Association
1931 North Meacham Road, Suite 100
Schaumburg, IL 60173-4360
(847) 925-8070
http://www.avma.org/

Board Certified Feline Specialists

American Board of Veterinary Practitioners
530 Church Street Ste 700
Nashville, TN 37219-2394
(615) 254-3687
www.abvp.com

Centers for Disease Control and Prevention
1600 Clifton Road NE
Atlanta, GA 30333
(404) 639-3311
www.cdc.gov

Feline Heartworm
American Heartworm Society
P.O. Box 667
Batavia, IL 60510
(630) 844-9697

National Animal Poison Control Center
1717 S. Philo, Suite 36
Urbana, IL 61802
(888) 426 4435, $45 per case, with as many follow-up calls as necessary included. Have name, address, phone number, dog's breed, age, sex, and type of poison ingested, if known, available
www.napcc.aspca.org

Orthopedic Foundation for Animals (OFA)
2300 E. Nifong Blvd.
Columbia, MO 65201-3856.
(573) 442-0418
www.offa.org/

Parasites Online
College of Veterinary Medicine
University of Missouri
W-203 Veterinary Medicine Bldg
Columbia, MO 65211
(573) 882-3554
http://208.33.51.55/

*Skin Diseases of Dogs and Cats: A
    Guide for Pet Owners and Profes-
    sionals,* Dr. Steven A. Melman
Dermapet, Inc.
P.O. Box 59713
Potomac, MD 20859

U.S. Pharmacopeia
vaccine reactions: (800) 487-7776
customer service: (800) 227-8772
www.usp.org

Veterinary Pet Insurance (VPI)
4175 E. La Palma Ave., #100
Anaheim, CA 92807-1846
(714) 996-2311
(800) USA PETS,
    (877) PET HEALTH in Texas
www.petplan.net/home.htm

Nutrition and Natural Foods

California Natural,
    Natural Pet Products
PO Box 271
Santa Clara, CA 95052
(800) 532-7261
www.naturapet.com

Home Prepared Dog and Cat Diets,
    Donald R. Strombeck
Iowa State University Press
(515) 292-0140

PHD Products Inc.
PO Box 8313
White Plains, NY 10602
(800) 863-3403
www.phdproducts.net/

Sensible Choice, Pet Products Plus
5600 Mexico Road
St. Peters, MO 63376
(800) 592-6687
www.sensiblechoice.com/

Pet Sitting, Traveling

Take Your Pet Too!: Fun Things to Do!,
    Heather MacLean Walters
M.C.E. Publishing
P.O. Box 84
Chester, NJ 07930-0084

*Traveling with Your Pet 1999: The AAA
    Petbook,* Greg Weeks, Editor
Guide to pet-friendly lodging in the
    U.S. and Canada

Vacationing With Your Pet!,
    Eileen Barish
Pet-Friendly Publications
P.O. Box 8459
Scottsdale, AZ 85252
(800) 496-2665

...other resources

Independent Pet and Animal
    Transportation Association
5521 Greenville Ave., Ste 104-310
Dallas, TX 75206
(903) 769-2267
www.ipata.com

National Association of Professional Pet
    Sitters
1200 G St. N.W., Suite 760
Washington, DC 20005
(800) 286-PETS
www.petsitters.org

Pet Sitters International
418 East King Street
King, NC 27021-9163
(336)-983-9222
www.petsit.com

Index